TARGET YOUR MATHS

Year 6

Stephen Pearce

First published 2014 by
Elmwood Education
Unit 5 Mallow Park
Watchmead
Welwyn Garden City
Herts. AL7 1GX
Tel. 01707 333232

ISBN 9781 906 622 305

Numerical answers are published in a separate book.

Typeset and illustrated by Tech-Set Ltd., Gateshead, Tyne and Wear.

PREFACE

Target your Maths has been written for pupils in Year 6 and their teachers.

The intention of the book is to provide teachers with material to teach the statutory requirements set out in the Year 6 Programme of Study for Mathematics in the renewed 2014 National Curriculum Framework

In the renewed Framework the Year 6 Programme of Study has been organised into nine domains or sub-domains.

Number – number and place value
Number – addition, subtraction, multiplication and division
Number – fractions (including decimals and percentages)
Ratio and Proportion
Algebra
Measurement
Geometry – properties of shapes
Geometry – position and direction
Statistics

The structure of **Target your Maths 6** corresponds to that of the Year 6 Programme of Study. There are also Review and Extension sections at the end of the book.

All the statutory requirements of the Year 6 Programme of Study are covered in **Target your Maths 6**. Appendix I of the Teacher's Answer Book matches the statutory requirements and some essential non-statutory guidance with the relevant pages in this book. Most requirements are covered by more than one page. The author believes it is important that teachers have ample material from which to select.

Each single or double page lesson in this book is divided into four sections:

Introduction: the learning intention expressed as a target and, where necessary, clearly worked examples.

Section A: activities based upon work previously covered. This generally matches the requirements for Year 5 pupils. This section can be used to remind children of work previously covered, as well as providing material for the less confident child.

Section B: activities based upon the requirements for Year 6 pupils. Most children should be able to work successfully at this level.

Section C: activities providing extension material for the faster workers and for those who need to be moved quickly onto more challenging tasks. Problems in Section C can also provide useful material for discussion in the plenary session.

The correspondence of the three sections A–C to the requirements for different year groups provides a simple, manageable structure for planning differentiated activities and for both the formal and informal assessment of children's progress. The commonality of the content pitched at different levels also allows for progression within the lesson. Children acquiring confidence at one level find they can successfully complete activities at the next level.

There is, of course, no set path through either the Year 6 Programme of Study or **Target your Maths 6** but teachers may find Appendices II and III in the Teacher's Answer Book useful for planning purposes. In these tables one possible approach is given to the planning of the curriculum throughout the year.

In Appendix II the **Target your Maths** pages for each domain are organised into a three term school year. In Appendix III the work for each term is arranged into twelve blocks, each approximately corresponding to one week's work. For the sake of simplicity blocks are generally based upon one domain only.

The structure as set out in Appendices II and III enables teachers to develop concepts progressively throughout the year and provides pupils with frequent opportunities to consolidate previous learning.

The author is indebted to many colleagues who have assisted him in this work. He is particularly grateful to Sharon Granville and Davina Tunkel for their invaluable advice and assistance.

Stephen Pearce

CONTENTS

TARGET   To read and write numbers up to 10 million.

Numbers are made up from digits.
472 is a three-digit number, 5472 is a four-digit number, and so on.

The way we read a digit depends upon its place in the number.

5472 is five thousand four hundred and seventy-two.

85 472 is eighty-five thousand four hundred and seventy-two.

685 472 is six hundred and eighty-five thousand four hundred and seventy-two.

3 685 472 is three million six hundred and eighty-five thousand four hundred and seventy-two.

TAKE CARE when a number has zeros in it.

4051 is four thousand and fifty-one.

20 008 is twenty thousand and eight.

1 060 400 is one million sixty thousand four hundred.

9 207 030 is nine million two hundred and seven thousand and thirty.

1 Copy the table, writing each area in figures.

Country	Area (square miles)
UK	ninety-four thousand five hundred and twenty-five
Egypt	three hundred and eighty-six thousand six hundred
Mongolia	six hundred and three thousand nine hundred and five
Finland	one hundred and thirty thousand five hundred and fifty
Netherlands	sixteen thousand and thirty-four
Ukraine	two hundred and thirty-three thousand and eighty-nine
Dem. Rep. of Congo	nine hundred and five thousand five hundred and sixty
South Africa	four hundred and seventy-one thousand and eight

2 Write the area of each of the following countries in words.

a) Guyana   83 000 sq miles
b) Afghanistan   250 000 sq miles
c) South Korea   38 023 sq miles
d) Peru   496 220 sq miles
e) Sudan   728 215 sq miles
f) Cambodia   69 900 sq miles

g) France   211 208 sq miles
h) Zimbabwe   150 803 sq miles
i) Turkey   301 383 sq miles
j) Czech Rep.   30 450 sq miles
k) South Sudan   400 367 sq miles
l) Mexico   761 602 sq miles

B

1 Copy the table, writing the population of each European capital city in figures.

Capital	Population
Paris	two million one hundred and eighty-seven thousand
Brussels	one million fifty-nine thousand four hundred and eighty
Moscow	eleven million five hundred thousand
Prague	one million one hundred and eighty-five thousand three hundred
Amsterdam	seven hundred and sixty thousand nine hundred and forty-nine
Stockholm	one million two hundred and eighty thousand and thirty-one
Berlin	three million four hundred and forty-eight thousand five hundred
Bucharest	one million nine hundred and eighteen thousand two hundred and sixty

2 Write the population of each of the following European capital cities in words.

a) Budapest 1 645 091
b) Madrid 3 173 083
c) Copenhagen 1 080 638
d) Oslo 900 017
e) Istanbul 13 600 000

f) Warsaw 1 709 578
g) London 8 174 100
h) Zagreb 706 353
i) Dublin 1 069 861
j) Rome 2 473 972

C

1 Copy the table, writing the population of each European country in figures.

Country	Population
UK	sixty-two million two hundred and sixty-two thousand
Hungary	ten million seventy-five thousand and thirty-four
Spain	forty-six million seven hundred and seventy-seven thousand
Romania	nineteen million forty-three thousand seven hundred and sixty-seven
Poland	thirty-eight million six hundred and twenty-five thousand
Belgium	eleven million seven thousand and twenty
Russia	one hundred and forty-three million one hundred thousand
Czech Rep.	ten million six hundred and seventy-five thousand and seventeen

2 Write the population of each of the following European countries in words.

a) Portugal 10 617 192
b) Ukraine 45 396 470
c) Switzerland 7 302 000
d) Italy 59 715 625
e) Germany 82 199 600

f) Greece 11 606 813
g) Turkey 70 000 987
h) Netherlands 16 829 400
i) Belarus 10 335 382
j) France 63 601 002

TARGET   To compare and order numbers.

Example

Arrange 76 053, 104 760, 75 063 in ascending order.

Compare the highest value digits first, then the next highest and so on.

The correct order is 75 063, 76 053, 104 760.

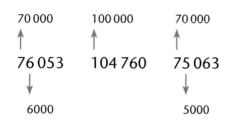

A

Put these sets of numbers in order, starting with the smallest.

1 13 173   17 313   11 737   13 337

2 24 229   22 492   22 924   24 292

3 18 555   15 585   18 518   15 558

4 66 727   67 276   67 627   66 772

5 39 353   35 593   35 935   39 335

Copy and complete.

6 23 750 + ☐ = 29 750

7 56 018 − ☐ = 16 018

8 92 843 + ☐ = 93 543

9 14 307 − ☐ = 13 807

10 45 962 + ☐ = 105 962

11 182 610 − ☐ = 174 610

B

Put these numbers in ascending order.

1 116 017   117 106   11 670   11 607

2 483 383   433 838   438 388   438 338

3 744 774   747 747   744 747   747 477

4 2 739 379   2 733 937   2 937 397   2 737 793

5 5 265 256   5 256 565   5 255 665   5 262 525

6 1 001 010   1 010 010   1 101 001   1 001 001

Copy and complete.

7 721 386 − ☐ = 715 386

8 530 274 + ☐ = 1 330 274

9 2 104 509 − ☐ = 2 095 509

10 1 649 328 + ☐ = 1 719 328

11 3 015 694 − ☐ = 15 694

12 6 908 830 + ☐ = 6 913 830

C

Work out the halfway number.

1 83 960 ◄——☐——► 84 100

2 217 500 ◄——☐——► 220 000

3 1 560 000 ◄——☐——► 1 630 000

4 493 900 ◄——☐——► 500 000

5 9 850 000 ◄——☐——► 10 850 000

6 3 400 000 ◄——☐——► 6 000 000

Copy and complete.

7 2 380 000 − ☐ = 2 375 800

8 14 175 937 − ☐ = 13 905 937

9 30 572 100 − ☐ = 10 272 100

10 6 059 283 − ☐ = 5 999 283

11 24 366 150 − ☐ = 22 866 150

12 10 000 000 − ☐ = 6 999 990

TARGET   To identify the place value of each digit in a number.

The value of a digit depends upon its place in the number.

		M	HTh	TTh	Th	H	T	U
Example		3	5	7	9	2	6	8
3 579 268		↓	↓	↓	↓	↓	↓	↓
	Value of digits	3 000 000	500 000	70 000	9000	200	60	8

A

Copy and complete by writing the missing number in the box.

1 23 735 = 20 000 + 3000 + ☐ + ☐ + 5

2 15 267 = ☐ + 5000 + ☐ + 60 + ☐

3 42 491 = ☐ + ☐ + 400 + ☐ + 1

4 78 024 = ☐ + 8000 + ☐ + ☐

5 31 986 = 30 000 + ☐ + ☐ + ☐ + ☐

Give the value of each digit as in the first five problems.

6 86 182
7 97 043
8 54 578
9 29 310
10 63 659

11 48 021
12 30 486
13 12 903
14 85 237
15 73 194

B

Write down the value of the digit underlined.

1 749 1<u>5</u>3
2 14 <u>6</u>37
3 1 <u>2</u>82 482
4 961 <u>7</u>90
5 <u>2</u> 438 014
6 4 8<u>3</u>0 569
7 1 377 9<u>2</u>1
8 123 <u>2</u>46
9 5 006 47<u>8</u>
10 1 665 <u>7</u>05
11 2 512 <u>3</u>34
12 497 6<u>9</u>7
13 <u>7</u> 045 022
14 3 <u>7</u>80 856
15 9 2<u>5</u>9 180

Add 4000 to:

16 1 185 360
17 329 511
18 2 477 362

Add 2 000 000 to:

19 15 178
20 5 209 364
21 37

Take 500 from:

22 1 937 820
23 275 138
24 3 420 000

Take 30 000 from:

25 2 625 000
26 130 070
27 5 000 000

C

Write the answers only.

1 2 384 700 + 50 000
2 11 509 264 − 3 000 000
3 23 167 535 + 8000
4 19 384 000 − 600 000
5 52 186 + 2 000 000
6 17 000 000 − 90 000
7 9 999 999 + 13
8 32 500 000 − 4000
9 17 968 019 + 70 000

Add 60 000 to:

10 1 053 827
11 15 992 310
12 86 247 200

Take 7000 from:

13 27 312 649
14 18 085 130
15 2 000 000

Add 9 000 000 to:

16 7 809 157
17 23 790
18 31 583 104

Take 800 000 from:

19 11 390 000
20 17 523 169
21 20 000 000

TARGET   To round whole numbers to the required degree of accuracy.

Examples

Rounding to the nearest 10	427 536 → 427 540	(6 > 5, round up)
Rounding to the nearest 100	427 536 → 427 500	(3 < 5, round down)
Rounding to the nearest 1000	427 536 → 428 000	(5 so round up)
Rounding to the nearest 10 000	427 536 → 430 000	(7 > 5, round up)

A

Round the following numbers to the nearest:

(10)	(100)	(1000)	(10 000)	(100 000)
1 3276	**7** 5048	**13** 3710	**19** 51 829	**25** 183 500
2 4853	**8** 22 290	**14** 38 265	**20** 25 060	**26** 647 039
3 11 308	**9** 79 917	**15** 42 537	**21** 49 512	**27** 462 746
4 59 762	**10** 51 884	**16** 329 641	**22** 103 700	**28** 928 907
5 28 195	**11** 116 452	**17** 157 490	**23** 607 188	**29** 354 158
6 43 417	**12** 208 735	**18** 860 823	**24** 580 936	**30** 993 600

B

Round to the nearest:
a) 10   b) 1000.

1 65 934
2 34 207
3 181 673
4 409 045
5 3 730 498
6 1 027 521

Round to the nearest:
a) 100   b) 100 000.

7 336 829
8 682 192
9 905 360
10 561 947
11 819 653
12 953 270

13 4 248 038
14 2 727 416
15 6 070 350
16 3 994 083
17 1 457 109
18 9 303 456

Round to the nearest:
a) 10 000   b) million.

19 2 826 000
20 8 591 370
21 1 387 294
22 7 405 068
23 9 940 952
24 5 269 107

C

Give the area of each ocean rounded
to the nearest:
a) 1 million square kilometres
b) 10 million square kilometres.

1 Pacific Ocean   155 557 000 km²
2 Atlantic Ocean   76 762 000 km²
3 Indian Ocean   68 556 000 km²
4 Southern Ocean   20 327 000 km²
5 Arctic Ocean   14 056 000 km²

Write the world population for each
of the following years rounded to:
a) 10 million   b) 100 million.

6 1960   3 038 413 000
7 1970   3 696 186 000
8 1980   4 453 007 000
9 1990   5 306 425 000
10 2000   6 122 770 000
11 2010   6 895 889 000

TARGET　To use negative numbers and calculate intervals across zero.

Examples

Find the temperature which is 10°C more than −6°C.

Answer 4°C.

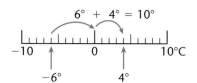

A

Copy and complete.

1　−4　−3　−2　☐　☐　☐　2

2　6　4　2　0　☐　☐　☐

3　−12　−9　−6　−3　☐　☐　☐

4　3　2　1　☐　☐　☐　−3

5　−5　☐　☐　☐　3　5　7

6　16　12　8　4　☐　☐　☐

Put each set of numbers in order, smallest first.

7　1　−6　−5　3　8　−2

8　−3　4　0　−1　2　−6

9　−3　6　2　1　0　−7

10　3　−8　−4　2　−2　5

B

Copy and complete.

1　10　7　4　☐　☐　☐

2　−6　−4　☐　☐　☐　4

3　−15　☐　−5　☐　5　☐

4　☐　☐　☐　2　6　10

5　5　3　1　☐　☐　☐

6　☐　☐　☐　2　5　8

Find the temperature which is:

7　5°C more than −2°C

8　8°C more than −10°C

9　7°C more than −3°C

10　4°C more than −4°C

11　9°C more than −7°C

12　6°C more than −8°C

13　10°C less than 6°C

14　7°C less than 2°C

15　9°C less than 0°C

16　12°C less than 4°C

17　8°C less than 7°C

18　6°C less than −5°C.

C

1　What temperatures are shown by the letters?

2　Give the difference in temperature between:

　a)　C and D　　　　b)　B and C　　　　c)　A and E　　　　d)　B and D

3　What would the temperature be if it was:

　a)　at A and rose 24°C　　　　　　c)　at C and fell 18°C

　b)　at D and fell 30°C　　　　　　d)　at B and rose 32°C?

TARGET   To use negative numbers in the context of temperature and calculate across zero.

Example

Find the difference in temperature between A and B.

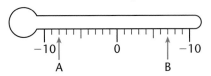

$A = -8°C$ $-8°C \rightarrow 0°C = 8°C$
$B = 7°C$ $0°C \rightarrow 7°C = 7°C$
           $-8°C \rightarrow 7°C = (8 + 7)°C = 15°C$

Answer *15°C*

A

Write the temperature shown by each letter.

1
    (A B C D on scale −10 0 10 20 30)

2 (E F G H on scale −10 −5 0 5 10)

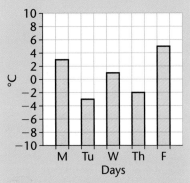

3 What was the coldest temperature recorded?

4 On which days was the temperature below 0°C?

5 What was the fall in temperature from:
   a) Monday to Tuesday
   b) Wednesday to Thursday?

6 What was the rise in temperature from:
   a) Tuesday to Wednesday
   b) Thursday to Friday?

B

For each thermometer, find the difference between:

a) X and Z
b) W and Y
c) X and Y
d) W and Z.

1 (W X Y Z on scale −20 0 20)

2 (W X Y Z on scale −10 −5 0 5 10)

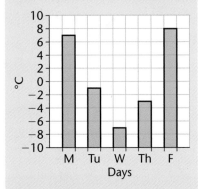

3 What was the fall in temperature from:
   a) Monday to Tuesday
   b) Tuesday to Wednesday?

4 What was the rise in temperature from:
   a) Wednesday to Thursday
   b) Thursday to Friday?

C

1 Copy and complete this table showing the maximum and minimum temperatures for different places.

Max.	Range	Min.
17°C	22°C	−5°C
28°C	46°C	
11°C	54°C	
−4°C	23°C	
46°C	52°C	
2°C		−37°C
35°C		−16°C
53°C		−7°C
−9°C		−23°C
	66°C	−35°C
	47°C	−54°C
	53°C	−28°C
	28°C	−41°C

2 Find the range between the highest and lowest temperature ever recorded in each UK country.

Country	High	Low
England	38·5°C	−26·1°C
Scotland	32·9°C	−27·2°C
Wales	35·2°C	−23·3°C
N.I.	30·8°C	−18·7°C

TARGET To solve number puzzles involving the addition and subtraction of positive and negative numbers.

In a magic square the sum of each row, column and diagonal is the same.

-7	2	-1
4	-2	-8
-3	-6	3

Example
Row 4 + -2 + -8 = -6
Column 2 + -2 + -6 = -6
Diagonal 3 + -2 + -7 = -6

Copy and complete the following magic squares.

A

1

		11
	14	
17	6	

2

26		
32	17	20

3

25		
	18	
17		11

4

	29	
	25	
	21	34

5

12		
57		
18		46

B

1

1		
-4	3	-2

2

		-5
		4
5		1

3

-1		
	-2	
-5		-3

4

	-7	8
	1	
-6		

5

-2		
5		
6		8

C

1

1			2
-6	7	4	-7
	-5		
		3	-2

2

	3		8
9		2	
	1	5	
-5		0	7

3

4			3
-5	-2	1	-4
	-6		
		2	-9

4

5			4
	3	6	
		-4	1
-5	2		-2

TARGET   To practise addition and subtraction for larger numbers.

Examples

```
    3 4 5  6 8 5
  + 2 6 9  2 1 7
    6 1 4  9 0 2
      1 1    1 1
```

```
  4 10 12 13 1
    5 3 4 0
  − 2 8 5 4 7
    2 2 7 9 3
```

```
  6 11 15  9 1
    7 2 6  0 3 5
  − 1 4 9  5 7 1
    5 7 6  4 6 4
```

A

Copy and complete.

1   2747   **7**   1284
   + 579   − 907

2   4885   **8**   5431
   + 2626   − 3685

3   3539   **9**   3125
   + 2872   − 1650

4   2673   **10**   6372
   + 1749   − 5713

5   6396   **11**   9540
   + 1605   − 4892

6   4968   **12**   7213
   + 4895   − 3724

13 There are 3594 passengers on board a cruise ship. 1768 more passengers come on board. How many passengers are there now on the ship? *5362*

14 Between 10 am and 11 am, 8130 people enter a shopping mall and 6143 people leave. How many more people are in the mall at 11 am than at 10 am? *1987*

B

Copy and complete.

1   16 794   **7**   44 256
   + 14 618   − 35 873

2   53 479   **8**   82 512
   + 35 635   − 40 574   *M1988*

3   27 856   **9**   56 434
   + 27 348   − 27 693   *55205*

4   45 645   **10**   93 185
   + 19 657   − 13 986   *65302* *79199*

5   38 928   **11**   65 341
   + 33 457   − 29 588

6   54 563   **12**   31 620
   + 19 638   − 24 926   *6691*

13 Rangers play Rovers both at home and away. The matches are watched by crowds of 49 384 and 37 957. What is the total attendance for the two matches? *87341*

14 In one year a delivery van is driven 61 380 miles. This is 16 487 miles further than during the previous year. What was the van's mileage in the first year? *77867*

C

Set out as in the example.

1 374 948 + 126 954

2 293 895 + 206 835

3 535 767 + 293 872

4 966 574 + 359 869

5 759 486 + 472 594

6 688 659 + 217 696

7 715 423 − 597 464   *117959*

8 604 635 − 326 690

9 453 242 − 196 597   *256645*

10 860 317 − 283 718

11 542 160 − 479 577   *62583*

12 937 054 − 739 486   *197568*

13 A manufacturing company has annual sales of £851 602 and expenses of £164 918. How much profit is made? *686684*

14 In ten years the population of a city increases from 457 485 to 537 240. By how much has the population increased? *79755*

TARGET To practise short multiplication of whole numbers and decimals.

Examples

Work from the
right and carry.

```
    3 9 7 5
  ×       7
  2 7 8 2 5
    6 5 3
```

```
  4 0 · 2 8
  ×       6
  2 4 1 · 6 8
      1   4
```

Align decimal
points.

A

Copy and complete.

1 138
× 3

7 90·5
× 4

2 746
× 2

8 87·2
× 8

3 295
× 6

9 94·2
× 3

4 327
× 9

10 73·5
× 5

5 680
× 5

11 51·9
× 9

6 194
× 7

12 17·4
× 6

Work out

13 827 × 4   **21** 31·9 × 2

14 263 × 7   **22** 46·3 × 4

15 508 × 2   **23** 65·2 × 9

16 436 × 8   **24** 20·8 × 7

17 657 × 3   **25** 38·4 × 5

18 386 × 6   **26** 9·5 × 8

19 840 × 9   **27** 5·39 × 3

20 924 × 5   **28** 72·6 × 6

B

Copy and complete.

1 2067
× 5
10 335

7 84·35
× 3
253·05

2 1859
× 4
7 436

8 376·2
× 9
3385·8

3 4283
× 8
34 264

9 253·8
× 7
1776·6

4 6174
× 7
43 218

10 39·26
× 4
157·04

5 7398
× 11
81 378

11 94·07
× 12
1128·84

6 5916
× 6
35 496

12 617·5
× 8
4940·0

Work out

13 2348 × 6   **21** 46·52 × 11 511·72

14 7290 × 3   **22** 704·8 × 6

15 3582 × 5   **23** 65·37 × 4   261·480

16 1594 × 9   **24** 91·24 × 5

17 7408 × 4   **25** 428·6 × 7

18 6815 × 12   **26** 37·05 × 12 444·6

19 2936 × 8   **27** 285·7 × 9

20 5049 × 7   **28** 50·79 × 8   406·32

C

Work out

1 13 269 × 6

2 54 706 × 3

3 29 548 × 12 354 575

4 161 437 × 5

5 47 095 × 8   360 766

6 135 176 × 7

7 269 840 × 9

8 183 501 × 11 2018 511

9 392·19 × 4

10 73·867 × 2

11 9267·4 × 11 92614

12 24·908 × 7

13 613·57 × 9

14 52·836 × 8   422·688

15 36·179 × 12

16 274·85 × 6

17 A delivery firm
buys seven new
vans, each costing
£16 549. What is
the total cost of the
vans?   15847

18 One box of tiles
weighs 23·875 kg.
What is the total
weight of six boxes?   143·25

TARGET   To practise short multiplication of whole numbers and decimals.

Examples

Work from the
right and carry.

```
      5 7 0 4
    ×       8
    ─────────
    4 5 6 3 2
      5     3
```

```
      6 2 · 5 8
    ×         9
    ───────────
    5 6 3 · 2 2
      2 5   7
```

Align decimal
points.

A

Copy and complete.

1.   364
  ×   2

2.   173
  ×   8

3.   429
  ×   5

4.   246
  ×   7

5.   9·7
  ×   4

6.   5·8
  ×   6

7.   6·4
  ×   3

8.   2·6
  ×   9

Work out

9.   587 × 2

10.   175 × 9

11.   346 × 5

12.   285 × 8

13.   9·7 × 3

14.   7·4 × 6

15.   3·8 × 4

16.   5·9 × 7

17. One biscuit weighs 8·2 g. What do seven biscuits weigh?

18. On one day 258 people visit a stately home. The entrance fee is £9. How much is taken in entrance fees?

B

Copy and complete.

1.   1564
  ×   5

2.   3916
  ×   11

3.   4638
  ×   8

4.   3739
  ×   9

5.   195·3
  ×   12

6.   24·65
  ×   6

7.   63·28
  ×   4

8.   230·7
  ×   7

Work out

9.   4795 × 3

10.   1824 × 9

11.   5237 × 11

12.   8578 × 4

13.   40·26 × 7

14.   209·1 × 8

15.   78·39 × 6

16.   64·07 × 12

17. One side of a square picture frame is 37·25 cm. What is its perimeter?

18. Stacey earns £2947 each month. How much does she earn in six months?

C

Work out

1.   61 527 × 6

2.   14 936 × 7

3.   159 318 × 3

4.   237 284 × 11

5.   25 179 × 9

6.   490 567 × 2

7.   143 658 × 8

8.   26 745 × 12

9.   82·092 × 4

10.   582·74 × 7

11.   30·498 × 6

12.   195·63 × 11

13.   63·084 × 9

14.   197·356 × 5

15.   71·902 × 8

16.   84·039 × 12

17. There are eight stock cubes in each box. How many cubes are there in 176 245 boxes?

18. Basil earns £2719·50 per month. How much does he earn in 12 months?

TARGET   To use a formal written method for long multiplication.

Examples

```
    5 4 5
    1 7 5 8
  ×     2 7
  1 2 3 0 6   (1758 × 7)
  3₅5₁1₁6 0   (1758 × 20)
  4 7 4 6 6
```

```
        2 5 1
    4 3 9 2
  ×     3 6
  2 6 3 5 2
  1 3₁1₂7 6 0
  1 5 8 1 1 2
        1   1
```

A

Copy and complete.

1
```
      68
  ×   13
          (68 × 3)
  ____    (68 × 10)

  ____
```

2
```
     492
  ×   18
          (492 × 8)
  ____    (492 × 10)

  ____
```

3
```
      36
  ×   24
          (36 × 4)
  ____    (36 × 20)

  ____
```

4
```
     267
  ×   35
          (267 × 5)
  ____    (267 × 30)

  ____
```

Work out

5 63 × 42   **9** 174 × 34

6 57 × 26   **10** 219 × 28

7 49 × 19   **11** 438 × 17

8 85 × 23   **12** 365 × 45

B

Copy and complete.

1
```
    1247
  ×   26
          (1247 × 6)
  ____    (1247 × 20)

  ____
```

2
```
    2538
  ×   14
          (2538 × 4)
  ____    (2538 × 10)

  ____
```

3
```
    1673
  ×   38
          (1673 × 8)
  ____    (1673 × 30)

  ____
```

4
```
    3496
  ×   25
          (3496 × 5)
  ____    (3496 × 20)

  ____
```

Work out

5 5728 × 16   **9** 6257 × 43

6 4359 × 37   **10** 1985 × 24

7 2584 × 29   **11** 4874 × 39

8 3046 × 35   **12** 7169 × 48

C

Work out

1 24 135 × 28

2 57 248 × 19

3 42 186 × 34

4 16 259 × 45

5 35 367 × 26

6 49 526 × 37

7 21 687 × 85

8 52 958 × 64

9 249 × 183

10 376 × 256

11 458 × 149

12 864 × 572

13 327 × 265

14 483 × 174

15 739 × 328

16 562 × 437

17 One can weighs 387 g. There are 36 cans in a box. What is the total weight of 25 boxes in kilograms?

TARGET To practise a formal written method for long multiplication.

Examples

```
        3 1 2
      1 8 2 7
  ×       2 4
  ─────────────
      7 3 0 8   (1827 × 4)
  3₁6₁5₁4 0     (1827 × 20)
  ─────────────
  4 3 8 4 8
        1
```

```
            1 7 3
      5 1 9 · 4
  ×         4 8
  ─────────────
      4 1 5 5 · 2
    2 0 7 7 6 · 0
  ─────────────
    2 4 9 3 1 · 2
          1  1
```

A

Copy and complete.

1
```
      39
  ×   25
  ─────────
          (39 × 5)
          (39 × 20)
  ─────────

  ─────────
```

2
```
      6·2
  ×    43
  ─────────
          (6·2 × 3)
          (6·2 × 40)
  ─────────

  ─────────
```

3
```
     183
  ×   17
  ─────────
          (183 × 7)
          (183 × 10)
  ─────────

  ─────────
```

4
```
    41·5
  ×   38
  ─────────
          (41·5 × 8)
          (41·5 × 30)
  ─────────

  ─────────
```

Work out

5 28 × 24   **9** 135 × 23

6 74 × 19   **10** 549 × 18

7 5·7 × 36   **11** 32·6 × 45

8 9·6 × 72   **12** 47·3 × 27

B

Copy and complete.

1
```
    1536
  ×   34
  ─────────
          (1536 × 4)
          (1536 × 30)
  ─────────

  ─────────
```

2
```
    4872
  ×   29
  ─────────
          (4872 × 9)
          (4872 × 20)
  ─────────

  ─────────
```

3
```
   239·4
  ×   52
  ─────────
          (239·4 × 2)
          (239·4 × 50)
  ─────────

  ─────────
```

4
```
   60·27
  ×   47
  ─────────
          (60·27 × 7)
          (60·27 × 40)
  ─────────

  ─────────
```

Work out

5 1853 × 63   **9** 41·86 × 27

6 5419 × 26   **10** 750·2 × 39

7 27·68 × 35   **11** 16·93 × 54

8 394·5 × 48   **12** 82·54 × 46

C

Work out

1 35 215 × 28

2 14 793 × 45

3 294·08 × 36

4 16·359 × 53

5 53·826 × 19

6 470·54 × 24

7 1293·7 × 37

8 30·682 × 65

9 476 × 233

10 923 × 458

11 65·4 × 192

12 3·89 × 356

13 0·547 × 429

14 8·15 × 657

15 79·2 × 284

16 0·438 × 378

17 Each can of paint holds 2·35 litres. How much paint is needed to fill 346 cans?

TARGET To practise written methods for short and long multiplication.

Examples

$$
\begin{array}{r}
4\,9\,5{\cdot}7 \\
\times\ \ \ \ \ \ \ 6 \\
\hline
2\,9\,7\,4{\cdot}2 \\
\scriptstyle 5\ 3\ 4
\end{array}
\qquad
\begin{array}{r}
\scriptstyle 2\ 1\ 1 \\
2\,8\,3\,6 \\
\times\ \ \ \ \ \ 4\,3 \\
\hline
8\,5\,0\,8 \\
1\,1_3\,3_1\,4_2\,4\,0 \\
\hline
1\,2\,1\,9\,4\,8 \\
\scriptstyle 1
\end{array}
\qquad
\begin{array}{r}
\scriptstyle 6\ 2\ \ \ 4 \\
3\,7\cdot2\,5 \\
\times\ \ \ \ \ \ 2\,9 \\
\hline
3\,3\,5\cdot2\,5 \\
7_1\,4\,5_1\cdot0\,0 \\
\hline
1\,0\,8\,0\cdot2\,5 \\
\scriptstyle 1
\end{array}
$$

A

Work out

1. 258×6
2. 437×5
3. 31.5×9
4. 59.6×7
5. 475×11
6. 763×4
7. 28.4×8
8. 34.9×12

Copy and complete.

9.
$$
\begin{array}{r}
165 \\
\times\ \ \ 35 \\
\hline
(165 \times 5) \\
(165 \times 30) \\
\hline
 \\
\hline
\end{array}
$$

10.
$$
\begin{array}{r}
36.2 \\
\times\ \ \ 24 \\
\hline
(36.2 \times 4) \\
(36.2 \times 20) \\
\hline
 \\
\end{array}
$$

Work out

11. 37×18
12. 91×23
13. 5.8×47
14. 6.3×16
15. 146×72
16. 507×19
17. 23.9×36
18. 38.4×25

B

Work out

1. 3297×4
2. 2518×7
3. 164.3×12
4. 70.69×3
5. 4825×9
6. 57.03×8
7. 619.2×5
8. 30.84×6
9. 1736×42
10. 3285×37
11. 290.4×64
12. 15.67×26
13. 58.43×83
14. 261.9×39
15. 63.72×45
16. 34.58×58
17. The mean weight of 72 sacks of coal is 39·47 kg. What is the total weight of the sacks?

C

Work out

1. $14\,673 \times 8$
2. $28\,509 \times 11$
3. 817.42×5
4. 39.065×9
5. 4239.7×6
6. 56.184×4
7. 608.29×12
8. 13.956×7
9. $15\,637 \times 53$
10. 274.29×29
11. 40.985×65
12. 315.06×48
13. 394×169
14. 8.72×346
15. 0.759×674
16. 9.68×525
17. Each pipe is 6·95 m long. What is the total length of 258 pipes?

TARGET   To practise short division of whole numbers and decimals.

Examples $4138 \div 9$ $289 \cdot 6 \div 8$ $370 \cdot 6 \div 4$

$$\begin{array}{r} 4\ 5\ 9\ r\ 7 \\ 9\overline{)4\ 1^5 3^8 8} \end{array} \qquad \begin{array}{r} 3\ 6 \cdot 2 \\ 8\overline{)2\ 8^4 9 \cdot {}^1 6} \end{array} \qquad \begin{array}{r} 9\ 2 \cdot 6\ 5 \\ 4\overline{)3\ 7^1 0 \cdot {}^2 6^2 0} \end{array}$$

A

Work out

1. $143 \div 2$
2. $115 \div 8$
3. $109 \div 3$
4. $122 \div 9$
5. $104 \div 6$
6. $369 \div 5$
7. $158 \div 4$
8. $184 \div 8$
9. $261 \div 9$
10. $226 \div 3$
11. $28 \cdot 0 \div 5$
12. $31 \cdot 8 \div 6$
13. $26 \cdot 0 \div 4$
14. $31 \cdot 2 \div 8$
15. $20 \cdot 4 \div 3$
16. $15 \cdot 2 \div 2$
17. $19 \cdot 6 \div 7$
18. $30 \cdot 4 \div 4$
19. $46 \cdot 8 \div 9$
20. $75 \cdot 2 \div 8$

B

Work out

1. $4585 \div 3$
2. $2843 \div 6$
3. $6123 \div 8$
4. $3356 \div 4$
5. $5295 \div 2$
6. $1358 \div 7$
7. $3142 \div 5$
8. $3211 \div 9$
9. $254 \cdot 8 \div 4$
10. $199 \cdot 2 \div 8$
11. $11 \cdot 72 \div 2$
12. $507 \cdot 5 \div 7$
13. $24 \cdot 65 \div 5$
14. $25 \cdot 02 \div 9$
15. $110 \cdot 1 \div 3$
16. $49 \cdot 8 \div 6$

17. There are eight ink cartridges in each pack. How many packs can be filled from 7538 cartridges?

18. Astra has £43·75. She spends one fifth of her money. How much does she have left?

19. Each bag holds seven oranges. How many bags are needed for 4795 oranges?

20. The total length of a long jumper's six jumps is 41·4 m. What is the mean length of his jumps?

C

Work out

1. $17\,477 \div 7$
2. $40\,789 \div 5$
3. $44\,416 \div 9$
4. $19\,173 \div 11$
5. $40\,979 \div 6$
6. $28\,624 \div 8$
7. $16\,490 \div 3$
8. $84\,753 \div 12$
9. $187 \cdot 7 \div 2$
10. $40 \cdot 012 \div 7$
11. $9381 \cdot 9 \div 11$
12. $185 \cdot 82 \div 6$
13. $5632 \cdot 2 \div 9$
14. $39 \cdot 715 \div 5$
15. $227 \cdot 28 \div 12$
16. $36 \cdot 952 \div 8$

17. One ninth of a shop's 24,111 customers spent more than £50. How many customers spent more than £50?

18. Six classroom tables cost £173·70 altogether. How much does one table cost?

19. Each box holds 12 pencils. How many boxes can be filled from 5720 pencils?

20. Seven packing cases have a total weight of 481·25 kg. What is the mean weight of the cases?

TARGET To practise short division of whole numbers and decimals.

Examples $4451 \div 7$ $525{\cdot}6 \div 6$ $2791 \div 4$

$$7\overline{)4\ 4^25^41} = 635\tfrac{6}{7}$$

$$6\overline{)5\ 2^45{\cdot}^36} = 87{\cdot}6$$

$$4\overline{)2\ 7^39^31{\cdot}^30^20} = 697{\cdot}75$$

A

Work out

1. $259 \div 4$
2. $147 \div 6$
3. $301 \div 7$
4. $292 \div 5$
5. $331 \div 9$
6. $355 \div 4$
7. $216 \div 8$
8. $263 \div 3$
9. $267 \div 7$
10. $275 \div 6$
11. $33{\cdot}6 \div 7$
12. $39{\cdot}5 \div 5$
13. $50{\cdot}4 \div 6$
14. $29{\cdot}1 \div 3$
15. $19{\cdot}6 \div 2$
16. $60{\cdot}8 \div 8$
17. $41{\cdot}3 \div 7$
18. $34{\cdot}8 \div 4$
19. $61{\cdot}2 \div 9$
20. $45{\cdot}6 \div 6$

B

Work out

1. $1941 \div 3$
2. $264{\cdot}6 \div 7$
3. $4851 \div 9$
4. $28{\cdot}96 \div 8$
5. $180{\cdot}24 \div 4$
6. $16\,098 \div 6$
7. $2473{\cdot}2 \div 9$
8. $100{\cdot}52 \div 7$

Work out to two decimal places.

9. $93{\cdot}1 \div 2$
10. $251{\cdot}4 \div 4$
11. $178 \div 8$
12. $587{\cdot}3 \div 5$
13. $3875 \div 4$
14. $319{\cdot}5 \div 6$
15. $296{\cdot}4 \div 5$
16. $142 \div 8$

17. Four friends share a bingo prize of £750. How much do they each receive?

18. Five identical crates weigh 134·3 kg altogether. How much does one crate weigh?

19. One in every seven of the 20 832 patients treated at a hospital in one year has a bone fracture. How many patients were treated for fractures?

20. In eight training runs Melissa runs a total distance of 110 km. What is the mean distance of her runs?

C

Work out

1. $34\,713 \div 9$
2. $283{\cdot}56 \div 6$
3. $90{\cdot}468 \div 12$
4. $15\,473{\cdot}6 \div 8$
5. $370{\cdot}23 \div 7$
6. $302{\cdot}038 \div 11$
7. $377{\cdot}658 \div 9$
8. $1125{\cdot}11 \div 7$

Work out to three decimal places.

9. $26{\cdot}07 \div 5$
10. $235{\cdot}4 \div 8$
11. $183{\cdot}73 \div 2$
12. $269{\cdot}38 \div 4$
13. $314{\cdot}85 \div 6$
14. $110{\cdot}12 \div 8$
15. $323{\cdot}7 \div 4$
16. $714{\cdot}86 \div 5$

17. Five identical steel bars weigh 78·84 kg altogether. How much does each bar weigh?

18. 39·88 litres of paint exactly fills five equal sized pots. What is the capacity of each pot?

19. A precision engineering firm is required to cut a 16·5 m length of cable into 12 equal lengths to the nearest millimetre. How long should each length be?

20. A jet flies 88·05 km in six minutes. How far does it fly in one minute?

TARGET To use the formal written method of long division.

Examples

$$853 \div 24$$

$$\begin{array}{r} 35 \\ 24\overline{)853} \\ 720 \quad (24 \times 30) \\ \hline 133 \\ 120 \quad (24 \times 5) \\ \hline 13 \end{array}$$

Answer   *35 r 13*

or $35\frac{13}{24}$

$$4259 \div 18$$

$$\begin{array}{r} 236 \\ 18\overline{)4259} \\ 36\downarrow \\ \hline 65 \\ 54\downarrow \\ \hline 119 \\ 108 \\ \hline 11 \end{array}$$

Answer   *236 r 11*

or $236\frac{11}{18}$

$$5091 \div 35$$

$$\begin{array}{r} 145\frac{16}{35} \\ 35\overline{)5091} \\ 35 \\ \hline 159 \\ 140 \\ \hline 191 \\ 175 \\ \hline 16 \end{array}$$

Answer   *145 r 16*

or $145\frac{16}{35}$

A

Work out

1. $325 \div 25$
2. $312 \div 13$
3. $400 \div 18$
4. $709 \div 22$
5. $720 \div 31$
6. $514 \div 24$
7. $550 \div 17$
8. $680 \div 29$
9. $378 \div 27$
10. $588 \div 14$
11. $390 \div 19$
12. $442 \div 26$
13. $529 \div 15$
14. $560 \div 42$
15. $672 \div 21$
16. $481 \div 33$

B

Work out

1. $1997 \div 13$
2. $3925 \div 32$
3. $4080 \div 17$
4. $5568 \div 24$
5. $6783 \div 41$
6. $4900 \div 35$
7. $6764 \div 19$
8. $9247 \div 28$
9. $7973 \div 36$
10. $9182 \div 52$
11. $8004 \div 23$
12. $9527 \div 45$
13. $5076 \div 39$
14. $6951 \div 27$
15. $7544 \div 46$
16. $10\,825 \div 29$

17. There are 16 sausages in each pack. How many packs can be made from 8750 sausages?

18. A group booking of 36 plane tickets costs £6696. What does each ticket cost?

19. Each bag holds 25 coins. How many bags are needed for 6784 coins?

C

Work out

1. $18\,600 \div 15$
2. $10\,469 \div 24$
3. $12\,043 \div 37$
4. $65\,284 \div 26$
5. $84\,637 \div 18$
6. $92\,421 \div 27$
7. $14\,589 \div 34$
8. $10\,607 \div 16$
9. $91\,276 \div 38$
10. $13\,618 \div 43$
11. $79\,054 \div 29$
12. $120\,268 \div 36$
13. $68\,379 \div 54$
14. $90\,240 \div 42$
15. $114\,044 \div 28$
16. $105\,888 \div 65$

TARGET   To practise long division of whole numbers and decimals.

Examples

8937 ÷ 25

$$357\tfrac{12}{25}$$
$$25\overline{)8937}$$
75	(300 × 25)
143	
125	(50 × 25)
187	
175	(7 × 25)
12	

790·4 ÷ 19

$$41·6$$
$$19\overline{)790·4}$$
76	(40 × 19)
30	
19	(1 × 19)
11·4	
11·4	(0·6 × 19)
0·0	

82·08 ÷ 24

$$3·42$$
$$24\overline{)82·08}$$
72	(3 × 24)
10·0	
9·6	(0·4 × 24)
0·48	
0·48	(0·02 × 24)
0·0	

A

Work out

1 286 ÷ 22

2 378 ÷ 14

3 850 ÷ 25

4 616 ÷ 28

5 396 ÷ 33

6 744 ÷ 16

7 672 ÷ 31

8 528 ÷ 42

9 40·5 ÷ 15

10 47·6 ÷ 34

11 73·6 ÷ 23

12 85·5 ÷ 19

13 69·7 ÷ 41

14 93·6 ÷ 24

15 81·0 ÷ 18

16 76·8 ÷ 32

B

Work out

1 1848 ÷ 14

2 4725 ÷ 21

3 8690 ÷ 33

4 5959 ÷ 42

5 3828 ÷ 29

6 7257 ÷ 16

7 7499 ÷ 51

8 8362 ÷ 37

9 556·6 ÷ 22

10 478·8 ÷ 38

11 63·24 ÷ 17

12 709·5 ÷ 43

13 81·94 ÷ 34

14 3523 ÷ 26

15 941·4 ÷ 18

16 91·85 ÷ 55

17 A jug holding 4·5 litres of juice is poured equally into 25 glasses. How much juice is in each glass?

18 Usama saves the same amount of money each week. In one year he saves £351. How much does he save each week?

19 The total weight of 32 identical parcels is 81·92 kg. What does each parcel weigh?

20 Each pin is made from 18 mm of wire. How many pins can be made from a 3·2 m wire?

C

Work out

1 222·25 ÷ 35

2 2901·3 ÷ 19

3 14·842 ÷ 41

4 33 840 ÷ 27

5 21·736 ÷ 52

6 3565·9 ÷ 13

7 15 000 ÷ 24

8 543·66 ÷ 39

9 62 437 ÷ 15

10 47·554 ÷ 31

11 2041·2 ÷ 28

12 617·32 ÷ 44

13 13·752 ÷ 36

14 58 465 ÷ 23

15 123·75 ÷ 45

16 77·064 ÷ 57

TARGET To practise the written method for short and long division.

Examples

$5717 \div 12$

$$12)\overline{5\ 7^9 1^7 7}$$
$$4\ 7\ 6\ r\ 5$$

Remainders can also be written as fractions and decimals.

$5590 \div 34$

$$34)\overline{5590} \quad 164\tfrac{14}{34}\ \tfrac{7}{17}$$
$$\underline{34} \quad (100 \times 34)$$
$$219$$
$$\underline{204} \quad (60 \times 34)$$
$$150$$
$$\underline{136} \quad (4 \times 34)$$
$$14$$

$845 \div 26$

$$26)\overline{845\cdot0} \quad 32\cdot5$$
$$\underline{78} \quad (30 \times 26)$$
$$65$$
$$\underline{52} \quad (2 \times 26)$$
$$13\cdot0$$
$$\underline{13\cdot0} \quad (0\cdot5 \times 26)$$
$$0\cdot0$$

A

Work out

1. $238 \div 4$
2. $509 \div 8$
3. $374 \div 5$
4. $794 \div 2$
5. $16\cdot8 \div 6$
6. $13\cdot8 \div 3$
7. $15\cdot3 \div 9$
8. $26\cdot6 \div 7$
9. $544 \div 16$
10. $312 \div 24$
11. $675 \div 27$
12. $624 \div 13$
13. $54\cdot4 \div 32$
14. $77\cdot5 \div 25$
15. $94\cdot3 \div 41$
16. $64\cdot8 \div 18$

B

Work out

1. $5189 \div 3$
2. $2974 \div 6$
3. $7530 \div 11$
4. $7651 \div 7$
5. $31\cdot32 \div 9$
6. $41\cdot85 \div 5$
7. $23\cdot76 \div 8$
8. $98\cdot28 \div 12$
9. $3690 \div 15$
10. $2495 \div 33$
11. $6890 \div 21$
12. $3301 \div 19$
13. $26\cdot46 \div 54$
14. $76\cdot44 \div 42$
15. $159\cdot6 \div 28$
16. $48\cdot24 \div 36$

17. In an eight hour day Tricia earns £91·60. How much does she earn per hour?

18. Each box holds 48 packets of rice. How many boxes are needed for 7500 packets?

19. An automatic handwash uses 34·84 litres of water in 26 washes. How much water is used in each wash?

C

Work out

1. $24\,537 \div 5$
2. $32\,664 \div 9$
3. $52\,981 \div 7$
4. $24\,548 \div 12$
5. $29\cdot752 \div 4$
6. $37\cdot782 \div 6$
7. $104\cdot94 \div 11$
8. $36\cdot688 \div 8$
9. $33\,792 \div 22$
10. $12\,389 \div 29$
11. $28\,647 \div 34$
12. $88\,304 \div 17$
13. $49\cdot704 \div 38$
14. $470\cdot73 \div 51$
15. $7556\cdot5 \div 35$
16. $75\cdot035 \div 43$

TARGET To practise written methods for multiplication and division.

Examples

$476·8 \times 9$

```
    4 7 6·8
×         9
  4 2 9 1·2
    6 6 7
```

2935×36

```
  5 2 3
  2 9 3 5
×      3 6
  1 7 6 1 0   (2935 × 6)
8₂8₁0₁5 0     (2935 × 30)
1 0 5 6 6 0
        1
```

$459·2 \div 8$

```
      5 7 · 4
8)4 5⁵9 ·³2
```

$9837 \div 27$

```
       364 9/27 1/3
27)9837
   81      (300 × 27)
   173
   162     (60 × 27)
   117
   108     (4 × 27)
     9
```

A

Work out

1. 347×9
2. 294×8
3. $61·8 \times 5$
4. $74·6 \times 7$

5. 518×17
6. 437×36
7. $79·2 \times 25$
8. $86·4 \times 43$

9. $440 \div 6$
10. $527 \div 9$
11. $20·3 \div 7$
12. $37·6 \div 8$

13. $786 \div 31$
14. $821 \div 19$
15. $68·8 \div 43$
16. $62·4 \div 24$

B

Work out

1. 5048×6
2. 2859×9
3. $39·65 \times 12$
4. $73·86 \times 8$

5. 1425×24
6. 3659×19
7. $29·37 \times 53$
8. $528·4 \times 37$

9. $3839 \div 11$
10. $4397 \div 7$
11. $248·4 \div 9$
12. $84·48 \div 12$

13. $2049 \div 14$
14. $1561 \div 48$
15. $73·37 \div 29$
16. $60·9 \div 35$

17. Each packet of pasta weighs 0·28 kg. There are 64 packets in each box. What is the total weight of the packets in 34 boxes in kilograms?

18. An 18 hole golf course is 6642 m long. What is the mean length of the holes?

19. A party of 48 Year 6 children attend a residential weekend at an Adventure Centre. Each place costs £43·69. What is the total cost for the party of 48?

20. A 4·75 litre vat of ice cream mixture is poured equally into 25 tubs. How much ice cream is in each tub?

C

Work out

1. $60\,753 \times 9$
2. $15\,729 \times 11$
3. $28·364 \times 7$
4. $490·27 \times 12$

5. $67\,418 \times 46$
6. $38\,029 \times 35$
7. $946·53 \times 18$
8. $56·278 \times 27$

9. $35\,098 \div 6$
10. $72\,296 \div 8$
11. $4543·2 \div 12$
12. $13·825 \div 7$

13. $51\,187 \div 18$
14. $35\,130 \div 23$
15. $23·706 \div 54$
16. $84·045 \div 39$

TARGET To practise written methods for long multiplication and long division.

Examples

5379×42

$$
\begin{array}{r}
{\scriptstyle 1\ 1}\\
5\ 3\ 7\ 9\\
\times \qquad 4\ 2\\
\hline
1\ 0\ 7\ 5\ 8\\
2\ 1_{1}5_{3}1_{3}6\ 0\\
\hline
2\ 2\ 5\ 9\ 1\ 8\\
\hline
{\scriptstyle 1}
\end{array}
$$

$72 \cdot 68 \times 29$

$$
\begin{array}{r}
{\scriptstyle 2\ 6\quad 7}\\
7\ 2\cdot 6\ 8\\
\times \qquad 2\ 9\\
\hline
6\ 5\ 4\cdot 1\ 2\\
1\ 4\ 5_{1}3_{1}\cdot 6\ 0\\
\hline
2\ 1\ 0\ 7\cdot 7\ 2\\
\hline
{\scriptstyle 1\ 1}
\end{array}
$$

$7084 \div 28$

$$
\begin{array}{r}
253\\
28{\overline{)7084}}\\
56\\
\hline
148\\
140\\
\hline
84\\
84\\
\hline
0
\end{array}
$$

$57 \cdot 75 \div 35$

$$
\begin{array}{r}
1\cdot 65\\
35{\overline{)57\cdot 75}}\\
35\\
\hline
22\cdot 7\\
21\cdot 0\\
\hline
1\cdot 75\\
1\cdot 75\\
\hline
0
\end{array}
$$

A

Work out

1. 427×13
2. 658×27
3. 139×52
4. 582×31

5. $27 \cdot 4 \times 42$
6. $81 \cdot 6 \times 15$
7. $79 \cdot 3 \times 38$
8. $36 \cdot 5 \times 24$

9. $437 \div 23$
10. $510 \div 15$
11. $980 \div 36$
12. $571 \div 42$

13. $72 \cdot 8 \div 14$
14. $100 \cdot 8 \div 28$
15. $70 \cdot 2 \div 39$
16. $40 \cdot 8 \div 17$

B

Work out

1. 5283×26
2. 7149×58
3. 3625×45
4. 9706×34

5. $28 \cdot 14 \times 63$
6. $73 \cdot 59 \times 29$
7. $60 \cdot 78 \times 47$
8. $45 \cdot 92 \times 36$

9. $2236 \div 13$
10. $5478 \div 22$
11. $5270 \div 41$
12. $5581 \div 34$

13. $33 \cdot 75 \div 25$
14. $73 \cdot 08 \div 18$
15. $899 \cdot 1 \div 37$
16. $76 \cdot 93 \div 49$

17. Each barrel has a capacity of 38·65 litres. What is the capacity of 56 barrels?

18. The total of the weights of 28 children in a class is 982·8 kg. What is the mean weight of the children?

19. There are 128 straws in a packet and 48 packets in a box. How many straws are there in 16 boxes?

20. The annual subscription to receive 52 copies of a magazine is £96·20. How much does each copy cost?

C

Work out

1. $63\,549 \times 37$
2. $92\,806 \times 65$
3. $41\,732 \times 26$
4. $85\,694 \times 48$

5. $79 \cdot 125 \times 17$
6. $24 \cdot 368 \times 39$
7. $904 \cdot 73 \times 28$
8. $48 \cdot 659 \times 54$

9. $61\,161 \div 19$
10. $51\,018 \div 33$
11. $16\,398 \div 24$
12. $66\,276 \div 45$

13. $88 \cdot 128 \div 32$
14. $5148 \cdot 9 \div 27$
15. $84 \cdot 288 \div 16$
16. $188 \cdot 19 \div 51$

TARGET To use estimation to check answers to calculations.

Examples

576·48 + 381·75
rounds to
580 + 380 = 960
Answer ≈ 960

832·9 − 659·84
rounds to
830 − 660 = 170
Answer ≈ 170

74·85 × 7
rounds to
75 × 7 = 525
Answer ≈ 525

75·69 ÷ 9
rounds to
76 ÷ 9 = 8·4
Answer ≈ 8·4

(≈ means *is approximately equal to*)

A

Round to the nearest 10 and estimate. Work out and check your answer.

1. 756 + 263
2. 382 + 175
3. 627 − 458
4. 935 − 261

5. 244 × 3
6. 575 × 8
7. 752 ÷ 5
8. 539 ÷ 6

Round to the nearest 100 and estimate. Work out and check your answer.

9. 5974 + 1647
10. 8546 + 3495
11. 7359 − 1892
12. 6784 − 5829

13. 8636 × 4
14. 3164 × 7
15. 6848 ÷ 2
16. 2655 ÷ 9

B

Round to the nearest 1000 and estimate. Work out and check your answer.

1. 39 275 + 14 637
2. 94 836 + 27 908
3. 50 926 − 11 543
4. 84 362 − 56 497

5. 65 730 × 2
6. 19 385 × 6
7. 26 192 ÷ 4
8. 37 840 ÷ 8

Round to the nearest whole number and estimate. Work out and check your answer.

9. 47·35 + 36·59
10. 68·72 + 45·49
11. 95·24 − 35·87
12. 26·17 − 18·69

13. 26·94 × 5
14. 35·26 × 9
15. 68·53 ÷ 7
16. 52·62 ÷ 3

C

Round to the nearest tenth and estimate. Work out and check your answer.

1. 7·593 + 2·6495
2. 9·864 + 4·9377
3. 3·18 − 1·704
4. 5·3506 − 1·672

5. 4·326 × 7
6. 5·381 × 12
7. 6·753 ÷ 3
8. 8·295 ÷ 5

Estimate and then work out. Check your answer with your estimate.

9. 493·875 + 276·495
10. 727 469 + 192 683
11. 81 920·8 − 47 549·2
12. 6217·34 − 3983·58

13. 7362·45 × 8
14. 964·918 × 6
15. 697 122 ÷ 9
16. 40 527·6 ÷ 12

TARGET To write a remainder as a fraction in its simplest form.

Examples

$94 \div 8 = 11\frac{\cancel{6}}{8}\frac{3}{4}$

$80 \div 12 = 6\frac{\cancel{8}}{\cancel{12}}\frac{2}{3}$

$2454 \div 9$

$2\ 7\ 2\frac{\cancel{6}}{9}\frac{2}{3}$

$9\overline{)24^65^24}$

$5316 \div 15$

$354\frac{\cancel{6}}{\cancel{15}}\frac{2}{5}$

$15\overline{)5316}$

$\underline{45}$

81

$\underline{75}$

66

$\underline{60}$

6

A

Write the answer only, giving the remainder as a fraction.

1. $25 \div 4$
2. $67 \div 7$
3. $89 \div 10$
4. $31 \div 2$
5. $115 \div 12$
6. $43 \div 6$
7. $104 \div 9$
8. $40 \div 3$
9. $72 \div 11$
10. $84 \div 5$
11. $69 \div 8$
12. $52 \div 7$

Work out. Give the remainder as a fraction.

13. $257 \div 3$
14. $379 \div 8$
15. $602 \div 11$
16. $443 \div 6$
17. $191 \div 2$
18. $560 \div 9$
19. $917 \div 12$
20. $286 \div 5$
21. $453 \div 7$
22. $307 \div 4$
23. $599 \div 10$
24. $763 \div 8$

25. There are six eggs in each box. How many boxes is 233 eggs?

26. How many weeks is 200 days?

B

Give the remainder as a fraction in its simplest form.

1. $2075 \div 6$
2. $4254 \div 9$
3. $5721 \div 7$
4. $3783 \div 5$
5. $1918 \div 8$
6. $6764 \div 12$
7. $1784 \div 14$
8. $5365 \div 25$
9. $7857 \div 18$
10. $2836 \div 32$
11. $6620 \div 13$
12. $9930 \div 29$

13. In one year Shirley takes 1460 pills. Her pills are in boxes of 16. How many boxes has she used?

14. How many days are there in 1000 hours?

C

Give the remainder as a fraction in its simplest form.

1. $64\,200 \div 11$
2. $74\,190 \div 8$
3. $40\,246 \div 6$
4. $55\,389 \div 12$
5. $31\,936 \div 7$
6. $62\,958 \div 9$
7. $28\,700 \div 23$
8. $38\,358 \div 41$
9. $89\,036 \div 37$
10. $72\,264 \div 16$
11. $97\,383 \div 52$
12. $61\,468 \div 26$

13. There are 36 nails in each packet. How many packets is 22\,887 nails?

14. Each loaf makes 12 sandwiches. In one year a cafe makes 20\,742 sandwiches. How many loaves have they used?

TARGET To determine whether to round up or down after division.

Examples

There are 12 crayons in each packet.
How many packets are needed for 200 crayons?
200 ÷ 12 = 16 rem. 8 (round up)
Answer: *17 packets are needed.*

There are 12 crayons in each packet.
How many packets can be made from 200 crayons?
200 ÷ 12 = 16 rem. 8 (round down)
Answer: *16 packets can be made.*

A

1. How many pairs of socks can be made from 57 socks?

2. Ten children can sit on each bench. How many benches are needed for 184 children?

3. Each box holds six eggs. How many boxes are needed for 440 eggs?

4. There are 116 straws in a box. How many triangular prisms can be made without cutting any of the straws?

5. The 126 guests at a wedding sit at tables of 8. How many tables are needed?

6. How many groups of twelve can be made from 250 people?

7. Grace saves £50 each week. How many weeks will it take her to save £720?

B

1. Eugene reads 15 pages of his book every day. How many days will it take him to read all 207 pages?

2. A nursery sows 2340 seeds in trays of 8. How many trays are needed?

3. Each packet contains 12 sweets. How many packets can be made from 5000 sweets?

4. Hamish carefully measures out 30 g of porridge for his breakfast every morning. How many breakfasts will his 800 g packet provide?

5. A school needs 1860 exercise books. How many packets of 25 books will need to be bought?

6. Each trip, a river ferry carries 36 cars. How many trips are needed to carry 584 cars?

7. How many 45 ml bottles of perfume can be made from 8 litres?

C

1. Eighteen cans are packed into each box. How many boxes are needed for 27 612 cans?

2. Tables cost £29 each. How many can a school buy for £5000?

3. There are 24 biscuits in each packet. How many packets can be made from 15 150 biscuits?

4. The Royal Mint produces 10 000 new coins They are put into bags of 35. How many bags are needed?

5. Each ball bearing weighs 52 g. How many can be made from 12 kilograms of steel?

6. It will cost £20 000 to stage a concert. How many £37 tickets will need to be sold before the organisers begin to make a profit?

7. Cement is sold in 22 kg bags. How many bags can be filled from 16 400 kg?

TARGET   To practise and apply known multiplication/division facts.

A

What is

1. 3×11
2. 8×5
3. 6×12
4. 7×8
5. 5×6
6. 9×4
7. 80×11
8. 60×7
9. 30×8
10. 90×12
11. 80×9
12. 90×7
13. $66 \div 11$
14. $21 \div 7$
15. $28 \div 4$
16. $96 \div 12$
17. $35 \div 5$
18. $32 \div 8$
19. $180 \div 3$
20. $420 \div 7$
21. $200 \div 4$
22. $1100 \div 11$
23. $600 \div 12$
24. $480 \div 6$

B

Copy and complete.

1. $\square \times 5 = 45$
2. $\square \times 9 = 540$
3. $\square \div 4 = 60$
4. $\square \div 3 = 80$
5. $\square \times 7 = 28$
6. $\square \times 12 = 720$
7. $\square \div 9 = 30$
8. $\square \div 7 = 9$
9. $\square \times 11 = 1210$
10. $\square \times 8 = 48$
11. $\square \div 12 = 110$
12. $\square \div 8 = 8$

Write the answer only.

13. 90×110
14. 500×7
15. 80×6
16. 120×120
17. 7×20
18. 800×9
19. 30×80
20. 1100×11
21. 90×4
22. 60×60
23. 700×9
24. 8×1200
25. $2700 \div 3$
26. $720 \div 80$
27. $1320 \div 12$
28. $450 \div 9$
29. $400 \div 50$
30. $1800 \div 1$
31. $2400 \div 6$
32. $7700 \div 11$
33. $560 \div 8$
34. $4500 \div 90$
35. $1440 \div 120$
36. $5600 \div 7$

C

Copy and complete.

1. $\square \times 7 = 630$
2. $\square \times 12 = 10\,800$
3. $\square \div 60 = 90$
4. $\square \div 9 = 9000$
5. $\square \times 110 = 13\,200$
6. $\square \times 4 = 36\,000$
7. $\square \div 7 = 700$
8. $\square \div 30 = 80$
9. $\square \times 60 = 420$
10. $\square \times 9 = 7200$
11. $\square \div 120 = 12$
12. $\square \div 80 = 700$

Write the answer only.

13. 0.3×6
14. 0.8×4
15. 1.1×11
16. 0.5×9
17. 0.7×12
18. 0.6×7
19. 0.9×8
20. 0.6×6
21. 1.2×11
22. 0.4×7
23. 0.8×5
24. 0.4×12
25. $8.8 \div 11$
26. $2.1 \div 3$
27. $5.4 \div 9$
28. $13.2 \div 12$
29. $4.8 \div 6$
30. $1.8 \div 2$
31. $6.4 \div 8$
32. $12.1 \div 11$
33. $4.2 \div 7$
34. $6.3 \div 9$
35. $14.4 \div 12$
36. $4 \div 8$

TARGET To practise and apply known multiplication/division facts.

A

What is

1. 8×12
2. 60×3
3. 9×70
4. 30×90
5. 60×5
6. 7×800
7. 40×70
8. 6×110
9. 9×60
10. 500×12
11. 70×90
12. 30×8
13. $27 \div 3$
14. $240 \div 6$
15. $400 \div 80$
16. $720 \div 12$
17. $1400 \div 7$
18. $720 \div 9$
19. $8800 \div 11$
20. $480 \div 80$
21. $420 \div 6$
22. $1080 \div 12$
23. $56 \div 7$
24. $450 \div 90$

B

Copy and complete.

1. $\square \times 12 = 96$
2. $\square \times 8 = 720$
3. $\square \times 6 = 3600$
4. $\square \times 50 = 450$
5. $\square \times 90 = 7200$
6. $\square \times 11 = 1320$
7. $\square \div 3 = 7$
8. $\square \div 6 = 900$
9. $\square \div 12 = 120$
10. $\square \div 40 = 70$
11. $\square \div 80 = 8$
12. $\square \div 700 = 7$

Write the answer only.

13. 70×5
14. 60×70
15. 800×3
16. 90×9
17. 1100×120
18. 8×80
19. 50×90
20. 80×700
21. 9×400
22. 70×1100
23. 60×8
24. 4×1200
25. $121 \div 11$
26. $1800 \div 3$
27. $7200 \div 800$
28. $2800 \div 700$
29. $60\,000 \div 1200$
30. $630 \div 9$
31. $3000 \div 60$
32. $13\,200 \div 1100$
33. $14\,400 \div 12$
34. $4800 \div 80$
35. $400 \div 50$
36. $54\,000 \div 90$

C

Copy and complete.

1. $\square \times 12 = 360$
2. $\square \times 70 = 4200$
3. $\square \times 9 = 6300$
4. $\square \times 800 = 7200$
5. $\square \times 110 = 121\,000$
6. $\square \times 120 = 13\,200$
7. $\square \div 700 = 7$
8. $\square \div 1100 = 90$
9. $\square \div 8 = 500$
10. $\square \div 90 = 400$
11. $\square \div 1200 = 80$
12. $\square \div 60 = 90$

Write the answer only.

13. 7×0.8
14. 6×0.4
15. 9×1.2
16. 5×0.7
17. 11×1.1
18. 8×0.9
19. 0.5×5
20. 0.8×3
21. 0.6×8
22. 0.3×9
23. 1.1×12
24. 0.7×9
25. $8.4 \div 12$
26. $4.5 \div 5$
27. $4.2 \div 6$
28. $3.2 \div 8$
29. $13.2 \div 11$
30. $5.6 \div 7$
31. $8.1 \div 9$
32. $2.1 \div 3$
33. $6.4 \div 8$
34. $3.6 \div 4$
35. $14.4 \div 12$
36. $5.4 \div 6$

TARGET To practise and apply known multiplication/division facts.

A

What is

1. 6×4
2. 5×8
3. 2×11
4. 4×7
5. $30 \div 5$
6. $21 \div 7$
7. $48 \div 12$
8. $77 \div 11$
9. 9×30
10. 11×120
11. 7×600
12. 5×50
13. $540 \div 9$
14. $320 \div 4$
15. $12\,100 \div 11$
16. $8400 \div 12$
17. 60×7
18. 40×9
19. 700×11
20. 300×12
21. $450 \div 90$
22. $560 \div 70$
23. $7200 \div 80$
24. $3600 \div 60$

B

Copy and complete.

1. $\square \times 6 = 30$
2. $\square \times 3 = 24$
3. $\square \div 9 = 7$
4. $\square \div 11 = 11$
5. $\square \times 7 = 350$
6. $\square \times 12 = 10\,800$
7. $\square \div 80 = 4$
8. $\square \div 70 = 70$
9. $\square \times 110 = 1320$
10. $\square \times 80 = 6400$
11. $\square \div 6 = 80$
12. $\square \div 120 = 70$

Write the answer only.

13. 3×0.7
14. 8×0.9
15. 12×1.2
16. 9×0.5
17. 3×0.8
18. 9×0.6
19. 0.6×3
20. 0.8×7
21. 1.2×11
22. 0.7×4
23. 0.5×12
24. 0.9×9
25. $2.0 \div 5$
26. $4 \div 8$
27. $13.2 \div 12$
28. $2.4 \div 4$
29. $2.8 \div 7$
30. $6.6 \div 11$
31. $2.7 \div 3$
32. $4.2 \div 6$
33. $3.6 \div 9$
34. $12.1 \div 11$
35. $6.3 \div 7$
36. $14.4 \div 12$

C

Copy and complete.

1. $\square \times 9 = 2.7$
2. $\square \times 0.6 = 12$
3. $\square \div 5 = 0.6$
4. $\square \div 1.2 = 8$
5. $\square \times 11 = 13.2$
6. $\square \times 0.7 = 63$
7. $\square \div 6 = 0.4$
8. $\square \div 0.8 = 9$
9. $\square \times 12 = 6$
10. $\square \times 0.5 = 7$
11. $\square \div 11 = 0.9$
12. $\square \div 0.7 = 8$

Write the answer only.

13. 8×1.2
14. 11×0.11
15. 0.7×6
16. 0.9×0.4
17. 0.8×8
18. 0.12×12
19. 4×0.7
20. 8×0.09
21. 0.9×0.7
22. 0.08×6
23. 1.2×11
24. 0.7×0.7
25. $0.56 \div 0.07$
26. $7.2 \div 12$
27. $81 \div 0.9$
28. $5.4 \div 0.6$
29. $12.1 \div 11$
30. $0.4 \div 8$
31. $4.9 \div 0.7$
32. $32 \div 0.4$
33. $0.36 \div 6$
34. $1.32 \div 12$
35. $54 \div 0.9$
36. $6.4 \div 0.8$

TARGET To practise and apply known multiplication/division facts.

A

What is

1. 4×6
2. 7×9
3. 9×5
4. 3×8

5. 8×70
6. 5×30
7. 7×60
8. 6×40

9. 50×8
10. 90×2
11. 30×9
12. 60×7

13. $48 \div 8$
14. $18 \div 6$
15. $27 \div 3$
16. $28 \div 7$

17. $540 \div 9$
18. $280 \div 4$
19. $480 \div 6$
20. $160 \div 2$

21. $360 \div 90$
22. $630 \div 70$
23. $350 \div 50$
24. $720 \div 80$

B

Write the answer only.

1. 9×0.7
2. 6×0.2
3. 5×0.9
4. 8×0.8

5. 6×0.5
6. 9×0.6
7. 0.8×9
8. 0.9×4

9. 0.7×7
10. 0.6×3
11. 0.9×8
12. 0.8×6

13. $6.3 \div 9$
14. $3.6 \div 6$
15. $2.4 \div 3$
16. $5.6 \div 7$

17. $1.4 \div 2$
18. $4.8 \div 8$
19. $4.2 \div 6$
20. $4 \div 5$

21. $3.5 \div 7$
22. $5.4 \div 9$
23. $3.2 \div 4$
24. $5.6 \div 8$

Copy and complete.

25. $\square \times 6 = 4.8$
26. $\square \times 2 = 1.8$
27. $\square \times 9 = 2.7$
28. $\square \times 0.7 = 4.2$

29. $\square \times 0.4 = 2.4$
30. $\square \times 0.8 = 5.6$
31. $\square \div 9 = 0.9$
32. $\square \div 5 = 0.8$

33. $\square \div 6 = 0.6$
34. $\square \div 3 = 0.7$
35. $\square \div 8 = 0.9$
36. $\square \div 7 = 0.5$

C

Write the answer only.

1. 0.09×4
2. 0.6×7
3. 0.008×6
4. 0.04×8

5. 0.007×3
6. 0.6×9
7. 9×0.07
8. 8×0.2

9. 7×0.08
10. 9×0.005
11. 3×0.6
12. 8×0.09

13. $0.27 \div 9$
14. $4.8 \div 8$
15. $0.54 \div 6$
16. $0.3 \div 5$

17. $3.5 \div 7$
18. $0.81 \div 9$
19. $0.32 \div 4$
20. $4.2 \div 6$

21. $0.18 \div 3$
22. $0.4 \div 8$
23. $0.36 \div 4$
24. $0.56 \div 7$

Copy and complete.

25. $\square \times 5 = 0.4$
26. $\square \times 8 = 0.72$
27. $\square \times 7 = 2.8$
28. $\square \times 4 = 0.24$

29. $\square \times 9 = 0.63$
30. $\square \times 6 = 4.8$
31. $\square \div 7 = 0.07$
32. $\square \div 3 = 0.8$

33. $\square \div 9 = 0.03$
34. $\square \div 6 = 0.05$
35. $\square \div 8 = 0.8$
36. $\square \div 9 = 0.09$

TARGET   To develop strategies to work out mental calculations.

Examples

ADDITION AND SUBTRACTION

Partitioning	Adjusting
643 + 270	8·5 − 3·9
643 + 200 + 70	8·5 − 4·0 + 0·1
843 + 70	4·5 + 0·1
913	4·6

Counting Up	Near Doubles
7003 − 4964	6·9 + 7·2
4964 → 4970 6	(7 × 2) − 0·1 + 0·2
4970 → 5000 30	14 − 0·1 + 0·2
5000 → 7003 2003	14 + 0·1
7003 − 4964 = 2039	14·1

MULTIPLICATION AND DIVISION

Using factors	Partitioning
26 × 18	7·4 × 7
26 × 2 × 3 × 3	(7 × 7) + (0·4 × 7)
52 × 3 × 3	49 + 2·8
156 × 3	51·8
468	

Multiply By 49/51 etc.	Doubling/halving
19 × 51	36 × 15
(19 × 50) + (19 × 1)	(36 × 30) ÷ 2
950 + 19	1080 ÷ 2
969	540

A

Choose one method for each group of six problems.

1	7 × 19	25	39 + 42
2	13 × 21	26	73 + 68
3	15 × 19	27	47 + 51
4	18 × 21	28	3·4 + 3·3
5	22 × 19	29	2·3 + 2·1
6	16 × 21	30	4·9 + 5·2
7	2·4 + 1·1	31	24 × 5
8	5·8 − 1·1	32	35 × 5
9	8·3 + 0·9	33	28 × 50
10	6·7 − 0·9	34	17 × 50
11	3·5 − 1·1	35	6 × 15
12	9·2 + 0·9	36	14 × 15
13	403 − 195	37	37 × 4
14	807 − 472	38	56 × 5
15	702 − 281	39	29 × 6
16	5000 − 1991	40	45 × 7
17	9000 − 4984	41	24 × 8
18	6008 − 3996	42	38 × 9
19	13 × 6	43	134 + 52
20	16 × 8	44	327 + 44
21	17 × 9	45	265 + 38
22	180 ÷ 12	46	582 − 64
23	240 ÷ 15	47	337 − 46
24	216 ÷ 12	48	415 − 78

B

Choose one method for each group of six problems.

1. 27×15
2. 36×15
3. 23×25
4. 38×25
5. 14×26
6. 18×38

7. $304 + 298$
8. $197 + 202$
9. $403 + 395$
10. $3.9 + 3.7$
11. $4.8 + 5.3$
12. $3.3 + 2.9$

13. 22×14
14. 19×27
15. 23×21
16. $252 \div 18$
17. $408 \div 24$
18. $288 \div 16$

19. $705 - 477$
20. $921 - 394$
21. $617 - 272$
22. $8000 - 3588$
23. $5004 - 2963$
24. $9018 - 5949$

25. $5700 + 2800$
26. $0.4 + 0.32$
27. $0.57 + 0.26$
28. $9300 - 4600$
29. $0.7 - 0.24$
30. $0.82 - 0.58$

31. 13×49
32. 18×51
33. 22×49
34. 14×101
35. 17×99
36. 23×101

37. $4.5 + 1.9$
38. $7.3 - 2.9$
39. $5.6 + 4.1$
40. $9.8 - 2.1$
41. $3.4 + 3.9$
42. $6.7 - 4.1$

43. 54×6
44. 87×8
45. 73×9
46. 6.5×7
47. 4.9×8
48. 9.7×6

C

Choose one method for each group of six problems.

1. $\square - 30.5 = 29.7$
2. $\square - 18.3 = 20.1$
3. $\square - 41.2 = 39.5$
4. $\square - 48.9 = 51.4$
5. $\square - 29.4 = 31.6$
6. $\square - 38.2 = 40.3$

7. 34×14
8. 2.7×18
9. 4.9×15
10. 56×2.5
11. 35×4.8
12. 45×3.9

13. $\square + 3800 = 7100$
14. $\square + 7.6 = 18.35$
15. $\square + 0.53 = 2.17$
16. $\square - 4500 = 8800$
17. $\square - 5.7 = 9.46$
18. $\square - 0.38 = 0.92$

19. 16×5.4
20. 21×2.7
21. 12×0.63
22. $4.9 \div 14$
23. $50.4 \div 24$
24. $4.32 \div 18$

25. $\square + 4.2 = 7.4$
26. $\square + 5.9 = 9.6$
27. $\square + 4.8 = 5.3$
28. $\square + 6.1 = 11.7$
29. $\square + 3.9 = 4.8$
30. $\square + 7.2 = 8.5$

31. $\square \div 7 = 4.8$
32. $\square \div 9 = 7.6$
33. $\square \div 8 = 5.9$
34. $\square \div 6 = 6.7$
35. $\square \div 7 = 9.5$
36. $\square \div 9 = 8.3$

37. $6200 - \square = 2874$
38. $8100 - \square = 3762$
39. $9300 - \square = 5696$
40. $7200 - \square = 4783$
41. $8400 - \square = 3679$
42. $9100 - \square = 4885$

43. $\square \div 29 = 17$
44. $\square \div 41 = 13$
45. $\square \div 59 = 16$
46. $\square \div 31 = 19$
47. $\square \div 39 = 14$
48. $\square \div 61 = 18$

TARGET   To use mental methods to add and subtract large numbers.

A

Write the answer only.

1 1438 + 700
2 5307 + 2008
3 29 824 + 480
4 1125 − 500
5 76 350 − 20 800
6 8240 − 75

7 35 909 + 5300
8 46 713 + 5070
9 31 328 + 907
10 12 519 − 6400
11 508 250 − 302
12 173 490 − 6009

13 18 075 + 38
14 292 160 + 24 000
15 558 176 + 9009
16 26 125 − 970
17 314 008 − 5400
18 327 179 − 40 030

B

Write the answer only.

1 178 345 + 5006
2 2 046 913 + 80 400
3 527 830 + 970
4 65 204 + 35 000

5 139 090 − 70 006
6 9 712 451 − 5090
7 381 629 − 3600
8 1 044 372 − 180 000

9 579 144 + 40 009
10 305 817 + 200 300
11 127 266 + 48
12 39 588 + 5900

13 4 052 400 − 9030
14 7 163 425 − 200 900
15 235 897 − 26 000
16 418 200 − 740

C

Write the answer only.

1 350 247 + 80 800
2 6 109 081 + 2 000 060
3 237 425 + 2900
4 9 514 963 + 2 600 000

5 762 390 − 2009
6 1 480 152 − 800 600
7 2 736 879 − 97 000
8 941 500 − 58

9 3 708 654 + 3070
10 10 452 037 + 800 209
11 518 990 + 650
12 4 760 716 + 460 005

13 20 429 240 − 6 080 001
14 153 805 − 90 030
15 61 473 280 − 1 700 000
16 5 093 000 − 5420

TARGET To perform mental calculations involving large numbers and mixed operations.

A

Write the answer only.

1. $(17 + 43) \times 9$
2. $10 \div (109 - 89)$
3. $(80 \times 7) - 99$
4. $64 + (2100 \div 30)$
5. $(1000 - 250) \div 50$
6. $100 \times (5 - 1.9)$

7. $49\,237 + 60\,005$
8. $15\,982 + 4700$
9. $166\,830 + 180$
10. $85\,211 - 7040$
11. $93\,640 - 68$
12. $473\,000 - 370$

13. $(57 + 39) \div 8$
14. $11 \times (47 + 43)$
15. $(220 - 180) \times 12$
16. $840 \div (24 + 46)$
17. $(100 \div 4) + 38$
18. $150 - (13 \times 6)$

B

Write the answer only.

1. $62\,681 + 9050$
2. $1\,570\,354 + 60\,050$
3. $804\,739 + 71$
4. $3\,469\,048 + 570\,000$

5. $(3 \times 45) + (45 \div 3)$
6. $(76 + 124) \times (80 - 27)$
7. $(365 + 75) \div (48 + 62)$
8. $(90 \times 90) - (6000 \div 5)$

9. $235\,173 - 90\,700$
10. $4\,716\,926 - 5070$
11. $304\,052 - 6200$
12. $2\,155\,230 - 48\,000$

13. $(71 - 45) \times (50 - 29)$
14. $(480 \div 12) + (8 \times 14)$
15. $(111 - 39) \div (5.1 + 3.9)$
16. $(25 \times 16) - (0.25 \times 1000)$

C

Write the answer only.

1. $12\,823\,176 + 207\,000$
2. $26\,164\,509 + 9\,000\,502$
3. $5\,078\,943 + 980$
4. $8\,497\,082 + 59\,040$

5. $20\,136\,500 - 800\,070$
6. $9\,310\,417 - 60\,909$
7. $71\,265\,804 - 740\,020$
8. $3\,509\,550 - 599$

9. $(0.4 \times 15) - (12.5 \div 100)$
10. $(1 - 0.85) \times (1.8 \times 5)$
11. $(2 \div 8) + (0.025 \times 8)$
12. $(0.1 - 0.044) \div (0.35 \times 20)$

13. $4 + (7 \times 13) - (128 \div 8)$
14. $500 - (240 \div 16) + (16 \times 16)$
15. $10 - (0.038 \times 100) - (4 \div 5)$
16. $4.8 + (7.2 \div 6) + (1.2 \times 30)$

TARGET   To identify common multiples.

Multiples are the numbers in a multiplication table. If we make separate lists of the multiples of two numbers some of their multiples will be common to both lists.

Examples

Multiples of 4   4, 8, 12, 16, 20, 24, 28, 32, 36, 40, … 60, … 80, …

Multiples of 5   5, 10, 15, 20, 25, 30, 35, 40, 45, 50, 55, 60, … 80, …

Common Multiples   The common multiples of 4 and 5 are 20, 40, 60, 80 and so on.

Lowest Common Multiple   The lowest common multiple of 4 and 5 is 20.

A

Write down the first six multiples of:

1 5   **3** 11

2 8   **4** 20.

Write Yes or No.

5 Is 47 a multiple of 2?

6 Is 39 a multiple of 3?

7 Is 36 a multiple of 4?

8 Is 58 a multiple of 5?

9 Is 72 a multiple of 6?

10 Is 72 a multiple of 7?

11 Is 72 a multiple of 8?

12 Is 72 a multiple of 9?

13 Is 105 a multiple of 10?

14 Is 330 a multiple of 11?

15 Is 132 a multiple of 12?

16 Is 100 a multiple of 15?

17 Find
   a) the 20th multiple of 6
   b) the 8th multiple of 15.

B

Find two numbers that are common multiples of:

1 2 and 5   **5** 4 and 7

2 2 and 7   **6** 5 and 6

3 3 and 5   **7** 2 and 11

4 3 and 8   **8** 3 and 7.

Find the lowest common multiple of:

9 2 and 9   **13** 4 and 6

10 3 and 11   **14** 6 and 10

11 3 and 4   **15** 8 and 6

12 6 and 7   **16** 10 and 8.

Find the lowest common multiple of each group of numbers.

17 3, 6 and 12

18 4, 6 and 12

19 2, 3 and 4

20 2, 3 and 5

21 2, 4 and 8

22 3, 4 and 8

23 The 9th multiple of 16 is the 8th multiple of which number?

C

Find three numbers that are multiples of:

1 3 and 4   **5** 5 and 7

2 2 and 9   **6** 6 and 8

3 3 and 11   **7** 4 and 9

4 4 and 5   **8** 6 and 10.

Find the lowest common multiple of:

9 2 and 13   **13** 10 and 12

10 4 and 14   **14** 15 and 25

11 5 and 11   **15** 8 and 12

12 4 and 10   **16** 16 and 18.

Find the lowest common multiple of each group of numbers.

17 3, 5 and 6

18 4, 5 and 6

19 2, 4 and 7

20 3, 4 and 7

21 3, 4 and 8

22 3, 5 and 8

23 The 12th multiple of 44 is the 11th multiple of which number?

TARGET To identify common factors and prime numbers.

Examples

Factors of 16   1, 2, 4, 8, 16
Factors of 40   1, 2, 4, 5, 8, 10, 20, 40

Common factors   1, 2, 4, 8

Highest common factor   8

Prime numbers – 2 factors only e.g. 23
Composite numbers – more than 2 factors e.g. 24

Prime factors can be found by
using a factor tree.
Prime factors of 24: 2 × 2 × 2 × 3

A

Find all the factors of each number. The number of factors is shown in brackets.

1 12 (6)   7 55 (4)
2 28 (6)   8 18 (6)
3 25 (3)   9 100 (9)
4 30 (8)   10 54 (8)
5 32 (6)   11 49 (3)
6 27 (4)   12 60 (12)

Write down the number(s) in each group which are not prime numbers.

13 7 8 9 10
14 17 18 19 20
15 23 24 25 26
16 31 32 33 34

17 46 47 48 49
18 56 57 58 59
19 70 71 72 73
20 88 89 90 91

21 The first five prime numbers are:
    2, 3, 5, 7, 11
    Write down the next ten prime numbers.

B

For each pair of numbers find:
a) the common factors
b) the highest common factor.

1 6, 15   7 36, 96
2 16, 24   8 40, 100
3 45, 60   9 28, 70
4 12, 18   10 32, 72
5 8, 12   11 18, 30
6 27, 36   12 24, 60

13 List all the prime numbers below 100. There are 25.

Explain why these numbers are composite numbers.

14 738   18 1990
15 273   19 177
16 415   20 301
17 119   21 143

Find all the prime factors of:

22 50   26 52
23 36   27 132
24 28   28 90
25 60   29 72.

C

For each group of numbers find:
a) the common factors
b) the highest common factor.

1 20, 32, 60
2 225, 450, 600
3 32, 64, 80
4 9, 27, 33
5 56, 96, 120
6 36, 54, 108
7 30, 48, 84
8 45, 72, 135

Explain why these numbers are composite numbers.

9 253   11 1923
10 221   12 361

Find all the prime numbers between:

13 100 and 110
14 130 and 140
15 150 and 160
16 190 and 200.

Find the prime factors of:

17 200   21 182
18 144   22 375
19 162   23 252
20 264   24 440.

TARGET   To use knowledge of the order of operations.

Combining mathematical operations could lead to confusion unless there are clear rules about the order in which they are done.

Example $5 + 3 \times 2$

This could be $5 + 3 \times 2 = 8 \times 2$ or $5 + 3 \times 2 = 5 + 6$
$= 16$ $= 11$

For this reason mathematical operations must be done in this order.

1. Deal with brackets   *Examples* $18 + 4 \times (7 + 5)$ $(10 + 6) \div 2 + 3$
2. Divide and multiply $18 + 4 \times 12$ $16 \div 2 + 3$
3. Add and subtract $18 + 48$ $8 + 3$
                                                    66 11

A

Work out. Show your working.

Remember: $\div / \times$ before $+/-$

1. $3 + 2 \times 4$
2. $9 - 6 \div 3$
3. $4 \times 8 - 6$
4. $20 + 12 \div 4$

5. $15 - 3 \times 2$
6. $24 \div 4 + 2$
7. $60 - 20 \div 5$
8. $12 \times 3 + 7$

9. $97 - 8 \times 9 + 11$
10. $30 \div 6 + 4 \times 5$
11. $4 + 16 \div 2 + 15$
12. $10 \times 2 + 4 \times 3$

13. $120 - 40 \div 8 - 50$
14. $8 + 2 \times 6 - 13$
15. $100 \div 10 - 5 \div 5$
16. $15 - 3 \times 4 - 3$

B

Work out. Show your working.

Remember: Brackets first.

1. $(55 - 4) \times (5 + 5)$
2. $55 - 4 \times 5 + 5$ 46
3. $(20 + 12) \div 4 - 1$ 7
4. $20 + 12 \div 4 - 1$

5. $6 \times (6 - 2) + 9$
6. $6 \times 6 - (2 + 9)$
7. $(24 + 48) \div 8 + 4$ 13
8. $24 + 48 \div (8 + 4)$ 28

9. $42 - (6 + 9) \div 3$ 37
10. $(16 - 8) \times (10 - 6)$ 8
11. $10 + 20 + 30 \times 40$
12. $45 \div (9 - 6) - 6$

13. $(54 - 18) \div (4 + 5)$ 4
14. $16 + 4 \times (3 + 8)$
15. $200 - (5 + 7) \times 7$ 116
16. $(100 - 28) \div (18 - 2)$

72   26

C

Work out. Show your working.

1. $(2 + 7) \times 4 - 10 \div 2$
2. $12 \div 2 + (4 - 2) \times 6$ 18
3. $(40 - 10) \div 5 + 1 \times 12$
4. $16 \times 2 - (8 \times 8) \div 4$

5. $6 \times (3 + 5) - 18 \div 3$ 12
6. $(25 + 75) \div 5 - 4 \times 5$
7. $72 \div (12 - 3) + 6 \times 7$ 56
8. $(10 - 7) \times 9 + 12 \div 2$

Copy and complete by putting in any missing brackets.

9. $10 \times (2 + 6) = 80$
10. $(16 - 10) \div 2 = 3$
11. $(11 - 5) \times (7 + 2) = 54$
12. $9 + (6 \div 3) - 1 = 12$

13. $20 + (25 - 10) \div 3 = 23$
14. $17 - 2 \times (6 + 4) = 150$
15. $60 \div (4 + 8) - 3 = 2$
16. $9 + 15 - 9 \times 3 = 27$

TARGET　To explore the order of operations using brackets.

ORDER OF OPERATIONS　　　　　　***Examples***

1. Deal with brackets　　　$7 \times 8 - 5 + 3$　　　$7 \times 8 - (5 + 3)$　　　$7 \times (8 - 5) + 3$
2. Divide and multiply　　　$56 - 5 + 3$　　　　$7 \times 8 - 8$　　　　$7 \times 3 + 3$
3. Add and subtract　　　　54　　　　　　　$56 - 8$　　　　　$21 + 3$
　　　　　　　　　　　　　　　　　　　　　　48　　　　　　　24

A

Work out the brackets first.

1. $(6 \times 3) + 2$
2. $6 \times (3 + 2)$
3. $(60 \div 10) - 5$
4. $60 \div (10 - 5)$
5. $(12 + 6) \div 2$
6. $12 + (6 \div 2)$

7. $30 - (5 \times 3)$
8. $(30 - 5) \times 3$
9. $24 \div (3 \times 4)$
10. $(24 \div 3) \times 4$
11. $5 \times (8 - 2)$
12. $(5 \times 8) - 2$

13. $(7 + 4) \times 9$
14. $7 + (4 \times 9)$
15. $(50 - 20) \div 10$
16. $50 - (20 \div 10)$
17. $(45 \div 5) + 4$
18. $45 \div (5 + 4)$

B

Put the brackets in the right place to make the calculation correct.

1. $3 \times 8 - 5 = 9$
2. $8 + 12 \div 4 = 5$
3. $60 \div 10 - 4 = 2$
4. $36 - 9 \times 2 = 18$
5. $48 \div 4 \times 3 = 4$

6. $3 + 4 \times 5 = 35$
7. $20 \div 4 + 1 = 6$
8. $48 - 15 \div 3 = 11$
9. $7 \times 6 + 2 = 56$
10. $100 \div 20 \times 2 = 10$

11. $9 + 6 \div 3 = 11$
12. $3 \times 7 - 3 = 18$
13. $8 - 4 \times 2 = 8$
14. $84 \div 12 - 5 = 12$
15. $6 \times 5 + 2 = 42$

C

Place two pairs of brackets to make each calculation correct.

1. $11 - 3 \times 2 = 90 \div 15 + 3$
2. $28 + 12 \div 4 = 2 \times 9 - 4$
3. $5 \times 5 + 3 = 1000 \div 20 + 5$
4. $64 \div 8 - 4 = 3 \times 5 + 1$
5. $104 - 56 \div 4 = 42 - 12 \times 3$

6. $18 + 6 \times 6 = 8 \times 20 - 16$
7. $14 \times 5 - 3 = 10 + 36 \div 2$
8. $75 \div 3 \times 5 = 100 \div 10 - 5$
9. $23 - 7 \times 2 = 8 \times 6 - 2$
10. $36 + 36 \div 9 = 24 - 8 \times 2$

TARGET   To solve multi-step word problems.

Example

A tie shop has 684 ties for sale.
One ninth are sold on Friday.
129 are sold on Saturday.
How many ties are left?

$684 \div 9 = 76$
$129 + 76 = 205$
$684 - 205 = 479$
Answer   *479 ties are left.*

A

1 There are 227 children in a school. Five of the classes in the school have 28 children each. The other three classes each have the same number of children. How many children are there in each of these three classes?

2 There are 200 raffle tickets. Three quarters are sold. 27 more are sold. How many tickets are left?

3 A builder has 500 bricks. He uses 180 in the morning and 50 per cent of the rest in the afternoon. How many bricks has he used?

4 A holiday costs £65 per person per day. How much will it cost five people for two weeks?

5 A rectangle is three times longer than it is wide. It is 42 cm long. What is its perimeter?

B

1 In an election 177 people voted for one of three candidates. Tara received one third of the votes. Drew received 65 votes. How many people voted for Moira?

2 A corner shop opens for 15 hours every weekday, 12 hours on Saturdays and 9 hours on Sunday. How many hours is it open each week?

3 Leah and Nadia both earn £972 per week. Leah saves 30% of her earnings. Nadia saves one third. How much more does Nadia save?

4 During one weekend a store had 13 255 customers. 1879 more came on Saturday than on Sunday. How many customers came on each day?

5 In one week's training a triathlete runs five times further than he swims and cycles four times further than he runs. Altogether he runs 28·6 km. What is the total distance he travels in training?

C

1 In March Edwin earns £2680. In April he earns 7% more. How much does he earn in the two months altogether?

2 A lorry makes three return journeys from London to Holyhead and two return journeys from London to Hull. The distance from London to Holyhead is 246 miles and from London to Hull is 186 miles. What is the lorry's total mileage?

3 There are 1560 people at a concert. Three eighths are men. 45% are women. How many children are in the audience?

4 A rectangle has a perimeter of 23·6 cm. One side is 3·8 cm. What is the area of the rectangle?

5 A car costs £9500 or the buyer can pay a 15% deposit and make eighteen monthly payments of £495. How much is saved by buying the car for £9500?

TARGET   To solve multi-step word problems.

Example

A bicycle frame weighs 12·75 kg. Each wheel weighs 1·85 kg. What is the total weight of the frame and the wheels?

1·85 × 2 = 3·7
12·75 + 3·7 = 16·45
Answer
Total weight is 16·45 kg.

A

1. DVDs cost £9·50. Oscar takes advantage of a buy one and get another for half price offer. How much does he pay for two DVDs?

2. Malik buys three teas and one coffee for £5·40 altogether. Teas cost £1·25. What does the coffee cost?

3. A mobile library has 3268 books. During the week 1374 books are returned and 925 are borrowed. How many books does the library have now?

4. Flora has 1·5 litres of drink. She pours it equally into two jugs. 0·38 litres is used from one jug. How much drink is left in this jug?

5. A wire is 4 m long. 10% is cut off. The rest is cut into four equal lengths. How long is each of these four lengths?

B ✓

1. T-shirts cost £4.35 each. Duane buys four for £12·79. How much has he saved? £3·61

2. Diana makes a muesli with 425 g of oat flakes, 220 g of nuts and 255 g of dried fruit. The mixture provides fifteen portions. How much muesli is in each portion? 60

3. A reel of cable is 62·8 m long. 27·26 m is cut off. A further 9·55 m is used. How much cable is left on the reel? 25·99m

4. There is 0·65 litres of pasta sauce in a jar. There are 12 jars in a box. How much sauce is in six boxes? 46·8L

5. The temperature is 2·6°C at midnight. It falls 3·9°C by dawn before rising 8·5°C by midday. What is the temperature at midday? 7·2

6. There are sixty questions in a test. Melvin gets 70% right. Miles gets five twelfths wrong. How many more questions does Melvin get right than Miles? 7

C ✓

1. A painting has a length of 17·5 cm and a perimeter of 63 cm. What is its area? 245cm²

2. Sadiq needs three planks 2·65 m long and twelve planks 3·4 m long. What is the total length of the planks he needs? 48·75m

3. Claire has read four ninths of the 162 pages in her book. How many more pages will she have to read before she is two thirds of the way through the book? 36

4. Fish costs £6·80 per kilogram. Todd buys 550 g. How much change does he receive from £10? 6·26

5. Four cartons of fruit juice hold 0·74 litres altogether. How many litres of juice are needed for fifty cartons? 9·25

6. One 16·5 kg bag of dog food feeds three corgis for a week. How many kilograms of dog food are needed to feed the 72 corgis in a kennel for a week? 396

TARGET To use common factors to simplify fractions.

To simplify a fraction to its lowest terms divide both the numerator and the denominator by the highest common factor.

Example

$$\frac{12\ (\div 4)}{20\ (\div 4)} = \frac{3}{5}$$

This process is called cancelling. It is shown like this: $\frac{\cancel{12}}{\cancel{20}}\frac{3}{5}$

A

Write the equivalent fractions shown in each diagram.

1

2

3

4

Copy and complete to simplify the fraction to its lowest terms.

5 $\dfrac{6\ (\div 6)}{12\ (\div 6)} = \dfrac{1}{\boxed{}}$

6 $\dfrac{3\ (\div 3)}{9\ (\div 3)} = \dfrac{\boxed{}}{3}$

7 $\dfrac{9\ (\div 3)}{12\ (\div 3)} = \dfrac{\boxed{}}{\boxed{}}$

8 $\dfrac{4\ (\div 2)}{10\ (\div 2)} = \dfrac{\boxed{}}{\boxed{}}$

9 $\dfrac{8\ (\div 4)}{12\ (\div 4)} = \dfrac{\boxed{}}{\boxed{}}$

10 $\dfrac{4\ (\div 4)}{8\ (\div 4)} = \dfrac{\boxed{}}{\boxed{}}$

B

Simplify the fraction shown in each diagram to its lowest terms.

1 **5**

2 **6**

3 **7**

4 **8**

Cancel each fraction to its lowest terms.

9 $\dfrac{8}{10}$ **15** $\dfrac{12}{18}$

10 $\dfrac{3}{9}$ **16** $\dfrac{6}{8}$

11 $\dfrac{10}{25}$ **17** $\dfrac{10}{12}$

12 $\dfrac{8}{12}$ **18** $\dfrac{16}{20}$

13 $\dfrac{2}{8}$ **19** $\dfrac{7}{21}$

14 $\dfrac{70}{100}$ **20** $\dfrac{6}{9}$

C

Cancel each fraction to its lowest terms.

1 $\dfrac{4}{16}$ **11** $\dfrac{16}{40}$

2 $\dfrac{30}{100}$ **12** $\dfrac{80}{100}$

3 $\dfrac{15}{20}$ **13** $\dfrac{15}{18}$

4 $\dfrac{6}{18}$ **14** $\dfrac{14}{24}$

5 $\dfrac{85}{100}$ **15** $\dfrac{15}{25}$

6 $\dfrac{42}{48}$ **16** $\dfrac{35}{50}$

7 $\dfrac{21}{35}$ **17** $\dfrac{30}{96}$

8 $\dfrac{44}{100}$ **18** $\dfrac{54}{81}$

9 $\dfrac{16}{24}$ **19** $\dfrac{14}{16}$

10 $\dfrac{20}{36}$ **20** $\dfrac{32}{72}$

Write >, < or = in each box.

21 $\dfrac{12}{24}\ \boxed{}\ \dfrac{3}{5}$ **25** $\dfrac{12}{30}\ \boxed{}\ \dfrac{3}{8}$

22 $\dfrac{4}{5}\ \boxed{}\ \dfrac{16}{20}$ **26** $\dfrac{2}{3}\ \boxed{}\ \dfrac{15}{20}$

23 $\dfrac{12}{36}\ \boxed{}\ \dfrac{1}{4}$ **27** $\dfrac{8}{32}\ \boxed{}\ \dfrac{2}{10}$

24 $\dfrac{3}{4}\ \boxed{}\ \dfrac{21}{24}$ **28** $\dfrac{3}{5}\ \boxed{}\ \dfrac{24}{40}$

TARGET   To use the highest common factor to simplify fractions.

To cancel a fraction divide both the numerator and the denominator by the highest common factor (HCF).

Examples

$\frac{8}{\cancel{12}}$ $\frac{2}{3}$ (HCF is 4) $\frac{\cancel{9}}{\cancel{15}}$ $\frac{3}{5}$ (HCF is 3)

A

Complete each pair of fractions.

1 $\frac{4}{8} = \frac{1}{\square}$ **2** $\frac{2}{8} = \frac{1}{\square}$

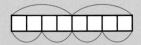

3 $\frac{4}{12} = \frac{1}{\square}$ **4** $\frac{3}{12} = \frac{1}{\square}$

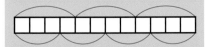

5 $\frac{2}{10} = \frac{1}{\square}$ **6** $\frac{6}{10} = \frac{\square}{\square}$

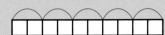

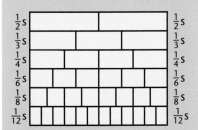

Use the fraction chart.
Copy and complete.

7 $\frac{2}{12} = \frac{\square}{6}$ **11** $\frac{9}{12} = \frac{\square}{4}$

8 $\frac{4}{12} = \frac{\square}{3}$ **12** $\frac{3}{6} = \frac{\square}{2}$

9 $\frac{2}{8} = \frac{\square}{4}$ **13** $\frac{8}{12} = \frac{\square}{3}$

10 $\frac{4}{6} = \frac{\square}{3}$ **14** $\frac{6}{8} = \frac{\square}{4}$

B

1

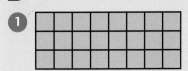

What fraction of 24 is:

a) 3   c) 8
b) 9   d) 16?

2

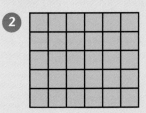

What fraction of 30 is:

a) 6   c) 5
b) 24   d) 25?

Cancel each fraction into its simplest form.

3 $\frac{3}{12}$ **11** $\frac{5}{10}$

4 $\frac{6}{9}$ **12** $\frac{10}{12}$

5 $\frac{4}{8}$ **13** $\frac{12}{16}$

6 $\frac{6}{15}$ **14** $\frac{75}{100}$

7 $\frac{90}{100}$ **15** $\frac{6}{10}$

8 $\frac{2}{6}$ **16** $\frac{14}{20}$

9 $\frac{2}{16}$ **17** $\frac{30}{100}$

10 $\frac{12}{18}$ **18** $\frac{20}{25}$

C

1 What fraction of 20 is:

a) 2   c) 5
b) 14   d) 15?

2 What fraction of 80 is:

a) 8   c) 10
b) 4   d) 50?

3 What fraction of 45 is:

a) 9   c) 27
b) 5   d) 20?

4 What fraction of £1 is:

a) 5p   c) 20p
b) 95p   d) 80p?

5 What fraction of 1 km is:

a) 50 m   c) 25 m
b) 650 m   d) 175 m?

6 Julia has £48.
She spends £18.
What fraction of her money is left?

7 A bottle of lemonade holds 1 litre.
350 ml is used.
What fraction is left?

8 A bag holds 75 kg of potatoes. 45 kg is used.
What fraction is left?

TARGET To use common multiples to find equivalent fractions and common factors to simplify fractions.

Examples A fraction can be changed to an equivalent fraction by:

cancelling using common factors $\dfrac{\cancel{18}^{\,3}}{\cancel{30}_{\,5}}$

multiplying using common multiples. $\dfrac{2\ (\times 5)}{3\ (\times 5)} = \dfrac{10}{15}$

A

Write the equivalent fractions shown by the shaded area in each pair of diagrams.

1
3
5

2
4
6

B

Continue these fraction chains for five further terms.

1 $\dfrac{1}{4} = \dfrac{2}{8} = \dfrac{3}{12}$

2 $\dfrac{2}{3} = \dfrac{4}{6} = \dfrac{6}{9}$

3 $\dfrac{1}{6} = \dfrac{2}{12} = \dfrac{3}{18}$

4 $\dfrac{3}{10} = \dfrac{6}{20} = \dfrac{9}{30}$

5 $\dfrac{5}{12} = \dfrac{10}{24} = \dfrac{15}{36}$

Copy and complete these equivalent fractions.

6 $\dfrac{2}{3} = \dfrac{8}{\square}$

7 $\dfrac{3}{4} = \dfrac{15}{\square}$

8 $\dfrac{3}{7} = \dfrac{6}{\square}$

9 $\dfrac{5}{6} = \dfrac{15}{\square}$

10 $\dfrac{7}{8} = \dfrac{42}{\square}$

11 $\dfrac{2}{5} = \dfrac{\square}{100}$

12 $\dfrac{4}{9} = \dfrac{\square}{36}$

13 $\dfrac{8}{25} = \dfrac{\square}{200}$

14 $\dfrac{7}{12} = \dfrac{\square}{60}$

15 $\dfrac{3}{4} = \dfrac{\square}{100}$

Simplify each fraction by cancelling.

16 $\dfrac{12}{14}$

17 $\dfrac{15}{25}$

18 $\dfrac{44}{48}$

19 $\dfrac{35}{100}$

20 $\dfrac{16}{24}$

21 $\dfrac{25}{30}$

22 $\dfrac{750}{1000}$

23 $\dfrac{12}{16}$

24 $\dfrac{9}{24}$

25 $\dfrac{68}{100}$

C

Pick out the letters above the fractions equivalent to the fraction in the brackets.
Rearrange these letters to find a European capital city.

1

D	I	S	E	N	O	L	R	M	B	
$\frac{12}{15}$	$\frac{9}{12}$	$\frac{4}{6}$	$\frac{27}{36}$	$\frac{15}{20}$	$\frac{60}{100}$	$\frac{21}{28}$	$\frac{6}{8}$	$\frac{10}{15}$	$\frac{12}{16}$	$\left(\frac{3}{4}\right)$

2

A	T	S	P	N	A	W	I	R	W	
$\frac{4}{8}$	$\frac{12}{20}$	$\frac{7}{14}$	$\frac{20}{50}$	$\frac{8}{15}$	$\frac{3}{6}$	$\frac{50}{100}$	$\frac{6}{10}$	$\frac{15}{30}$	$\frac{9}{18}$	$\left(\frac{1}{2}\right)$

3

A	E	M	G	N	D	I	N	R	V	
$\frac{8}{20}$	$\frac{14}{35}$	$\frac{12}{25}$	$\frac{20}{60}$	$\frac{4}{10}$	$\frac{15}{40}$	$\frac{10}{25}$	$\frac{18}{45}$	$\frac{25}{80}$	$\frac{6}{15}$	$\left(\frac{2}{5}\right)$

4

S	A	L	I	N	P	E	T	R	H	
$\frac{25}{30}$	$\frac{10}{12}$	$\frac{40}{45}$	$\frac{50}{54}$	$\frac{20}{24}$	$\frac{45}{50}$	$\frac{75}{90}$	$\frac{15}{18}$	$\frac{25}{36}$	$\frac{35}{42}$	$\left(\frac{5}{6}\right)$

5 Now make up a similar problem of your own.

TARGET To compare and order fractions, including improper fractions.

Examples

Which fraction is larger:

1 $\frac{4}{5}$ or $\frac{7}{10}$

$\frac{8}{10}$ or $\frac{7}{10}$

$\frac{4}{5}$ is larger

2 $\frac{7}{4}$ or $\frac{11}{6}$

$\frac{21}{12}$ or $\frac{22}{12}$

$\frac{11}{6}$ is larger

Arrange $\frac{3}{4}, \frac{3}{2}, \frac{4}{3}, \frac{5}{6}$ in ascending order.

$\frac{3}{4} = \frac{9}{12}$ $\frac{3}{2} = \frac{18}{12}$ $\frac{4}{3} = \frac{16}{12}$ $\frac{5}{6} = \frac{10}{12}$

The correct order is $\frac{3}{4}, \frac{5}{6}, \frac{4}{3}, \frac{3}{2}$.

A

1 Which of the fractions in the box are:
   a) less than half
   b) one half
   c) between half and 1
   d) greater than 1?

| $\frac{40}{100}$ | $\frac{4}{6}$ | $\frac{13}{12}$ | $\frac{10}{40}$ | $\frac{25}{50}$ |
| $\frac{19}{16}$ | $\frac{8}{14}$ | $\frac{4}{8}$ | $\frac{25}{20}$ | $\frac{3}{7}$ |

Copy and complete to find the larger fraction.

2 $\frac{5}{8}$ or $\frac{1}{2} \rightarrow \frac{5}{8}$ or $\frac{\square}{8}$

   $\square$ is larger.

3 $\frac{3}{10}$ or $\frac{2}{5} \rightarrow \frac{3}{10}$ or $\frac{\square}{10}$

   $\square$ is larger.

4 $\frac{7}{12}$ or $\frac{3}{4} \rightarrow \frac{7}{12}$ or $\frac{\square}{12}$

   $\square$ is larger.

5 $\frac{1}{3}$ or $\frac{2}{9} \rightarrow \frac{\square}{9}$ or $\frac{2}{9}$

   $\square$ is larger.

Write > or < in each box.

6 $\frac{1}{2} \square \frac{4}{10}$ **10** $\frac{2}{12} \square \frac{1}{4}$

7 $\frac{3}{4} \square \frac{7}{8}$ **11** $\frac{4}{7} \square \frac{1}{2}$

8 $\frac{1}{3} \square \frac{3}{6}$ **12** $\frac{6}{12} \square \frac{2}{3}$

9 $\frac{4}{5} \square \frac{15}{20}$ **13** $\frac{7}{10} \square \frac{3}{5}$

B

Write > or < in each box.

1 $\frac{2}{10} \square \frac{1}{4}$ **5** $\frac{7}{6} \square \frac{10}{8}$

2 $\frac{2}{3} \square \frac{4}{7}$ **6** $\frac{5}{3} \square \frac{8}{5}$

3 $\frac{5}{6} \square \frac{3}{4}$ **7** $\frac{9}{4} \square \frac{20}{9}$

4 $\frac{3}{8} \square \frac{5}{12}$ **8** $\frac{17}{10} \square \frac{21}{12}$

Arrange in ascending order.

9 $\frac{3}{4}, \frac{7}{12}, \frac{2}{3}$

10 $\frac{11}{20}, \frac{6}{10}, \frac{1}{2}$

11 $\frac{5}{12}, \frac{1}{3}, \frac{1}{6}, \frac{1}{4}$

12 $\frac{3}{5}, \frac{1}{2}, \frac{2}{3}, \frac{8}{15}$

13 $\frac{1}{4}, \frac{3}{8}, \frac{1}{2}, \frac{3}{16}$

14 $\frac{74}{100}, \frac{4}{5}, \frac{5}{4}, \frac{7}{10}$

15 $\frac{5}{3}, \frac{9}{6}, \frac{7}{4}, \frac{17}{12}$

16 $\frac{7}{5}, \frac{3}{2}, \frac{13}{10}, \frac{145}{100}$

Find the number which lies halfway between:

17 $\frac{1}{5}$ and $\frac{2}{5}$

18 $\frac{3}{8}$ and $\frac{1}{4}$

19 $\frac{1}{3}$ and $\frac{1}{2}$

20 $\frac{7}{10}$ and $\frac{4}{5}$

21 $\frac{5}{6}$ and 1

22 $\frac{3}{4}$ and $\frac{2}{3}$

23 1 and $\frac{11}{8}$

24 $\frac{3}{2}$ and $\frac{9}{5}$

C

Arrange in ascending order.

1 $\frac{2}{6}, \frac{1}{5}, \frac{2}{7}, \frac{1}{4}$

2 $\frac{3}{4}, \frac{2}{3}, \frac{7}{8}, \frac{7}{12}$

3 $\frac{1}{4}, \frac{2}{5}, \frac{2}{9}, \frac{3}{10}$

4 $\frac{11}{12}, \frac{5}{6}, \frac{2}{3}, \frac{4}{5}$

5 $\frac{3}{2}, \frac{10}{7}, \frac{7}{4}, \frac{25}{16}$

6 $\frac{13}{9}, \frac{9}{6}, \frac{11}{8}, \frac{5}{4}$

7 $\frac{9}{5}, \frac{7}{4}, \frac{15}{8}, \frac{17}{10}$

8 $\frac{19}{12}, \frac{14}{9}, \frac{5}{3}, \frac{13}{8}$

Find the number which lies halfway between:

9 $\frac{1}{5}$ and $\frac{1}{4}$

10 $\frac{1}{3}$ and $\frac{5}{9}$

11 $\frac{3}{2}$ and $\frac{7}{4}$

12 $\frac{13}{10}$ and $\frac{7}{5}$

13 $\frac{7}{6}$ and $\frac{4}{3}$

14 $\frac{3}{2}$ and $\frac{5}{3}$

15 $\frac{1}{4}$ and $\frac{2}{7}$

16 $\frac{23}{12}$ and $\frac{15}{8}$

Write > or < in each box.

17 $\frac{7}{10} + \frac{1}{3} \square \frac{2}{5} + \frac{2}{3}$

18 $\frac{3}{4} + \frac{2}{5} \square \frac{3}{5} + \frac{1}{2}$

19 $\frac{3}{4} - \frac{2}{3} \square \frac{5}{6} - \frac{3}{4}$

20 $\frac{5}{9} + \frac{5}{6} \square \frac{1}{2} + \frac{11}{12}$

TARGET To add and subtract fractions and mixed numbers with different denominators.

Examples $\dfrac{3}{5} + \dfrac{7}{10} = \dfrac{6+7}{10} = \dfrac{13}{10} = 1\dfrac{3}{10}$ $\dfrac{11}{12} - \dfrac{3}{4} = \dfrac{11-9}{12} = \dfrac{\cancel{2}}{\cancel{12}}\dfrac{1}{6}$

$2\dfrac{3}{7} + 1\dfrac{5}{7} = 3\dfrac{8}{7} = 4\dfrac{1}{7}$ $5\dfrac{3}{4} - 1\dfrac{1}{8} = 4\dfrac{6-1}{8} = 4\dfrac{5}{8}$

If the numerators cannot be subtracted change one whole one into a fraction.

$4\dfrac{3}{10} - 2\dfrac{1}{2} = 2\dfrac{3-5}{10} = 1\dfrac{13-5}{10} = 1\dfrac{\cancel{8}}{\cancel{10}}\dfrac{4}{5}$

A

Copy and complete.

1 $\dfrac{4}{9} + \dfrac{1}{9} = \dfrac{\square + \square}{9} = \dfrac{\square}{9}$

2 $\dfrac{23}{100} + \dfrac{39}{100} = \dfrac{\square + \square}{100} = \dfrac{\square}{100}$

3 $\dfrac{3}{4} - \dfrac{1}{4} = \dfrac{\square - \square}{4} = \dfrac{\square}{4}$

4 $\dfrac{5}{8} - \dfrac{3}{8} = \dfrac{\square - \square}{8} = \dfrac{\square}{8}$

5 $\dfrac{3}{5} + \dfrac{4}{5} = \dfrac{\square}{5} = 1\dfrac{\square}{5}$

6 $\dfrac{7}{12} + \dfrac{7}{12} = \dfrac{\square}{12} = 1\dfrac{\square}{12}$

7 $1\dfrac{1}{6} - \dfrac{5}{6} = \dfrac{\square}{6} - \dfrac{5}{6} = \dfrac{\square}{6}$

8 $1\dfrac{3}{10} - \dfrac{7}{10} = \dfrac{\square}{10} - \dfrac{7}{10} = \dfrac{\square}{10}$

Work out

9 $\dfrac{1}{5} + \dfrac{2}{5}$ 13 $\dfrac{6}{7} + \dfrac{4}{7}$

10 $\dfrac{3}{8} + \dfrac{3}{8}$ 14 $\dfrac{3}{4} + \dfrac{3}{4}$

11 $\dfrac{99}{100} - \dfrac{12}{100}$ 15 $1\dfrac{1}{3} - \dfrac{2}{3}$

12 $\dfrac{7}{9} - \dfrac{5}{9}$ 16 $1\dfrac{4}{11} - \dfrac{9}{11}$

B

Continue to complete. Write answers in lowest terms or as mixed numbers where necessary.

1 $\dfrac{1}{2} + \dfrac{3}{8} = \dfrac{\square}{8} + \dfrac{3}{8} = \dfrac{\square}{8}$

2 $\dfrac{11}{12} - \dfrac{5}{6} = \dfrac{11}{12} - \dfrac{\square}{12} = \dfrac{\square}{12}$

3 $\dfrac{5}{9} + \dfrac{1}{3} = \dfrac{5 + \square}{9} = \dfrac{\square}{9}$

4 $\dfrac{4}{5} - \dfrac{7}{10} = \dfrac{\square - 7}{10} = \dfrac{\square}{10}$

5 $3\dfrac{2}{7} + 1\dfrac{3}{7} = 4\dfrac{\square + \square}{7} = \dots$

6 $1\dfrac{7}{11} + 2\dfrac{10}{11} = 3\dfrac{\square + \square}{11} = \dots$

7 $4\dfrac{61}{100} - 1\dfrac{37}{100} = 3\dfrac{\square - \square}{100} = \dots$

8 $7\dfrac{4}{9} - 3\dfrac{5}{9} = 4\dfrac{\square - \square}{9} = \dots$

Work out

9 $\dfrac{4}{10} + \dfrac{1}{2}$ 13 $1\dfrac{43}{100} + 5\dfrac{79}{100}$

10 $\dfrac{3}{4} + \dfrac{5}{12}$ 14 $3\dfrac{2}{9} + 1\dfrac{7}{9}$

11 $\dfrac{7}{8} - \dfrac{1}{4}$ 15 $4\dfrac{4}{5} - 2\dfrac{3}{5}$

12 $1\dfrac{1}{3} - \dfrac{5}{6}$ 16 $6\dfrac{7}{12} - 3\dfrac{11}{12}$

C

Work out

1 $\dfrac{1}{4} + \dfrac{1}{3}$

2 $\dfrac{2}{7} + \dfrac{1}{2}$

3 $\dfrac{2}{3} + \dfrac{3}{5}$

4 $\dfrac{9}{10} + \dfrac{2}{3}$

5 $\dfrac{7}{12} - \dfrac{1}{5}$

6 $\dfrac{9}{10} - \dfrac{3}{4}$

7 $1\dfrac{1}{6} - \dfrac{5}{8}$

8 $1\dfrac{1}{2} - \dfrac{4}{5}$

9 $2\dfrac{1}{3} + 1\dfrac{5}{12}$

10 $3\dfrac{57}{100} + 3\dfrac{3}{4}$

11 $5\dfrac{2}{5} + 2\dfrac{3}{10}$

12 $1\dfrac{3}{4} + 1\dfrac{7}{8}$

13 $3\dfrac{1}{2} - 1\dfrac{21}{100}$

14 $4\dfrac{3}{8} - 3\dfrac{5}{16}$

15 $2\dfrac{1}{2} - 1\dfrac{2}{3}$

16 $5\dfrac{125}{1000} - 2\dfrac{4}{5}$

TARGET To add and subtract mixed numbers.

Examples

$$3\frac{2}{3} + 1\frac{4}{5} = 4\frac{10 + 12}{15} = 4\frac{22}{15} = 5\frac{7}{15}$$

$$6\frac{3}{4} - 2\frac{7}{10} = 4\frac{15 - 14}{20} = 4\frac{1}{20}$$

If the numerators cannot be subtracted convert one whole one into a fraction.

$$5\frac{3}{8} - 3\frac{5}{6} = 2\frac{9 - 20}{24} = 1\frac{33 - 20}{24} = 1\frac{13}{24}$$

A

Copy and complete.

1. $\frac{1}{2} + \frac{1}{6} = \frac{\square}{6} + \frac{1}{6} = \frac{\square}{6}$

2. $\frac{2}{5} + \frac{3}{10} = \frac{\square}{10} + \frac{3}{10} = \frac{\square}{10}$

3. $\frac{3}{4} - \frac{5}{12} = \frac{\square}{12} - \frac{5}{12} = \frac{\square}{12}$

4. $\frac{1}{3} - \frac{1}{6} = \frac{\square}{6} - \frac{1}{6} = \frac{\square}{6}$

Work out

5. $\frac{1}{6} + \frac{5}{12}$

6. $\frac{2}{10} + \frac{1}{2}$

7. $\frac{1}{12} + \frac{2}{3}$

8. $\frac{23}{100} + \frac{4}{10}$

9. $\frac{3}{12} + \frac{2}{6}$

10. $\frac{1}{2} + \frac{1}{8}$

11. $\frac{1}{3} + \frac{4}{9}$

12. $\frac{5}{8} + \frac{1}{4}$

13. $\frac{9}{10} - \frac{2}{5}$

14. $\frac{1}{2} - \frac{1}{12}$

15. $\frac{7}{12} - \frac{1}{4}$

16. $\frac{5}{6} - \frac{1}{3}$

17. $\frac{11}{12} - \frac{5}{6}$

18. $\frac{3}{4} - \frac{1}{8}$

19. $\frac{8}{10} - \frac{1}{2}$

20. $\frac{7}{9} - \frac{2}{3}$

B

Copy and complete.

1. $4\frac{1}{3} + 2\frac{5}{12} = 6\frac{\square + 5}{12} = 6\frac{\square}{12}$

2. $1\frac{1}{4} + 2\frac{3}{5} = 3\frac{\square + \square}{20} = 3\frac{\square}{20}$

3. $3\frac{1}{2} - 1\frac{3}{8} = 2\frac{\square - 3}{8} = 2\frac{\square}{8}$

4. $2\frac{3}{5} - 1\frac{1}{3} = 1\frac{\square - \square}{15} = 1\frac{\square}{15}$

Work out

5. $5\frac{7}{10} + 1\frac{19}{100}$

6. $2\frac{1}{12} + 1\frac{5}{6}$

7. $1\frac{1}{2} + 4\frac{3}{10}$

8. $3\frac{2}{3} + 2\frac{1}{9}$

9. $4\frac{2}{5} + 1\frac{5}{6}$

10. $1\frac{3}{4} + 3\frac{2}{3}$

11. $2\frac{5}{8} + 4\frac{9}{10}$

12. $5\frac{4}{7} + 2\frac{1}{2}$

13. $3\frac{3}{4} - 2\frac{1}{12}$

14. $2\frac{2}{3} - 1\frac{1}{6}$

15. $4\frac{1}{2} - 2\frac{5}{12}$

16. $7\frac{57}{100} - 4\frac{2}{10}$

17. $3\frac{2}{5} - 1\frac{1}{2}$

18. $5\frac{5}{9} - 2\frac{1}{4}$

19. $6\frac{2}{3} - 1\frac{9}{10}$

20. $8\frac{7}{8} - 3\frac{3}{5}$

C

Work out

1. $3\frac{5}{7} + 3\frac{1}{2}$

2. $5\frac{3}{10} + 4\frac{5}{6}$

3. $2\frac{4}{5} + 3\frac{5}{8}$

4. $6\frac{5}{9} + 2\frac{3}{4}$

5. $4\frac{2}{3} + 7\frac{6}{11}$

6. $9\frac{3}{4} + 5\frac{2}{7}$

7. $1\frac{7}{8} + 6\frac{1}{6}$

8. $7\frac{11}{12} + 2\frac{2}{5}$

9. $4\frac{1}{6} + 1\frac{3}{4}$

10. $5\frac{3}{10} - 3\frac{7}{12}$

11. $2\frac{3}{5} - 1\frac{2}{3}$

12. $8\frac{2}{7} - 4\frac{4}{5}$

13. $9\frac{1}{2} - 2\frac{8}{9}$

14. $6\frac{1}{4} - 3\frac{9}{10}$

15. $3\frac{2}{3} - 1\frac{6}{7}$

16. $7\frac{5}{12} - 2\frac{5}{8}$

TARGET To multiply pairs of fractions, writing the answer in its simplest form.

Examples

METHOD 1
Multiply and then cancel.

1. $\frac{3}{4} \times \frac{8}{9} = \frac{24}{36}\,\frac{2}{3}$

2. $\frac{5}{12} \times \frac{3}{10} = \frac{15}{120} = \frac{3}{24} = \frac{1}{8}$

METHOD 2
Cancel and then multiply.

1. $\frac{3^1}{4_1} \times \frac{8^2}{9_3} = \frac{2}{3}$ (cancel 3 and 9, 4 and 8)

2. $\frac{5^1}{12_4} \times \frac{3^1}{10_2} = \frac{1}{8}$ (cancel 5 and 10, 3 and 12)

A

Copy and complete.

1. $\frac{1}{2} \times \frac{1}{5} = \frac{1}{\Box}$

2. $\frac{1}{4} \times \frac{1}{6} = \frac{1}{\Box}$

3. $\frac{1}{2} \times \frac{1}{2} = \frac{1}{\Box}$

4. $\frac{1}{3} \times \frac{1}{4} = \frac{1}{\Box}$

5. $\frac{4}{5} \times \frac{1}{7} = \frac{\Box}{35}$

6. $\frac{1}{2} \times \frac{3}{4} = \frac{3}{\Box}$

7. $\frac{1}{5} \times \frac{2}{3} = \frac{\Box}{\Box}$

8. $\frac{3}{4} \times \frac{1}{10} = \frac{\Box}{\Box}$

Work out

9. $\frac{1}{2} \times \frac{1}{3}$ 13. $\frac{1}{2} \times \frac{5}{6}$

10. $\frac{1}{5} \times \frac{1}{10}$ 14. $\frac{1}{3} \times \frac{2}{3}$

11. $\frac{1}{2} \times \frac{1}{4}$ 15. $\frac{7}{10} \times \frac{1}{2}$

12. $\frac{1}{3} \times \frac{1}{5}$ 16. $\frac{3}{8} \times \frac{1}{4}$

B

Copy and complete.

1. $\frac{2}{3} \times \frac{2}{3} = \frac{\Box}{9}$

2. $\frac{3}{4} \times \frac{4}{5} = \frac{12}{\Box} = \frac{3}{\Box}$

3. $\frac{1}{3} \times \frac{11}{12} = \frac{\Box}{\Box}$

4. $\frac{5}{6} \times \frac{4}{5} = \frac{\Box}{30} = \frac{\Box}{3}$

5. $\frac{3}{4} \times \frac{3}{8} = \frac{\Box}{\Box}$

6. $\frac{3}{6} \times \frac{4}{6} = \frac{\Box}{\Box} = \frac{\Box}{\Box}$

7. $\frac{9}{10} \times \frac{5}{12} = \frac{\Box}{\Box} = \frac{\Box}{\Box}$

8. $\frac{4}{5} \times \frac{3}{8} = \frac{\Box}{\Box} = \frac{\Box}{\Box}$

Multiply and then cancel as in METHOD 1.

9. $\frac{1}{2} \times \frac{4}{7}$ 13. $\frac{3}{4} \times \frac{4}{9}$

10. $\frac{2}{5} \times \frac{5}{6}$ 14. $\frac{3}{10} \times \frac{5}{10}$

11. $\frac{2}{3} \times \frac{3}{4}$ 15. $\frac{3}{5} \times \frac{5}{12}$

12. $\frac{4}{5} \times \frac{7}{12}$ 16. $\frac{2}{3} \times \frac{9}{10}$

17. Do 9 to 16 again using METHOD 2.

C

Cancel and then multiply as in METHOD 2.

1. $\frac{7}{10} \times \frac{4}{5}$ 5. $\frac{3}{4} \times \frac{5}{12}$

2. $\frac{2}{5} \times \frac{3}{4}$ 6. $\frac{3}{10} \times \frac{8}{9}$

3. $\frac{99}{100} \times \frac{2}{9}$ 7. $\frac{7}{12} \times \frac{4}{7}$

4. $\frac{7}{8} \times \frac{2}{3}$ 8. $\frac{5}{6} \times \frac{39}{100}$

Change the first number into an improper fraction and work out.

9. $1\frac{3}{8} \times \frac{6}{11}$ 17. $2\frac{1}{12} \times \frac{4}{5}$

10. $3\frac{3}{5} \times \frac{1}{6}$ 18. $5\frac{1}{4} \times \frac{6}{7}$

11. $3\frac{1}{3} \times \frac{2}{5}$ 19. $6\frac{2}{3} \times \frac{9}{10}$

12. $4\frac{1}{2} \times \frac{11}{12}$ 20. $2\frac{4}{9} \times \frac{5}{11}$

13. $5\frac{4}{7} \times \frac{2}{9}$ 21. $4\frac{4}{5} \times \frac{3}{6}$

14. $2\frac{7}{10} \times \frac{2}{3}$ 22. $3\frac{5}{9} \times \frac{7}{8}$

15. $3\frac{7}{11} \times \frac{5}{8}$ 23. $6\frac{5}{12} \times \frac{8}{11}$

16. $3\frac{3}{8} \times \frac{4}{9}$ 24. $8\frac{1}{6} \times \frac{3}{7}$

TARGET To divide fractions by whole numbers.

To divide a fraction by a whole number multiply the denominator by the divisor.

Examples

$$\frac{1}{2} \div 3 = \frac{1}{2 \times 3} = \frac{1}{6}$$

$$\frac{2}{5} \div 4 = \frac{\cancel{2}^1}{5 \times \cancel{4}^2} = \frac{1}{10}$$

  $\frac{1}{2} \div 3 = \frac{1}{6}$

 $\frac{2}{5} \div 4 = \frac{2}{20} \ \frac{1}{10}$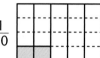

A

Copy and complete.

1. $\frac{1}{2} \div 3 = \frac{1}{2 \times 3} = \frac{1}{\square}$

2. $\frac{1}{4} \div 5 = \frac{1}{4 \times \square} = \frac{1}{\square}$

3. $\frac{1}{6} \div 2 = \frac{1}{\square \times \square} = \frac{1}{\square}$

4. $\frac{1}{3} \div 6 = \frac{\square}{\square \times \square} = \frac{\square}{\square}$

5. $\frac{3}{4} \div 4 = \frac{3}{4 \times 4} = \frac{3}{\square}$

6. $\frac{2}{5} \div 3 = \frac{2}{5 \times \square} = \frac{2}{\square}$

7. $\frac{3}{7} \div 2 = \frac{3}{\square \times \square} = \frac{3}{\square}$

8. $\frac{5}{6} \div 6 = \frac{\square}{\square \times \square} = \frac{\square}{\square}$

Work out

9. $\frac{1}{2} \div 8$ 13. $\frac{5}{8} \div 2$

10. $\frac{1}{5} \div 2$ 14. $\frac{2}{3} \div 5$

11. $\frac{1}{4} \div 3$ 15. $\frac{3}{5} \div 4$

12. $\frac{1}{10} \div 4$ 16. $\frac{4}{11} \div 3$

B

Simplify before multiplying.

1. $\frac{3}{4} \div 9 = \frac{\cancel{3}^1}{4 \times \cancel{9}^3} = \frac{\square}{\square}$

2. $\frac{8}{9} \div 2 = \frac{8}{9 \times 2} = \frac{\square}{\square}$

3. $\frac{2}{3} \div 7 = \frac{\square}{\square \times 7} = \frac{\square}{\square}$

4. $\frac{9}{10} \div 12 = \frac{9}{\square \times \square} = \frac{\square}{\square}$

5. $\frac{3}{5} \div 5 = \frac{\square}{\square \times \square} = \frac{\square}{\square}$

6. $\frac{6}{7} \div 8 = \frac{\square}{\square \times \square} = \frac{\square}{\square}$

7. $\frac{2}{9} \div 4 = \frac{\square}{\square \times \square} = \frac{\square}{\square}$

8. $\frac{2}{3} \div 10 = \frac{\square}{\square \times \square} = \frac{\square}{\square}$

Work out

9. $\frac{5}{8} \div 11$ 13. $\frac{5}{6} \div 10$

10. $\frac{9}{10} \div 6$ 14. $\frac{3}{4} \div 7$

11. $\frac{6}{7} \div 9$ 15. $\frac{6}{11} \div 3$

12. $\frac{4}{5} \div 12$ 16. $\frac{4}{9} \div 8$

C

Change to an improper fraction and divide.

1. $5\frac{3}{5} \div 4$

2. $7\frac{1}{2} \div 5$

3. $2\frac{4}{7} \div 6$

4. $4\frac{3}{8} \div 7$

5. $2\frac{8}{11} \div 3$

6. $7\frac{1}{5} \div 12$

7. $3\frac{5}{9} \div 2$

8. $6\frac{2}{3} \div 8$

Work out the bracket and divide.

9. $\left(\frac{1}{5} + \frac{7}{10}\right) \div 3$

10. $\left(\frac{7}{9} - \frac{1}{3}\right) \div 2$

11. $\left(\frac{3}{4} \times \frac{1}{2}\right) \div 6$

12. $\left(4\frac{8}{9} \div 11\right) \div 8$

13. $\left(\frac{2}{3} + \frac{1}{12}\right) \div 9$

14. $\left(\frac{6}{7} - \frac{2}{5}\right) \div 4$

15. $\left(\frac{2}{3} \times \frac{9}{10}\right) \div 12$

16. $\left(2\frac{5}{8} \div 7\right) \div 3$

TARGET To find a whole quantity given the quantity represented by a unit fraction.

To find a unit fraction of a whole quantity we divide the quantity by the denominator. (Ex. 1.)
To find the whole quantity given the quantity represented by a unit fraction we use the inverse method, which is multiplication. (Ex. 2, 3 and 4.)

Example 1
$\frac{1}{5}$ of 75p
75p ÷ 5 = 15p
Answer 15p

Example 2
$\frac{1}{5}$ of ☐ = 15p
15p × 5 = 75p
Answer 75p

Example 3
$\frac{1}{8}$ of ☐ = 60 g
60 g × 8 = 480 g
Answer 480 g

Example 4
$\frac{1}{100}$ of ☐ = 0·125 litres
0·125 litres × 100 = 12·5
Answer 12·5 litres

A

Copy and complete.

1. $\frac{1}{5}$ of 30 = 30 ÷ 5 = ☐
2. $\frac{1}{8}$ of 24 = 24 ÷ 8 = ☐
3. $\frac{1}{4}$ of 48 = 48 ÷ ☐ = ☐
4. $\frac{1}{6}$ of 42 = ☐ ÷ ☐ = ☐
5. $\frac{1}{3}$ of 30 = ☐
6. $\frac{2}{3}$ of 30 = ☐ × 2 = ☐
7. $\frac{1}{9}$ of 36 = ☐
8. $\frac{4}{9}$ of 36 = ☐ × 4 = ☐
9. $\frac{1}{7}$ of 56 = ☐
10. $\frac{5}{7}$ of 56 = ☐ × ☐ = ☐
11. $\frac{1}{10}$ of 50 = ☐
12. $\frac{3}{10}$ of 50 = ☐ × ☐ = ☐

Work out

13. $\frac{3}{8}$ of 80
14. $\frac{4}{5}$ of 45
15. $\frac{5}{12}$ of 72
16. $\frac{3}{4}$ of 32
17. $\frac{2}{11}$ of 33
18. $\frac{5}{6}$ of 30
19. $\frac{7}{10}$ of 90
20. $\frac{6}{7}$ of 28

B

Copy and complete.

1. $\frac{1}{4}$ of ☐ = 6p
2. $\frac{1}{3}$ of ☐ = 12 cm
3. $\frac{1}{9}$ of ☐ = 5 litres
4. $\frac{1}{10}$ of ☐ = 400 m
5. $\frac{1}{5}$ of ☐ = 0·7 cm
6. $\frac{1}{8}$ of ☐ = 90 ml
7. $\frac{1}{12}$ of ☐ = £11
8. $\frac{1}{7}$ of ☐ = 60 g
9. $\frac{1}{6}$ of ☐ = 24 m
10. $\frac{1}{11}$ of ☐ = £0·90
11. $\frac{1}{3}$ of ☐ = 2400 km
12. $\frac{1}{100}$ of ☐ = 100 g

13. Asif has read 56 pages of his book. This is one third of the book. How many pages does it have altogether?

14. Colleen has painted 4·8 m of a fence. This is one sixth of the fence's length. How long is the fence?

C

Copy and complete.

1. $\frac{5}{6}$ of ☐ = 400 ml
2. $\frac{3}{10}$ of ☐ = £3000
3. $\frac{4}{7}$ of ☐ = 4·8 kg
4. $\frac{7}{12}$ of ☐ = 56p
5. $\frac{8}{9}$ of ☐ = 720 km
6. $\frac{2}{5}$ of ☐ = 2·4 litres
7. $\frac{9}{11}$ of ☐ = £1·08
8. $\frac{7}{8}$ of ☐ = 2800 ml
9. $\frac{3}{4}$ of ☐ = 0·27 kg
10. $\frac{2}{3}$ of ☐ = 1·4 cm
11. $\frac{5}{1000}$ of ☐ = 0·015 kg
12. $\frac{11}{12}$ of ☐ = 880 m

13. Four ninths of the visitors to a museum are children. 348 children visited the museum. How many people visited the museum?

14. Three eighths of a cake has been eaten. 375 g is left. What was the weight of the whole cake?

TARGET To calculate the decimal equivalent of a fraction by division.

Examples

1 To find the decimal equivalent of $\frac{3}{8}$ divide 3 by 8.

$$8\overline{)3.^30^60^40} \quad 0.\ 3\ 7\ 5 \qquad \frac{3}{8} = 0.375$$

2 Use a calculator to find the decimal equivalent of $\frac{3}{7}$ rounded to 3 decimal places.

$\boxed{3}\ \boxed{\div}\ \boxed{7}\ \boxed{=} \rightarrow 0.428571428$

Answer = *0.429*

A

Copy and complete.

1 $\frac{2}{5} = 2 \div 5 = 0.\square$

2 $\frac{3}{12} = \square \div 12 = 0.\square$

3 $\frac{1}{2} = 1 \div \square = \square$

4 $\frac{6}{10} = \square \div \square = \square$

5 $\square = 3 \div 4 = \square$

6 $\frac{4}{8} = \square \div \square = \square$

7 $\frac{30}{100} = \square \div \square = \square$

8 $\square = 5 \div \square = 0.05$

For each fraction write the decimal equivalent.

9 $\frac{1}{10}$ **13** $\frac{3}{5}$

10 $\frac{6}{12}$ **14** $\frac{2}{4}$

11 $\frac{75}{100}$ **15** $\frac{8}{10}$

12 $\frac{2}{8}$ **16** $\frac{1}{1000}$

17 Use a calculator to check your answers.

B

For each fraction:
a) write the decimal equivalent
b) calculate as in Example 1 above to check your answer.

1 $\frac{4}{10}$ **7** $\frac{9}{12}$

2 $\frac{5}{8}$ **8** $\frac{3}{6}$

3 $\frac{3}{4}$ **9** $\frac{4}{5}$

4 $\frac{1}{5}$ **10** $\frac{1}{4}$

5 $\frac{2}{8}$ **11** $\frac{6}{8}$

6 $\frac{1}{8}$ **12** $\frac{7}{10}$

Use a calculator to find the decimal equivalent. Round to 3 decimal places where necessary.

13 $\frac{1}{3}$ **19** $\frac{7}{15}$

14 $\frac{9}{16}$ **20** $\frac{4}{6}$

15 $\frac{7}{9}$ **21** $\frac{8}{11}$

16 $\frac{1}{12}$ **22** $\frac{5}{12}$

17 $\frac{5}{11}$ **23** $\frac{4}{9}$

18 $\frac{2}{7}$ **24** $\frac{5}{7}$

C

For each fraction:
a) calculate the decimal equivalent as in Example 1 above, rounding to 3 decimal places where necessary
b) use a calculator to check your answers.

1 $\frac{5}{9}$ **7** $\frac{2}{3}$

2 $\frac{11}{12}$ **8** $\frac{5}{6}$

3 $\frac{2}{6}$ **9** $\frac{1}{9}$

4 $\frac{3}{11}$ **10** $\frac{6}{7}$

5 $\frac{1}{7}$ **11** $\frac{2}{12}$

6 $\frac{7}{12}$ **12** $\frac{6}{11}$

Use a calculator to find the decimal equivalent. Round to 3 decimal places where necessary.

13 $\frac{5}{16}$ **19** $\frac{1}{18}$

14 $\frac{10}{13}$ **20** $\frac{49}{99}$

15 $\frac{1}{15}$ **21** $\frac{9}{28}$

16 $\frac{39}{40}$ **22** $\frac{15}{24}$

17 $\frac{6}{19}$ **23** $\frac{31}{36}$

18 $\frac{9}{14}$ **24** $\frac{3}{52}$

TARGET To identify the value of each digit to three decimal places.

The value of a digit depends upon its position in the number.

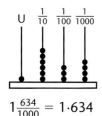

$1\frac{634}{1000} = 1\cdot634$

$1 + \frac{6}{10} + \frac{3}{100} + \frac{4}{1000}$

$1 + 0\cdot6 + 0\cdot03 + 0\cdot004$

Give the value of the 5 in each number.

$0\cdot513 \rightarrow \frac{5}{10}$ $1\cdot359 \rightarrow \frac{5}{100}$

$5\cdot247 \rightarrow 5$ $0\cdot085 \rightarrow \frac{5}{1000}$

A

Write as decimals.

1. $\frac{9}{10}$
2. $\frac{27}{100}$
3. $\frac{1}{2}$
4. $\frac{3}{100}$
5. $\frac{7}{10}$
6. $\frac{135}{1000}$
7. $\frac{1}{4}$
8. $\frac{89}{100}$
9. $\frac{3}{10}$
10. $\frac{11}{1000}$
11. $\frac{3}{4}$
12. $\frac{8}{1000}$

Write as fractions.

13. 0·25
14. 0·1
15. 0·634
16. 0·98
17. 0·02
18. 0·309
19. 0·81
20. 0·4
21. 0·562
22. 0·07
23. 0·19
24. 0·057

Give the value of the underlined figure.

25. 13·<u>5</u>
26. 8·1<u>6</u>
27. <u>2</u>·4
28. 0·3<u>2</u>8
29. 5·0<u>9</u>
30. 2<u>9</u>·7
31. 6·2<u>7</u>
32. <u>1</u>1·036
33. 37·<u>6</u>
34. 0·<u>9</u>4
35. 4·5<u>8</u>5
36. 4<u>2</u>·81

B

Write as decimals.

1. $4\frac{713}{1000}$
2. $7\frac{28}{1000}$
3. $\frac{36}{100}$
4. $2\frac{7}{1000}$
5. $1\frac{539}{1000}$
6. $8\frac{98}{100}$
7. $\frac{41}{1000}$
8. $9\frac{485}{1000}$
9. $13\frac{19}{100}$
10. $5\frac{6}{1000}$
11. $\frac{147}{1000}$
12. $6\frac{53}{1000}$

Write as mixed numbers.

13. 3·839
14. 8·075
15. 12·42
16. 6·901
17. 4·06
18. 9·548
19. 1·082
20. 27·7
21. 5·643
22. 3·02
23. 16·317
24. 2·49

Give the value of the underlined figure.

25. 4·9<u>2</u>3
26. 0·16<u>5</u>
27. <u>5</u>9·014
28. 17·<u>8</u>07
29. 32·6<u>8</u>
30. 5·07<u>2</u>
31. 43·2<u>9</u>6
32. 6·03<u>8</u>
33. 21·4<u>5</u>
34. 9·<u>7</u>41
35. <u>4</u>·309
36. 8·5<u>6</u>3

C

Copy and complete.

1. $1\cdot392 + 0\cdot04 = \square$
2. $4\cdot79 + 0\cdot035 = \square$
3. $0\cdot224 + 0\cdot28 = \square$
4. $0\cdot581 + \square = 1\cdot181$
5. $6\cdot953 + \square = 7\cdot001$
6. $5\cdot437 + \square = 5\cdot54$
7. $2\cdot356 - 0\cdot09 = \square$
8. $0\cdot844 - 0\cdot45 = \square$
9. $9\cdot862 - 0\cdot106 = \square$
10. $8\cdot295 - \square = 7\cdot895$
11. $3\cdot003 - \square = 2\cdot98$
12. $0\cdot108 - \square = 0\cdot099$

Give the answer as a decimal.

13. $\frac{43}{100} + 0\cdot209$
14. $\frac{1}{4} + 0\cdot277$
15. $\frac{187}{1000} + 0\cdot65$
16. $\frac{3}{4} - 0\cdot075$
17. $\frac{1}{5} - 0\cdot099$
18. $\frac{1}{2} - 0\cdot125$

TARGET To round decimals to the nearest tenth or hundredth.

Examples

Rounding to the nearest whole number. $4.93 \rightarrow 5$ $97.286 \rightarrow 97$
Rounding to the nearest tenth. $10.34 \rightarrow 10.3$ $0.284 \rightarrow 0.3$
Rounding to the nearest hundredth. $5.481 \rightarrow 5.48$ $6.1552 \rightarrow 6.16$
Rounding to the nearest thousandth. $0.3716 \rightarrow 0.372$ $8.5193 \rightarrow 8.519$

A

Copy and complete by choosing one of the numbers in the brackets.

1. $2.4 \rightarrow (2, 3)$
2. $6.6 \rightarrow (6, 7)$
3. $12.9 \rightarrow (12, 13)$
4. $1.1 \rightarrow (1, 2)$
5. $9.5 \rightarrow (9, 10)$
6. $4.37 \rightarrow (4.3, 4.4)$
7. $1.92 \rightarrow (1.9, 2.0)$
8. $2.75 \rightarrow (2.7, 2.8)$
9. $5.48 \rightarrow (5.4, 5.5)$
10. $1.63 \rightarrow (1.6, 1.7)$

Round to the nearest:
a) pound
b) 10p.

11. £5.26   17. £1.05
12. £8.94   18. £96.68
13. £7.45   19. £2.44
14. £11.72   20. £81.56
15. £9.39   21. £5.03
16. £3.21   22. £10.99

B

Round to the nearest tenth.

1. 1.37   6. 8.427
2. 6.536   7. 2.883
3. 4.26   8. 91.109
4. 31.95   9. 1.692
5. 7.74   10. 13.36

Round to the nearest hundredth.

11. 0.759   16. 0.523
12. 4.394   17. 5.976
13. 1.162   18. 61.468
14. 17.285   19. 20.831
15. 3.007   20. 6.625

Round to the nearest:
a) 100 g
b) 10 g.

21. 1.348 kg
22. 10.782 kg
23. 9.145 kg
24. 21.096 kg
25. 152.563 kg
26. 0.177 kg
27. 34.459 kg
28. 273.105 kg

C

Round to the nearest hundredth.

1. 0.326   6. 6.737
2. 2.583   7. 0.175
3. 14.952   8. 51.249
4. 1.808   9. 3.761
5. 2.093   10. 8.454

Round to the nearest thousandth.

11. 1.7292   16. 0.1739
12. 0.3546   17. 6.1371
13. 2.1062   18. 2.8653
14. 3.4128   19. 5.2982
15. 1.0851   20. 0.5417

Round to the nearest:
a) $\frac{1}{100}$
b) $\frac{1}{1000}$.

21. 3.636363
22. 0.372519
23. 1.81912
24. 7.054806
25. 4.513513
26. 0.714285714
27. 6.157894737
28. 1.0053816

TARGET   To round decimals to up to three decimal places.

Examples

Rounding to the nearest whole number.	$4 \cdot 931 \to 5$	$97 \cdot 286 \to 97$
Rounding to 1 decimal place.	$10 \cdot 3473 \to 10 \cdot 3$	$0 \cdot 284 \to 0 \cdot 3$
Rounding to 2 decimal places.	$5 \cdot 48129 \to 5 \cdot 48$	$6 \cdot 1552 \to 6 \cdot 16$
Rounding to 3 decimal places.	$0 \cdot 3716 \to 0 \cdot 372$	$8 \cdot 51939 \to 8 \cdot 519$

A

Round to the nearest whole number.

1 1·6   7 22·62

2 7·83   8 18·45

3 35·17   9 49·514

4 63·5   10 3·13

5 6·38   11 184·7

6 24·05   12 50·909

Round to 1 decimal place.

13 0·64   19 1·436

14 4·39   20 15·76

15 3·552   21 0·915

16 12·108   22 6·28

17 28·07   23 11·153

18 0·829   24 2·547

Round to the nearest:
a) litre
b) 100 ml.

25 1·72 litres

26 8·382 litres

27 6·539 litres

28 0·26 litres

29 9·644 litres

30 5·918 litres

B

Round to 2 decimal places.

1 3·368   7 9·0572

2 0·9427   8 2·3719

3 25·625   9 68·234

4 7·1061   10 1·1986

5 0·5194   11 40·4137

6 14·8735   12 5·785

Round to 3 decimal places.

13 7·3281   19 0·53181

14 0·8079   20 9·6026

15 21·7245   21 3·36532

16 2·4932   22 10·2005

17 1·8567   23 1·1761

18 4·9194   24 5·06873

Round each number to:
a) 1 decimal place
b) 2 decimal places.

25 6·3691   31 2·0375

26 3·924   32 1·48253

27 7·5485   33 39·5284

28 0·69708   34 8·351

29 15·7554   35 0·9762

30 94·813   36 3·24507

C

Round each number to:
a) 2 decimal places
b) 3 decimal places.

1 1·2746   7 2·60072

2 6·50834   8 0·44633

3 0·189931   9 5·3526

4 43·9115   10 17·1275

5 9·68501   11 0·81438

6 0·73395   12 1·09592

Use a calculator.
Work out, giving each answer correct to:
a) 1 decimal place
b) 2 decimal places
c) 3 decimal places.

13 68 ÷ 9

14 93 ÷ 11

15 44 ÷ 7

16 71 ÷ 6

17 152 ÷ 3

18 30 ÷ 13

19 129 ÷ 16

20 65 ÷ 14

21 50 ÷ 19

22 83 ÷ 7

23 175 ÷ 11

24 91 ÷ 17

TARGET   To multiply and divide decimals by 10 and 100.

Multiplying   – digits move left
Dividing   – digits move right
×/÷ by 10   – digits move 1 place
×/÷ by 100 – digits move 2 places

Examples

$3.286 \times 10 = 32.86$ $49.2 \div 10 = 4.92$

$1.63 \times 100 = 163$ $7.8 \div 100 = 0.078$

A

Multiply by 10.

1. 0.4
2. 3.9
3. 21.6
4. 0.2
5. 10.7
6. 9.5
7. 0.12
8. 35.8
9. 4.35
10. 0.6
11. 17.41
12. 40.9

Divide by 10.

13. 92
14. 7
15. 181
16. 25
17. 203
18. 8
19. 71.9
20. 54
21. 386
22. 0.2
23. 3.5
24. 507

Copy and complete.

25. ☐ × 10 = 13
26. ☐ × 10 = 2.9
27. ☐ × 10 = 51.4
28. ☐ × 10 = 7

29. ☐ ÷ 10 = 0.33
30. ☐ ÷ 10 = 8.6
31. ☐ ÷ 10 = 0.2
32. ☐ ÷ 10 = 1.05

B

Multiply by 100.

1. 0.9
2. 5.38
3. 71.6
4. 0.44
5. 2.1
6. 0.05
7. 4.76
8. 9.032
9. 0.5
10. 10.891
11. 23.07
12. 0.255

Divide by 100.

13. 37
14. 2
15. 180
16. 6204
17. 853
18. 1710
19. 0.6
20. 3098
21. 20.7
22. 509
23. 1.4
24. 1002

Copy and complete.

25. 0.62 m = ☐ cm
26. 0.7 mm = ☐ cm
27. 6p = £ ☐
28. 40 cm = ☐ m

29. £1.38 = ☐ p
30. 1.1 m = ☐ cm
31. 11.6 cm = ☐ mm
32. 209p = £ ☐

C

Multiply by 1000.

1. 0.06
2. 0.309
3. 2.8
4. 1.43
5. 0.071
6. 0.02
7. 10.5
8. 6.7
9. 0.14
10. 0.558
11. 2.06
12. 0.009

Divide by 1000.

13. 710
14. 5
15. 4800
16. 26
17. 3940
18. 82 500
19. 4007
20. 936
21. 580
22. 6
23. 11
24. 300

Work out and write each answer as a decimal.

25. one tenth of a half
26. 100 times larger than three quarters
27. one hundredth of 10
28. 10 times larger than one and a quarter
29. one tenth of two and a tenth
30. 100 times larger than one and a half

TARGET   To multiply and divide decimals by 10, 100 and 1000.

Multiplying   – digits move left
Dividing   – digits move right

×/÷ by 10   – digits move 1 place
×/÷ by 100   – digits move 2 places
×/÷ by 1000 – digits move 3 places

Examples

$1 \cdot 327 \times 10 = 13 \cdot 27$ $5038 \div 10 = 503 \cdot 8$

$1 \cdot 327 \times 100 = 132 \cdot 7$ $5038 \div 100 = 50 \cdot 38$

$1 \cdot 327 \times 1000 = 1327$ $5038 \div 1000 = 5 \cdot 038$

A

Multiply by 10.

1.   0·3
2.   1·8
3.   0·64
4.   3·17
5.   0·02
6.   0·59
7.   2·07
8.   1·35
9.   6·9
10.   0·81
11.   5·44
12.   0·06

Divide by 10.

13.   5
14.   1·2
15.   28
16.   0·7
17.   15
18.   4·3
19.   39
20.   0·1
21.   6
22.   2·5
23.   74
24.   0·8

Copy and complete.

25. ☐ × 10 = 0·8
26. ☐ × 10 = 75
27. ☐ × 10 = 2·3
28. ☐ × 10 = 10·6

29. ☐ ÷ 10 = 4·7
30. ☐ ÷ 10 = 0·22
31. ☐ ÷ 10 = 0·9
32. ☐ ÷ 10 = 3·05

B

Multiply by:

(100)   (1000)

1.   3·15
2.   0·6
3.   1·024
4.   0·09
5.   5·8
6.   0·107
7.   0·3
8.   0·065
9.   0·01
10.   2·5
11.   0·002
12.   4·28

Divide by:

(100)   (1000)

13.   45
14.   1·2
15.   370
16.   9
17.   0·6
18.   1485
19.   290
20.   54
21.   6100
22.   327
23.   18 700
24.   3

Copy and complete.

25. ☐ × 10 = 0·06
26. ☐ ÷ 100 = 0·9
27. ☐ × 100 = 45
28. ☐ ÷ 1000 = 0·247

29. 0·02 × ☐ = 20
30. 83 ÷ ☐ = 8·3
31. 0·05 × ☐ = 5
32. 400 ÷ ☐ = 0·4

C

Copy and complete.

1. ☐ × 10 = 0·8
2. ☐ ÷ 100 = 0·4
3. ☐ × 1000 = 163
4. ☐ ÷ 10 = 0·207
5. ☐ × 100 = 0·9
6. ☐ ÷ 1000 = 0·055

7. 0·18 × ☐ = 18
8. 0·07 ÷ ☐ = 0·007
9. 0·06 × ☐ = 60
10. 1·2 ÷ ☐ = 0·012
11. 0·3 × ☐ = 3
12. 290 ÷ ☐ = 0·29

Work out and write each answer as a decimal.

13. one half of a tenth
14. one tenth of a tenth
15. one half of a hundredth

What number is:

16. 10 times larger than three quarters of 2
17. 100 times larger than a half of a quarter
18. 1000 times larger than a twentieth?

TARGET To multiply and divide decimals by 10, 100 and 1000.

Examples

×/÷ by 10	×/÷ by 100	×/÷ by 1000
digits move 1 place	digits move 2 places	digits move 3 places
$41.8 \times 10 = 418$	$1.075 \times 100 = 107.5$	$3.46 \times 1000 = 3460$
$0.057 \times 10 = 0.57$	$0.62 \times 100 = 62$	$0.273 \times 1000 = 273$
$2.9 \div 10 = 0.29$	$183 \div 100 = 1.83$	$5195 \div 1000 = 5.195$
$3.65 \div 10 = 0.365$	$950 \div 100 = 9.5$	$68 \div 1000 = 0.068$

A Work out.

1. 2.9×10
2. $0.2 \div 10$
3. 1.75×10
4. $38 \div 10$
5. 0.4×10
6. $5.5 \div 10$

7. 0.64×10
8. $7 \div 10$
9. 43.1×10
10. $118 \div 10$
11. 0.09×10
12. $67.3 \div 10$

13. 8.2×100
14. $6 \div 100$
15. 4.38×100
16. $17 \div 100$
17. 0.95×100
18. $30 \div 100$

19. 0.5×100
20. $210 \div 100$
21. 0.03×100
22. $8460 \div 100$
23. 40.9×100
24. $67 \div 100$

B Work out.

×10	÷10	×100	÷100	×1000	÷1000
1. 0.6	7. 2	13. 3.999	19. 56	25. 1.427	31. 338
2. 8.3	8. 5.05	14. 1.1	20. 187.4	26. 0.93	32. 29
3. 0.007	9. 0.6	15. 0.57	21. 30	27. 6.6	33. 7
4. 0.44	10. 19.2	16. 0.065	22. 8	28. 0.05	34. 1200
5. 6.2	11. 73	17. 8.04	23. 206	29. 4.82	35. 60
6. 0.195	12. 401	18. 29.2	24. 49.3	30. 1.115	36. 450

C Copy and complete.

1. $\square \times 10 = 0.07$
2. $\square \div 10 = 0.04$
3. $\square \times 100 = 28.1$
4. $\square \div 100 = 0.08$
5. $\square \times 1000 = 90$
6. $\square \div 1000 = 0.006$

7. $0.055 \times \square = 5.5$
8. $0.02 \times \square = 0.2$
9. $7.6 \times \square = 7600$
10. $41.4 \div \square = 4.14$
11. $38 \div \square = 0.038$
12. $909 \div \square = 9.09$

13. $\square \times 10 = 2.66$
14. $\square \div 10 = 0.035$
15. $\square \times 100 = 882$
16. $\square \div 100 = 9.504$
17. $\square \times 1000 = 707$
18. $\square \div 1000 = 1.5$

TARGET To multiply numbers with up to two decimal places by whole numbers.

When multiplying a decimal by a whole number you need to be careful that the answer has the correct number of decimal places. Generally there must be the same number of decimal places in the decimal being multiplied as in the answer.

Examples

$0.8 \times 3 = 2.4$

$0.83 \times 2 = 1.66$

$0.083 \times 2 = 0.166$

The exception, of course, is when the smallest value digit of the answer is a 0.

Examples

$0.06 \times 5 = 0.3 \quad (0.30)$

$1.25 \times 4 = 5 \quad (5.00)$

The same rules apply when using a written method. In practice this is straightforward providing you set out your calculation neatly and align decimal points.

Examples

1
$$\begin{array}{r} 15.37 \\ \times \quad 6 \\ \hline 92.22 \\ \hline \scriptstyle 3\,2\,4 \end{array}$$

2
$$\begin{array}{r} 276.9 \\ \times \quad 3 \\ \hline 830.7 \\ \hline \scriptstyle 2\,2\,2 \end{array}$$

However, it is always advisable to check that your answer is a sensible one.

Example 1   15.37 rounds to 15
$15 \times 6 = 90$
92.22 is a sensible answer.

Example 2   276.9 rounds to 280
$280 \times 3 = 840$
830.7 is a sensible answer.

A

1 One bathroom tile is 0.3 m long. How long is a row of:

a) 2 tiles   b) 5 tiles   c) 8 tiles?

2 One can of beans weighs 0.4 kg. What is the weight of:

a) 2 cans   b) 3 cans   c) 7 cans?

Work out

3 $0.6 \text{ km} \times 2$

4 $0.5 \text{ litres} \times 8$

5 $0.9 \text{ kg} \times 6$

6 $0.2 \text{ m} \times 9$

7 $0.8 \text{ litres} \times 7$

8 $0.7 \text{ cm} \times 3$

9 $0.5 \text{ m} \times 5$

10 $0.6 \text{ kg} \times 8$

11 One can of paint holds 3.5 litres. Copy and complete to find the capacity of:

a) 4 cans

$$\begin{array}{r} 3.5 \text{ litres} \\ \times \quad 4 \\ \hline \qquad \text{litres} \end{array}$$

b) 7 cans.

$$\begin{array}{r} 3.5 \text{ litres} \\ \times \quad 7 \\ \hline \qquad \text{litres} \end{array}$$

12 A bike race circuit is 2.8 km long. How long is a race of:

a) 3 circuits

$$\begin{array}{r} 2.8 \\ \times \quad 3 \\ \hline \qquad \text{km} \end{array}$$

b) 5 circuits?

$$\begin{array}{r} 2.8 \\ \times \quad 5 \\ \hline \qquad \text{km} \end{array}$$

Work out

13 $4.9 \text{ m} \times 5$

14 $6.7 \text{ km} \times 2$

15 $8.6 \text{ litres} \times 3$

16 $5.8 \text{ cm} \times 9$

17 $9.4 \text{ m} \times 6$

18 $7.2 \text{ kg} \times 8$

19 8.3×4

20 6.5×7

21 2.7×9

22 5.6×6

23 3.9×8

24 4.8×7

B

1 A tube of toothpaste holds 0·08 litres. What is the capacity of:

   a) 3 tubes   **b)** 5 tubes   **c)** 9 tubes?

2 One pot noodle weighs 0·09 kg. What is the weight of:

   a) 2 pots   **b)** 9 pots   **c)** 12 pots?

Work out

3 £0·04 × 8

7 0·09 kg × 3

4 0·07 km × 6

8 £0·03 × 6

5 0·06 m × 5

9 0·08 km × 4

6 0·05 litres × 9

10 0·07 m × 8

11 One bar of chocolate cost £1·39. Copy and complete to find the cost of:

   a) 3 bars   **b)** 8 bars.

$$\begin{array}{r} £1·39 \\ \times\ \underline{3} \\ £\ \underline{} \end{array} \qquad \begin{array}{r} £1·39 \\ \times\ \underline{8} \\ £\ \underline{} \end{array}$$

12 One inch is 2·54 cm. Copy and complete to find how many centimetres is:

   a) 6 inches   **b)** 9 inches.

$$\begin{array}{r} 2·54 \\ \times\ \underline{6} \\ \underline{}\ cm \end{array} \qquad \begin{array}{r} 2·54 \\ \times\ \underline{9} \\ \underline{}\ cm \end{array}$$

Work out

13 28·5 cm × 5

19 8·19 × 4

14 £1·76 × 6

20 6·27 × 8

15 43·9 kg × 8

21 61·3 × 7

16 5·64 m × 3

22 25·8 × 9

17 51·8 litres × 7

23 7·45 × 6

18 £3·92 × 9

24 9·07 × 3

25 Cans of paint hold 4·78 litres. What is the total capacity of 6 cans?

C

1 A dripping tap loses 0·006 litres every second. How much water is lost in:

   a) 5 seconds

   b) 12 seconds

   c) 40 seconds?

2 One coin weighs 0·012 kg. What is the weight of:

   a) 7 coins

   b) 11 coins

   c) 20 coins?

Work out

3 0·009 km × 7

7 0·006 × 9

4 0·005 litres × 11

8 0·004 × 12

5 0·008 m × 6

9 0·009 × 8

6 0·007 kg × 5

10 0·007 × 4

11 Train tickets cost £52·75 each. Copy and complete to find the cost of:

   a) 4 tickets   **b)** 9 tickets.

$$\begin{array}{r} £52·75 \\ \times\ \underline{4} \\ £\ \underline{} \end{array} \qquad \begin{array}{r} £52·75 \\ \times\ \underline{9} \\ £\ \underline{} \end{array}$$

12 One patio tile weighs 2·685 kg. Copy and complete to find the weight of:

   a) 5 tiles   **b)** 12 tiles.

$$\begin{array}{r} 2·685\ kg \\ \times\ \underline{5} \\ \underline{}\ kg \end{array} \qquad \begin{array}{r} 2·685\ kg \\ \times\ \underline{12} \\ \underline{}\ kg \end{array}$$

Work out

13 £71·82 × 6

19 5·963 × 8

14 2·594 m × 9

20 9·248 × 3

15 64·57 km × 5

21 14·87 × 9

16 4·278 kg × 8

22 85·74 × 7

17 £16·39 × 7

23 7·195 × 4

18 3·862 litres × 4

24 9·236 × 6

TARGET To divide numbers with up to two decimal places by one-digit whole numbers.

Examples

Check mental calculations with inverse multiplication.

$7 \cdot 2 \, km \div 8 = 0 \cdot 9 \, km$
$0 \cdot 9 \, km \times 8 = 7 \cdot 2 \, km$

$£0 \cdot 48 \div 12 = £0 \cdot 04$
$£0 \cdot 04 \times 12 = £0 \cdot 48$

With written calculations align decimal points.

$34.2 \, kg \div 6$

$$6 \overline{) 34 \cdot {}^4 2} \quad \begin{array}{c} 5 \cdot 7 \end{array}$$

Answer *5·7 kg*

Check by rounding and inverse multiplication.

5·7 kg rounds to 6 kg
6 kg × 6 = 36 kg   5·7 kg is a sensible answer.

A

Work out

1. $1 \cdot 2 \, cm \div 4$
2. $3 \cdot 5 \, m \div 7$
3. $1 \cdot 8 \, kg \div 9$
4. $1 \cdot 6 \, litres \div 2$
5. $5 \cdot 4 \, km \div 6$
6. $1 \cdot 8 \, cm \div 3$
7. $5 \cdot 6 \, kg \div 8$
8. $4 \cdot 0 \, m \div 5$

Copy and complete.

9. $2 \overline{) 7 \cdot 4 \, km}$
10. $9 \overline{) 13 \cdot 5 \, litres}$
11. $4 \overline{) 6 \cdot 4 \, m}$
12. $5 \overline{) 6 \cdot 5 \, cm}$
13. $7 \overline{) 8 \cdot 4 \, kg}$
14. $3 \overline{) 5 \cdot 4 \, litres}$
15. $8 \overline{) 11 \cdot 2 \, m}$
16. $6 \overline{) 10 \cdot 2 \, km}$

B

Write the answer only.

1. $0 \cdot 24 \, m \div 3$
2. $£0 \cdot 48 \div 8$
3. $0 \cdot 28 \, kg \div 4$
4. $0 \cdot 63 \, cm \div 7$
5. $0 \cdot 3 \, km \div 5$
6. $0 \cdot 72 \, m \div 9$
7. $£1 \cdot 40 \div 2$
8. $0 \cdot 18 \, kg \div 6$
9. $0 \cdot 42 \div 7$
10. $0 \cdot 45 \div 5$
11. $0 \cdot 36 \div 9$
12. $0 \cdot 21 \div 3$
13. $0 \cdot 18 \div 2$
14. $0 \cdot 3 \div 6$
15. $0 \cdot 36 \div 4$
16. $0 \cdot 24 \div 8$

Work out.

17. $£24 \cdot 80 \div 4$
18. $23 \cdot 2 \, m \div 8$
19. $3 \cdot 9 \, kg \div 5$
20. $37 \cdot 1 \, cm \div 7$
21. $1 \cdot 7 \, km \div 2$
22. $2 \cdot 94 \, m \div 6$
23. $£1 \cdot 92 \div 3$
24. $3 \cdot 33 \, kg \div 9$
25. $43 \cdot 2 \div 6$
26. $17 \cdot 7 \div 3$
27. $47 \cdot 6 \div 7$
28. $33 \cdot 6 \div 4$
29. $5 \cdot 04 \div 9$
30. $1 \cdot 4 \div 5$
31. $3 \cdot 76 \div 8$
32. $2 \cdot 1 \div 6$

C

Write the answer only.

1. $0 \cdot 063 \, km \div 9$
2. $0 \cdot 024 \, m \div 4$
3. $0 \cdot 099 \, kg \div 11$
4. $0 \cdot 048 \, m \div 6$
5. $0 \cdot 072 \, km \div 8$
6. $0 \cdot 035 \, kg \div 5$
7. $0 \cdot 036 \, m \div 12$
8. $0 \cdot 056 \, km \div 7$
9. $0 \cdot 048 \div 6$
10. $0 \cdot 081 \div 9$
11. $0 \cdot 02 \div 5$
12. $0 \cdot 056 \div 8$
13. $0 \cdot 032 \div 4$
14. $0 \cdot 049 \div 7$
15. $0 \cdot 027 \div 3$
16. $0 \cdot 132 \div 12$

Work out

17. $£8 \cdot 25 \div 5$
18. $23 \cdot 03 \, m \div 7$
19. $1 \cdot 455 \, km \div 3$
20. $1 \cdot 242 \, kg \div 9$
21. $£16 \cdot 38 \div 6$
22. $21 \cdot 12 \, km \div 8$
23. $1 \cdot 428 \, kg \div 4$
24. $2 \cdot 82 \, m \div 12$
25. $23 \cdot 76 \div 9$
26. $19 \cdot 6 \div 5$
27. $0 \cdot 894 \div 6$
28. $2 \cdot 328 \div 3$
29. $30 \cdot 8 \div 8$
30. $11 \cdot 72 \div 4$
31. $4 \cdot 404 \div 12$
32. $1 \cdot 722 \div 7$

TARGET To use written division methods in cases where the answer has up to two decimal places.

Examples

$51.8 \div 7$ $86 \div 4$ $9.7 \div 5$

Align decimal points.

$$7 \overline{)51.^28} \quad \begin{array}{c} 7.4 \end{array}$$

$$4 \overline{)86.^20} \quad \begin{array}{c} 21.5 \end{array}$$

$$5 \overline{)9.^47^20} \quad \begin{array}{c} 1.94 \end{array}$$

Check answer. $7 \times 7 = 49$ $22 \times 4 = 88$ $1.9 \times 5 = 9.5$

A

Work out

1. $14.8 \div 2$
9. $23.4 \div 9$
2. $31.8 \div 6$
10. $37.2 \div 4$
3. $23.5 \div 5$
11. $52.2 \div 6$
4. $26.4 \div 4$
12. $20.4 \div 3$

5. $41.6 \div 8$
13. $36.4 \div 7$
6. $23.7 \div 3$
14. $17.8 \div 2$
7. $59.5 \div 7$
15. $37.6 \div 8$
8. $34.5 \div 5$
16. $65.7 \div 9$

17. Eight gravy cubes weigh 60·8 g. What does one cube weigh?

18. A back garden is three times the length of the front garden. The back garden is 26·1 m long. How long is the front garden?

19. An oil drum holds 32·9 litres. One seventh is used. How much oil has been used?

B

Work out to one decimal place.

1. $75 \div 2$
5. $384 \div 5$
2. $267 \div 5$
6. $119 \div 2$
3. $138 \div 4$
7. $141 \div 6$
4. $188 \div 8$
8. $174 \div 4$

Work out to two decimal places.

9. $3.7 \div 5$
13. $5.9 \div 2$
10. $6.7 \div 2$
14. $3.4 \div 4$
11. $5.2 \div 8$
15. $6.9 \div 5$
12. $4.6 \div 4$
16. $8.7 \div 6$

17. Celia buys 1·6 kg of cheese. One fifth is eaten. How much has been eaten?

18. A regular hexagon has a perimeter of 9·3 cm. What is the length of one side?

19. A hose uses 116 litres of water in 8 minutes. How much does it use in one minute?

20. Four laps of a cyclo-cross course is a total distance of 10·6 km. How long is one lap?

C

Work out to two decimal places.

1. $69 \div 4$
5. $50 \div 8$
2. $27 \div 4$
6. $94 \div 8$
3. $95 \div 4$
7. $70 \div 8$
4. $55 \div 4$
8. $38 \div 8$

Work out to three decimal places.

9. $3.14 \div 5$
13. $4.71 \div 6$
10. $1.67 \div 2$
14. $9.33 \div 5$
11. $4.6 \div 8$
15. $3.4 \div 8$
12. $6.9 \div 4$
16. $5.3 \div 4$

17. Four tiles weigh 2·5 kg. What does one tile weigh?

18. A plane flies 0·74 km in five seconds. How far does it fly in one second in kilometres?

19. A bottle holds 100 ml of medicine. It provides sixteen doses. How much is each dose?

TARGET To practice written methods for division giving remainders as decimals.

Example   6020 ÷ 8   7 5 2. 5
                        8)6 0⁴2²0.⁴0

4497 ÷ 12   3 7 4. 7 5
                        12)4 4⁸9⁵7.⁹0⁶0

A

Write the answer only giving the remainder as:

a) a fraction
b) a decimal.

1 37 ÷ 10   7 47 ÷ 4

2 25 ÷ 2   8 89 ÷ 10

3 43 ÷ 5   9 33 ÷ 2

4 29 ÷ 4   10 57 ÷ 6

5 76 ÷ 8   11 71 ÷ 5

6 52 ÷ 5   12 98 ÷ 8

Work out. Give the remainder as a decimal.

13 77 ÷ 2   19 226 ÷ 4

14 134 ÷ 5   20 343 ÷ 10

15 161 ÷ 10   21 549 ÷ 12

16 191 ÷ 4   22 173 ÷ 4

17 149 ÷ 2   23 463 ÷ 5

18 176 ÷ 5   24 298 ÷ 10

25 Graham saves one tenth of his pay.
He earns £639.
How much does he save?

26 Four identical barrels have a total capacity of 114 litres.
What is the capacity of one barrel?

B

Give the remainder as a decimal.

1 1176 ÷ 4

2 1347 ÷ 2

3 2694 ÷ 5

4 3674 ÷ 8

5 7213 ÷ 10

6 6990 ÷ 12

7 4837 ÷ 5

8 5726 ÷ 8

9 3947 ÷ 10

10 2588 ÷ 4

11 8372 ÷ 16

12 6440 ÷ 25

13 A lorry makes the same journey on five days. Altogether it travels 2847 km. How long is the journey?

14 Eight identical containers have a total weight of 3658 kg. What does each container weigh?

15 Four people share a prize of £2739. How much do they receive each?

C

Give the remainder as a decimal rounded to three decimal places where necessary.

1 50 981 ÷ 8

2 23 837 ÷ 3

3 32 400 ÷ 7

4 96 475 ÷ 12

5 62 967 ÷ 11

6 40 652 ÷ 9

7 34 765 ÷ 14

8 57 788 ÷ 32

9 88 750 ÷ 19

10 71 676 ÷ 45

11 90 929 ÷ 17

12 78 417 ÷ 24

13 Vanessa earns £35 217 per year. How much does she earn each month?

14 An island has an area of 70 000 km². One third of the island is rain forest. What is the area of the rain forest on the island?

15 A family uses 72 000 litres of water in 52 weeks. What is their mean weekly water usage?

TARGET To write remainders as fractions and decimals in the context of word problems.

Examples

How many years is 825 months?

$825 \div 12 = 68\frac{9}{12}\;\frac{3}{4}$

Answer

825 months is $68\frac{3}{4}$ years.

Twelve identical containers weigh 825 kg altogether. What does one weigh?

$825 \div 12 = 68 \cdot 75$

Answer   *One container weighs 68·75 kg.*

Write the remainder as either a fraction in its simplest form or as a decimal, whichever is most appropriate.

A

1 A rope is 55 m long. It is cut into 4 equal lengths. How long is each length?

2 How many times larger is £100 than £6?

3 A garden has an area of 345 m². Half of the garden is a lawn. What is the area of the lawn?

4 In five hours of driving a lorry used 112 litres of petrol. How much petrol did the lorry use on average each hour?

5 Each guest at a garden party is served one slice of cake. Each cake is cut into 12 slices. How many cakes are needed to serve 177 guests?

6 Eight bags hold 110 apples. What is the average number of apples in each bag?

7 Jason's time of 49 seconds for 400 m is five times longer than his best 100 m time. What is his best 100 m time?

B

1 The total of the ages of the 15 players in a rugby team is 355. What is the mean age?

2 Eight plane tickets cost £2902. What does one ticket cost?

3 Shayla earns £483 for working 35 hours. How much does she earn per hour?

4 The model of a bridge is 4 m long. The actual bridge has a length of 2145 m. How many times longer is the bridge than the model?

5 A leaking pipe loses 1641 litres of water in a day. How much does it lose every hour?

6 Vernon works out that tomorrow he will be 11 000 days old. How many weeks old will he be?

7 Eighty-five identical metal bars weigh 1394 kg. What does one bar weigh?

C

Round decimals to two decimal places where necessary.

1 A plane flies 1000 km in 73 minutes. What is the mean distance travelled by the plane per minute?

2 The 16 members of a lottery syndicate win £59 558. How much does each member receive?

3 There are 22 chocolates in each box. How many boxes can be made from 4015 chocolates?

4 In 75 days a bread factory used 12 020 bags of flour. What was the mean number of bags used per day?

5 In July a dairy produced 17 245 litres of milk. What was the mean milk production per day?

6 James weighs 84 kg. His lorry weighs 54 068 kg. How many times heavier is the lorry than James?

TARGET **To recall and use equivalences between fractions, decimals and percentages.**

Per cent means out of 100.
Percentages are fractions with a denominator of 100.
The symbol for per cent is %.

Example

$\frac{47}{100} = 47\% = 0.47$

To express fractions as percentages, change them to equivalent fractions with denominators of 100.

Examples

$\frac{3}{10} = \frac{30}{100} = 30\%$

$\frac{3}{4} = \frac{75}{100} = 75\%$

To express decimals as percentages, multiply by 100.

Examples

$0.2 = 20\% \quad (0.2 \times 100 = 20)$
$0.85 = 85\% \ (0.85 \times 100 = 85)$

It is useful to know that:

$\frac{1}{100} = 0.01 = 1\%, \ \frac{2}{100} = 0.02 = 2\%,$ etc.

$\frac{1}{10} = 0.1 = 10\%, \ \frac{2}{10} = 0.2 = 20\%,$ etc.

$\frac{1}{4} = 25\%, \ \frac{1}{2} = 50\%, \ \frac{3}{4} = 75\%$

A

Express each shaded area as:

a) a fraction
b) a decimal
c) a percentage.

1 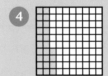   **6**

2   **7**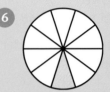

3 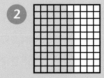   **8**

4    **9**

5 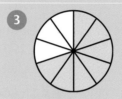   **10**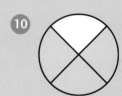

11 What percentage of the boxes contain:

    a) ticks   **c)** dots
    b) crosses   **d)** triangles?

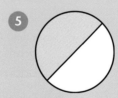

✗		✓	●	
✓	●			✓
		△	✓	●
●	✓		✗	

12 What percentage of the boxes are blank?

B

1. Copy and complete the table.

Fractions	Decimals	%ages
$\frac{1}{10}$	0·1	10%
		50%
		32%
		90%
	0·18	
	0·25	
	0·02	
	0·4	
$\frac{7}{50}$		
$\frac{3}{4}$		
$\frac{6}{100}$		
$\frac{11}{25}$		
		1%
	0·95	

What percentage could be used in each sentence.

2. Half the tissues in the box had been used.

3. Nineteen of the twenty horses in the race were brown.

4. The basketball team won four in every five matches played.

5. Twenty-nine hundredths of the Earth's surface is water.

6. Ella and Elysia achieved full marks in the Maths Test.

7. Darren has read three quarters of his book.

8. Twenty-seven in every fifty visitors to the Museum stayed for more than two hours.

9. Nine out of the twenty-five balloons in the packet were yellow.

10. Three in every five chocolates had a soft centre.

C

Write each fraction as:

a) a decimal

b) a percentage.

1. $\frac{7}{10}$ 3. $\frac{87}{100}$ 5. $\frac{2}{5}$ 7. $\frac{23}{25}$

2. $\frac{4}{50}$ 4. $\frac{3}{20}$ 6. $\frac{126}{200}$ 8. $\frac{18}{40}$

Write each percentage as:

a) a fraction in its simplest form

b) a decimal.

9. 23%   13. 71%

10. 35%   14. 0·5%

11. 60%   15. 30%

12. 9%   16. 17·5%

17. Eight children competed for the title School Master Chef. Their task was to produce cakes for the School Fête. Complete the list of results.

Name	Cakes made	Cakes sold	%age sold	%age unsold
Ailsa	50	39		
Bilal	54		50%	
Carmen	40			30%
Digby	60	39		
Esmé	45		80%	
Fred	56			25%
Gail	48	30		
Harry	55		60%	

18. Use squared paper.
Draw a 6 × 10 grid of 60 boxes.

a) Colour 25% red.

b) Colour 20% blue.

c) Colour 9 boxes yellow.

d) Write down the percentage of the boxes not coloured.

TARGET   To solve number problems involving fractions, decimals and percentages mentally.

A

1. What is one tenth of a right angle?

2. What is the product of 5 and 0·9?

3. Divide 2·8 by 4.

4. Take two thirds from 3.

5. What is 10% larger than 80?

6. How many fifths make 6?

7. What is 50% of 19?

8. What is the difference between 2·7 and 4·1?

9. Increase 4 by 50%.

10. Add three sevenths and two sevenths.

11. Which number is ten times greater than 1·2?

12. Which number is ten times smaller than 2·5?

13. Subtract five eighths from 7.

14. What is 10% of 5?

15. Find one quarter of 10.

16. Increase 5·6 by 2·1.

B

1. Halve 4·6.

2. What is three tenths plus one and a half?

3. How much is £5 increased by 50%?

4. Find the difference between 1·5 and 0·15.

5. Find one quarter of 180°.

6. What needs to be added to 1·36 to make 2?

7. How many eighths are there in two and a half?

8. Divide 5·8 by 100.

9. Add three tenths to 0·64.

10. What is 1% of £50?

11. Multiply 0·77 by 100.

12. Find seven ninths of 27.

13. What is seven tenths minus one quarter?

14. What is the cost of a £19 jumper if the price is reduced by 10%?

15. What is twice 0·8?

16. Find 90% of £35.

C

1. What is one quarter of £55?

2. Find the number which is 100 times greater than 0·009.

3. What is half of 0·13?

4. What is the total of one half, three quarters and five eighths?

5. Find 11% of £2400.

6. Take nine tenths from 1·382.

7. What is the product of 8 and 0·25?

8. Find eleven twelfths of 60.

9. What is added to 1·06 to make 8?

10. Increase £180 by 5%.

11. Add three quarters to 0·839.

12. Find 25% of 0·1.

13. What is 20 times greater than 0·08?

14. What is 90% of 360°?

15. Subtract 0·315 from 1.

16. What is one fifth of 1·4?

TARGET   To solve problems involving the calculation of percentages of amounts.

Examples

10% of 800 m

$\frac{1}{10}$ of 800 m

800 m ÷ 10

80 m

30% of 800 m

(10% of 800 m) × 3

80 m × 3

240 m

5% of 800 m

(10% of 800 m) ÷ 2

80 m ÷ 2

40 m

75% of 800 m

$\frac{3}{4}$ of 800 m

(800 m ÷ 4) × 3

200 m × 3

600 m

A

Find 10% of:

1. 30
2. 80
3. 50
4. 100
5. 150
6. 200
7. 420
8. 500.

Find 10% of:

9. 40p
10. 70p
11. £1·00
12. £1·80
13. £2·00
14. £4·60
15. £12·00
16. 90p.

Find 10% of:

17. 20 cm
18. 60 cm
19. 400 g
20. 1000 g
21. 1 m
22. 5 m
23. 1 kg
24. 3 kg.

25. There are 240 trees in a wood. 10% are oak trees. How many oak trees are there in the wood?

26. A fridge costs £450. In a sale there is 10% off. What is the new price?

B

For each of the following amounts find:
a) 10%   b) 5%   c) 20%.

1. £2·00
2. 500 ml
3. 3 kg
4. 15 m

Find:

5. 20% of 300
6. 70% of 250
7. 30% of 600
8. 60% of 25

9. 5% of 500 g
10. 5% of 2 kg
11. 5% of 380 ml
12. 5% of 8 litres

13. Toyah makes 5 litres of soup. 70% is used. How much is left?

14. There are 140 rooms in a hotel. 20% have been decorated since the hotel opened. How many have not been redecorated?

15. A tracksuit costs £25. The price goes up by 5%. What is the new price?

C

Find:

1. 1% of £240
2. 4% of £8
3. 25% of 34 cm
4. 15% of 2 m

5. 11% of 500 g
6. 15% of 4 kg
7. 99% of 10 litres
8. 95% of 600 ml

Copy and complete:

9. 10% of ☐ = 25
10. 20% of ☐ = 7
11. 90% of ☐ = 18
12. 25% of ☐ = 13

13. 1% of ☐ = 1·4
14. 2% of ☐ = 0·8
15. 5% of ☐ = 12
16. 75% of ☐ = 360

17. Latrice has £15 000 in a savings account at the start of the year. How much will she have in her account at the end of the year if the annual interest rate is:
a) 1%   b) 5%   c) 7·5%?

TARGET To calculate fractions and percentages of amounts.

Examples

$\frac{1}{12}$ of 600

$600 \div 12$

50

$\frac{5}{12}$ of 600

$\left(\frac{1}{12} \text{ of } 600\right) \times 5$

50×5

250

10% of 350

$\frac{1}{10}$ of 350

35

70% of 350

$(10\% \text{ of } 350) \times 7$

35×7

245

1% of 350

$\frac{1}{100}$ of 350

$350 \div 100$

$3 \cdot 5$

A

Find:

1. $\frac{1}{3}$ of 18

2. $\frac{1}{5}$ of 35

3. $\frac{1}{6}$ of 24

4. $\frac{1}{4}$ of 36

5. $\frac{1}{8}$ of 40

6. $\frac{2}{3}$ of 24

7. $\frac{2}{5}$ of 15

8. $\frac{3}{4}$ of 16

9. $\frac{5}{6}$ of 36

10. $\frac{4}{7}$ of 28

11. 10% of 30

12. 10% of 150

13. 10% of 80

14. 10% of £1·00

15. 10% of 500 cm

16. 20% of 40

17. 30% of 200

18. 50% of 36

19. 30% of 50

20. 25% of 24

B

Work out:

1. $\frac{3}{4}$ of 32 **24**
2. $\frac{2}{3}$ of 21 **14**
3. $\frac{4}{5}$ of 100 **80**
4. $\frac{5}{8}$ of 64 **40**
5. $\frac{3}{7}$ of 42 **18**
6. $\frac{7}{9}$ of 45 **35**
7. 20% of 90 **18**
8. 30% of 140 **42**
9. 5% of 520 **26**
10. 75% of 480 **360**
11. 40% of 250 **100**
12. 1% of 110 **1·1**

13. Fifty 5 year olds were asked if they believed in Father Christmas. Three fifths said yes. 30% said no. How many were *don't knows*? **5** **10·5**

14. There are 80 straws in a box. 60% are used. How many are left? **32**

15. Ninety children were asked if they have any brothers or sisters. Five ninths have at least one sister. 20% have no sister but at least one brother. How many children have neither brother nor sister? **32**

16. A cinema has 400 seats. At the first screening of a film 78% of the seats were filled. At the second screening thirteen sixteenths were filled. Which screening had the bigger audience, and by how many? **300**

C

Work out:

1. $\frac{5}{6}$ of 180
2. $\frac{3}{8}$ of 400
3. $\frac{2}{7}$ of 6·3
4. $\frac{7}{12}$ of 600
5. $\frac{8}{15}$ of 90
6. $\frac{49}{50}$ of 1000
7. 4% of 150
8. 15% of 280
9. 2·5% of 5000
10. 7% of 40
11. 95% of 600
12. 21% of 500

13. There are 3700 books in a library. 21% of them are out on loan. How many books are on the shelves? **2923**

14. A town has a population of 24 000. Three eighths are women. 35% are men. How many children live in the town? **7006**

15. The School Choir consists of 25% of the children in the school. 135 children are not in the choir. How many children are there in the school? **188**

16. There were 12 600 runners registered to take part in a marathon. 3% were injured in training and unable to take part. One ninth dropped out during the race. How many runners completed the course?

TARGET   To calculate fractions and percentages of quantities.

Examples

$\frac{1}{7}$ of £630

£630 ÷ 7

£90

$\frac{3}{7}$ of £630

$\left(\frac{1}{7}\text{ of £630}\right) \times 3$

£90 × 3

£270

10% of 25 m

$\frac{1}{10}$ of 25 m

2·5 m

60% of 25 m

(10% of 25 m) × 6

2·5 m × 6

15 m

5% of 25 m

(10% of 25 m) ÷ 2

2·5 m ÷ 2

1·25 m

A
Find

1 $\frac{1}{4}$ of 28

2 $\frac{1}{3}$ of 24

3 $\frac{1}{5}$ of 30p

4 $\frac{1}{8}$ of 40 mm

5 $\frac{1}{6}$ of 48 kg

6 $\frac{2}{3}$ of 18

7 $\frac{3}{4}$ of 36

8 $\frac{5}{6}$ of 30 cm

9 $\frac{2}{5}$ of 35 g

10 $\frac{3}{7}$ of £21

11 10% of 50

12 10% of 120

13 10% of £2

14 10% of £3·20

15 10% of 1 m

16 20% of 40

17 30% of 70

18 50% of 34 cm

19 25% of 32 km

20 20% of 25p

B
Work out

1 $\frac{2}{3}$ of 600 g

2 $\frac{5}{8}$ of 72 cm

3 $\frac{7}{10}$ of 500 ml

4 $\frac{4}{5}$ of 60p

5 $\frac{6}{7}$ of 42 kg

6 $\frac{3}{4}$ of 120 km

7 $\frac{2}{9}$ of £45

8 $\frac{5}{6}$ of 54 m

9 30% of £250

10 25% of 30 m

11 40% of 75 kg

12 5% of 80p

13 90% of 360 ml

14 75% of 160 km

15 60% of 55 cm

16 5% of 10 g

17 Seventy-five per cent of a bag of sand has not been used. 4·5 kg has been used. How much sand was in the full bag?   13·5

18 Darnell has £160. He spends three eighths of his money in one shop and 30% of it in another. How much has he spent?   £112

19 One 150 ml glass of drink is 5% of the amount in a jug. How much drink is in the full jug?   3000

20 Shannon is cycling 70 km. She rides a quarter of the distance in the first hour and 20% in the second hour. How far has she cycled?

C
Work out

1 $\frac{4}{5}$ of £6·00

2 $\frac{33}{100}$ of 1 kg

3 $\frac{5}{9}$ of £126

4 $\frac{9}{20}$ of 400 g

5 $\frac{3}{8}$ of 96 cm

6 $\frac{13}{15}$ of 120

7 $\frac{9}{25}$ of 1 km

8 $\frac{7}{12}$ of 600 ml

9 1% of 500 g

10 3% of 150 m

11 5% of 1·8 kg

12 15% of £2·20

13 75% of 42 cm

14 2·5% of £7·20

15 95% of £3·00

16 99% of £68·00

17 Kizzy's bank account pays 4% interest. She has £640 in the account. How much interest will she earn?

18 A builder mixes 4·8 kg of materials to make concrete. 55% is gravel, 30% is sand and the rest is cement. How much does he use of each material?

19 Paul uses 5 litres of water washing up. This is 2% of the total amount of water he uses in a day. How much water does he use daily?   250

20 Pattie earns £800 per week. She receives a raise of 7·5%. How much does she now earn?

TARGET   To use and simplify the notation of ratio.

EXPRESSING RATIOS
Fractions compare part to whole.
Ratios compare part to part.

Example 1
A cake is cut into 8 equal slices.
3 slices are eaten.

$\frac{3}{8}$ eaten

$\frac{5}{8}$ uneaten

The ratio of eaten to uneaten slices is 3 to 5.
This is written as $3:5$.

Example 2
Seven of the footballers in a team are right-footed, four are left-footed.

The ratio of right- to left-footed players is $7:4$.

SIMPLIFYING RATIOS
Writing a ratio in its lowest terms makes it easier to use. As with cancelling fractions, ratios are simplified by dividing each number by the highest common factor.

Example 1
In a test Jamil gets 15 questions right and 5 questions wrong. The ratio of right to wrong answers is $15:5$, which can be simplified to $3:1$.

Example 2
Simplify these ratios:

$\quad 2:8 \;\rightarrow 1:4$
$21:6 \;\rightarrow 7:2$
$25:40 \rightarrow 5:8$

A

1. Jess has been on holiday for 4 days. He has 10 days left. Write the ratio of days gone to days left in its lowest terms.

2. In a hospital ward there are 2 doctors and 10 nurses. Write the ratio doctors : nurses in its lowest terms.

3. A builder mixes 12 kg of sand and 4 kg of cement. Write the ratio sand : cement in its lowest terms.

4. Terri takes 14 photos. She saves 8 and deletes 6. Write the ratio of photos saved to photos deleted in its lowest terms.

5. In a squad of 15 footballers, 3 are left-footed and 12 are right-footed. Write the ratio of left-footed to right-footed players in its lowest terms.

6. There are 25 adults and 20 children on a bus. Write the ratio adults : children in its lowest terms.

7. In a quiz Barnie gets 12 answers right and 8 wrong. Write the ratio of right to wrong answers in its lowest terms.

8. At playtime 6 teachers have a mug of tea and 14 have coffee. Write the ratio tea : coffee in its lowest terms.

9. Write these ratios in their lowest terms.

   a) $4:6$ e) $14:16$
   b) $15:20$ f) $40:10$
   c) $6:3$ g) $15:9$
   d) $10:12$ h) $8:20$

B

1. Six km² of a farm is used for cultivating crops and nine km² for grazing livestock. Write the ratio of cultivation : grazing land use in its lowest terms. *2:3*

2. Five of the pencils in a packet are blunt and 15 are sharp. Write the ratio of blunt to sharp pencils in its simplest form. *1:3*

3. Twenty people in a shoe shop are browsing and eight people make a purchase. Write the ratio browsers : purchasers in its lowest terms. *5:2*

4. Judy has spent £15. She has £18 left. Write the ratio of money spent : left in its lowest terms. *5:6*

5. A hockey club has 80 adult members and 30 juniors. Write the ratio adults : juniors in its simplest form. *8:3*

6. There are 6 instructors and 42 children at a gymnastics coaching session. Write the ratio of instructors to children in its lowest terms. *1:7*

7. Sixteen plain packets of crisps are sold and 36 flavoured packets. Write the ratio plain : flavoured in its lowest terms. *4:9*

8. Twelve slices of a loaf have been eaten. Nine are left. Write the ratio eaten : uneaten slices in its simplest form. *4:3*

9. There are 26 children in a class. 14 are girls. Write the ratio girls : boys in its simplest form. *7:6*

10. Simplify
    a) 6 : 24 *1:4*
    b) 18 : 10 *9:5*
    c) 100 : 30 *10:3*
    d) 16 : 28 *4:7*
    e) 40 : 60 *2:3*
    f) 24 : 21 *8:7*
    g) 50 : 300 *1:6*
    h) 40 : 24 *5:3*

C

1. A factory produces 60 cars. 25 are sprayed black. Write the ratio of black cars to cars of other colours in its lowest terms. *5:7*

2. A 60 cm length is cut from a 2 m plank. Write the ratio of this length to that of the remaining plank in its simplest form. *3:7*

3. When a river bursts its banks 24 of the 68 houses in a village are flooded. Write the ratio flooded : unflooded houses in its lowest terms. *6:11*

4. A greengrocer has 136 kg of potatoes. 80 kg are sold. Write the ratio of sold to unsold potatoes in its lowest terms. *10:7*

5. In two weeks Lamar eats 3 pears, 9 apples and 12 bananas. Write the ratio of pears to apples to bananas in its lowest terms. *1:3:4*

6. A set of crockery contains four small, ten medium-sized and ten large plates. Write the ratio small : medium : large in its simplest form. *2:5:5*

7. In one hour an office worker spends 12 minutes dealing with emails, 18 minutes answering letters and 30 minutes on the phone. Write the ratio time spent on emails : letters : phone calls in its lowest terms. *2:3:5*

8. In Year 6 24 children walk to school, 16 cycle and 4 come by car. Write the ratio walkers : cyclists : passengers in its simplest form. *6:4:1*

9. There are 200 marbles in a jar. 90 are green, 45 are red and 65 are blue. Write the ratio green : red : blue marbles in its simplest form. *18:9:14*

10. Simplify
    a) 48 : 18 *8:3*
    b) 24 : 60 *2:5*
    c) 20 : 45 *4:9*
    d) 36 : 21 *12:7*
    e) 2 : 4 : 10 *1:2:5*
    f) 32 : 12 : 8 *8:3:2*
    g) 5 : 25 : 20 *1:5:4*
    h) 21 : 9 : 18 *7:3:6*

TARGET To use ratio to solve problems involving the relative sizes of two quantities.

Example 1

A prize of £200 is shared 3 : 2 between Diane and Dave. How much should they receive each?

1 Find the number of shares.

5 (3 + 2 = 5)

2 Find the value of each share.

£40 (£200 ÷ 5 = £40)

3 Work out how much is received each.

Diane £120 (£40 × 3)
Dave £80 (£40 × 2)

Example 2

The ratio of boys to girls in a school is 6 : 5. There are 168 boys in the school. How many children are there altogether?

1 Find the total number of parts.

11 (6 + 5 = 11)

2 Find the value of one part.

28 (168 ÷ 6 = 28)

3 Work out the number of children.

308 (28 × 11 = 308)

Example 3

The ratio of adults to children at a cinema is 3 : 4. There are 111 adults in the cinema. How many children are there?

1 Find the number of parts.

7 (3 + 4 = 7)

2 Find the value of each part.

37 (111 ÷ 3 = 37)

3 Work out the number of children.

148 (37 × 4 = 148)

A

A row of tiles is laid with this repeating pattern.

1 How many blue tiles are there if there are:

a) 12 red tiles   b) 30 red tiles?

2 How many red tiles are there if there are:

a) 12 blue tiles   b) 40 blue tiles?

In a raffle there is one prize for every 20 tickets.

3 How many prizes are there if:

a) 120 tickets are sold

b) 500 tickets are sold?

4 How many tickets have been sold if there are:

a) 9 prizes   b) 17 prizes?

5 In Year 6 the ratio of dinners to packed lunches is 2 : 1. Forty children have a dinner. How many have a packed lunch?

6 In a class the ratio of boys to girls is 3 : 4. There are 16 girls. How many boys are there?

7 The ratio of red to green apples in a bowl is 3 : 1. If there are 15 red apples, how many apples are green?

8 At a market the ratio of blue jeans sold to black jeans sold is 7 : 2. If 6 black jeans are sold, how many blue jeans are sold?

B

1. In one season the ratio of goals for to goals against in Chelsea's matches was 5 : 3. If Chelsea scored 80 goals, how many did they let in?

2. In November the ratio of wet days to dry days was 4 : 1. How many days were wet?

3. In a survey of trees in a wood the ratio of beech trees to other trees was 2 : 5. If there were 14 beeches, how many other types of tree were there?

4. In a supermarket the ratio of male to female employees is 2 : 3. If there are 36 female employees, how many men work there?

5. During a lesson lasting one hour the ratio of the time Aidan spends working to the time he spends day-dreaming is 3 : 7. How long does he actually work?

6. In a hospital ward the ratio of nurses to patients is 2 : 9. If there are 63 patients, how many nurses are there?

7. A cashier in a bank counts £1300 in £10 and £20 notes only. The ratio £10 notes : £20 notes is 3 : 5. How many are there of each note?

8. Share:
   a) 21 sweets in the ratio 3 : 4
   b) £1·20 in the ratio 2 : 1
   c) 1 litre of drink in the ratio 2 : 3
   d) 36 strawberries in the ratio 4 : 5
   e) £90 in the ratio 3 : 15
   f) 480 g of nuts in the ratio 5 : 3.

C

1. A photocopier enlarges in a ratio of 5 : 7. If the original document was 30 cm long and 20 cm wide, what are the dimensions of the photocopy?

2. In a bakery the ratio of large loaves to small loaves is 8 : 3. If there are 96 large loaves, how many small loaves are there?

3. On a plane the ratio of adult to child passengers is 15 : 2. If there are 300 adult passengers, how many children are there on the plane?

4. In a necklace the ratio of black to red to green beads is 1 : 2 : 4. If there are 32 red beads, how many beads are:
   a) black
   b) green?

5. In an English exam the ratio of marks given for spelling to writing to reading is 2 : 8 : 5. If there are 48 marks for writing, how many are there for:
   a) spelling
   b) reading?

6. In a sports shop the ratio of large to medium to small running vests sold is 3 : 5 : 4. If 15 medium vests are sold, how many large vests and how many small vests are sold?

7. Three afternoon lessons last for 2 hours altogether. The lengths of the lessons are in the ratio 2 : 3 : 3. How long is each lesson?

8. Split:
   a) 1·32 m in the ratio 6 : 5
   b) £65 in the ratio 4 : 9
   c) 6 hours in the ratio 7 : 2
   d) 2 kg in the ratio 1 : 3 : 4
   e) £5·40 in the ratio 3 : 2 : 5
   f) 750 ml in the ratio 5 : 1 : 9.

TARGET   To solve problems involving proportion.

A proportion is a quantity that is part of a whole. In everyday life we often have to solve problems of proportion when dealing with recipes.

Example 1
A cake recipe requires 50 g of butter to be used for every cake. The amount of butter needed will increase in proportion to the number of cakes.

Cakes	Butter
1	50 g
2	100 g
3	150 g
⋮	⋮
7	350 g
8	400 g
and so on.	

Example 2
A recipe for 8 people requires 1000 g of fruit.

How much fruit is needed for 5 people?

Step 1   Find how much fruit is needed for 1 person.

125 g (1000 g ÷ 8 = 125 g)

Step 2   Find how much fruit is needed for 5.

625 g (125 g × 5 = 625 g)

 A

① In an art lesson lasting one and a half hours Keeley spends 15 minutes drawing and the rest of the time painting. Write as a fraction in its lowest terms the proportion of the lesson Keeley is:

a) drawing   b) painting.

② One litre of orange paint is made by mixing 200 ml of red paint with 800 ml of yellow. Write as a percentage the proportion of the mixture which is:

a) red   b) yellow.

③ Rex and Rover share a 600 g can of dog food. Rex eats 250 g. Rover eats 350 g. Write the proportion eaten by each dog as a fraction in its lowest terms.

④ There are 60 passengers on a bus. 45 are children. 15 are adults. Write as a percentage the proportion of passengers who are:

a) children   b) adults.

A necklace is made using this pattern of beads.

⑤ How many beads are there altogether if there are:

a) 36 red beads   b) 40 yellow beads?

⑥ How many red beads are there if there are 40 beads altogether?

⑦ How many yellow beads are there if there are 72 beads altogether?

⑧   **NUT BROWNIES**

100 g butter	2 eggs
120 g chocolate	80 g sugar
60 g flour	160 g nuts

Makes 8 brownies

Rewrite the above ingredients for:

a) 4 brownies   b) 24 brownies.

B

1 In a cafe three cups of tea cost £1·80 altogether. What would be the cost of:

a) 2 cups   b) 40 cups?

2 Four rolls cost £1·00. Find the cost of:

a) 3 rolls   b) 10 rolls.

3 £8 is worth 9·6 euros. How many euros will I be given in exchange for:

a) £5   b) £200?

4 A machine can make 300 pins in six minutes. How many pins can it make in:

a) 5 minutes   b) 14 minutes?

5 Five bricks weigh 4 kg altogether. What is the weight of:

a) 3 bricks   b) 16 bricks?

6 A plane travels 300 km in 15 minutes. How far does it travel in:

a) 8 minutes   b) 45 minutes?

7 Shaun uses 400 ml of squash to make ten glasses of drink. How much squash would he need to make:

a) 6 glasses   b) 38 glasses?

8 Twelve eggs cost £2·40. Find the cost of:

a) 7 eggs   b) 20 eggs.

9 Fish costs £7 for 1 kg. Find the cost of:

a) 600 g   b) 350 g.

C

1 Five cinema tickets cost £38. What is the cost of:

a) 4 tickets   b) 11 tickets?

2 A cyclist rides 6 km in 15 minutes. Travelling at the same speed how long would it take her to cycle:

a) 5 km

b) 19 km?

3 A farmer uses 96 m of wire to fence a 20 m length of field. How much wire will he need to fence a further:

a) 7 m   b) 150 m?

4 Nine biscuits cost £1·08. Find the cost of:

a) 4 biscuits   b) 30 biscuits.

5 Six litres of water runs from a tap in 30 seconds. At the same rate of flow how much water will run from the tap in:

a) 18 seconds

b) 1 minute 20 seconds?

6 Sixteen bags of flour weigh 44 kg. Find the weight of:

a) 2 bags   b) 50 bags.

7 £400 is worth 580 US dollars. At this exchange rate what is the value in dollars of:

a) £10   b) £30 000?

8 In 40 minutes Martin walks 3·6 km. Walking at the same speed how far would he walk in:

a) 2 minutes

b) 1 hour 25 minutes?

TARGET To solve problems involving ratio and proportion.

Ratio compares part to part.
Proportion compares part to whole.

Example 1
A necklace is made using this pattern of beads.

Ratios of blue to red beads	2 : 3
Proportion of blue beads	$\frac{2}{5}$
Proportion of red beads	$\frac{3}{5}$

Example 2
In a supermarket 2 large packets of cereal are put on the shelves for every 5 small packets. 40 small packets are put out. How many large packets are put on the shelves?

Find ratio of small to large packets.

5 : 2

Find value of one part.

8 (40 ÷ 5 = 8)

Work out the number of large packets put out on shelves.

16 (8 × 2 = 16)

Example 3
At a swimming gala 3 in every 8 swimmers receive a medal. How many medals are awarded if there are 72 swimmers altogether?

Find proportion of swimmers receiving a medal.

$\frac{3}{8}$ (3 in every 8)

Find the number of medals awarded.

27 (72 ÷ 8 = 9   9 × 3 = 27)

A

A necklace is made using this pattern of beads.

1. Write the ratio of green beads to black beads.

2. Write the proportion of the beads which is green.

3. If there are 20 green beads, how many black beads are there?

4. If there are 56 beads altogether, how many beads are:

    a) black   b) green?

5. A map has a scale of 1 cm to 2 km. Two castles are 23 cm apart on the map. What is the actual distance between the castles?

6. Lavinia makes jam. One jar in every 4 is plum jam. She makes 56 jars altogether. How many jars of plum jam does she make?

7. A shop sells 5 ice creams to every 2 lollies it sells. 35 ice creams are sold. How many lollies are sold?

8. Two in every three members of the audience at a concert are children. There are 1200 children at the concert. How many adults are in the audience?

9. In Year 4 the ratio of children with a pet to those with no pet is 5 : 4. If 36 children do not have a pet, how many do?

B

1. A bridge is 48 m tall. A scale model of the bridge is 37 cm long and 12 cm tall. How long is the actual bridge? *148*

2. In a cake recipe the ratio of dried fruit to nuts is 3 : 2. What quantity of dried fruit is required if 90 g of nuts is used? *135*

3. a) Five bars of chocolate cost £8·75. What do three bars cost? *5.25*

   b) The cost of all the bars in a box is £35. How many bars are in a box? *20*

4. The ratio of the weight of a large bag of potatoes to that of a small bag is 11 : 5. If a large bag weighs 5·5 kg, how much does a small bag weigh? *2.5 kg*

5. There are 360 passengers on a flight to Singapore from London. Five in every eight of the passengers are flying on to Sydney. How many of the passengers are bound for Sydney? *225*

6. A factory makes 7 single beds to every 4 double beds.
   a) How many double beds does it produce if it makes 91 single beds? *52*

   b) How many single beds does it produce if it makes 96 double beds? *168*

7. A car uses £8 worth of petrol for every 100 km it travels. What is the cost of the petrol used to travel:
   a) 70 km *5.60*   b) 240 km? *19·20*

8. The profits made by a shop are shared between the owner and her assistant in a ratio of 5 : 3, the owner receiving the larger share. How much does the assistant receive if:
   a) total profit is £20 000 *12 500*

   b) the owner receives £17 435? *160*

C

A row of tiles has this repeating pattern.

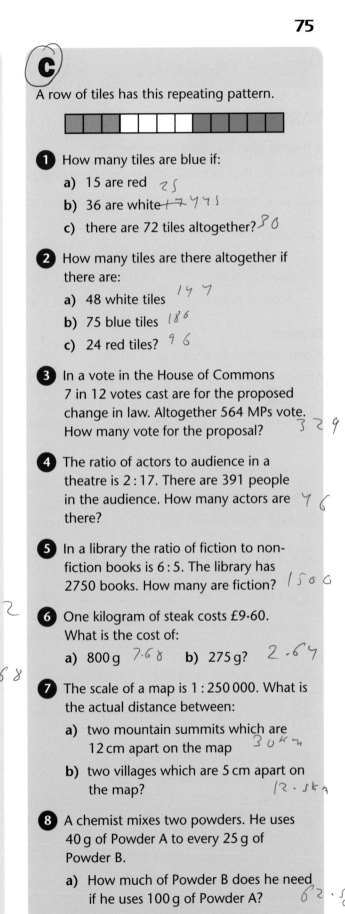

1. How many tiles are blue if:
   a) 15 are red *25*
   b) 36 are white *17 44 5*
   c) there are 72 tiles altogether? *30*

2. How many tiles are there altogether if there are:
   a) 48 white tiles *147*
   b) 75 blue tiles *180*
   c) 24 red tiles? *96*

3. In a vote in the House of Commons 7 in 12 votes cast are for the proposed change in law. Altogether 564 MPs vote. How many vote for the proposal? *329*

4. The ratio of actors to audience in a theatre is 2 : 17. There are 391 people in the audience. How many actors are there? *46*

5. In a library the ratio of fiction to non-fiction books is 6 : 5. The library has 2750 books. How many are fiction? *1500*

6. One kilogram of steak costs £9·60. What is the cost of:
   a) 800 g *7.68*   b) 275 g? *2·64*

7. The scale of a map is 1 : 250 000. What is the actual distance between:
   a) two mountain summits which are 12 cm apart on the map *30 km*

   b) two villages which are 5 cm apart on the map? *12·5 km*

8. A chemist mixes two powders. He uses 40 g of Powder A to every 25 g of Powder B.
   a) How much of Powder B does he need if he uses 100 g of Powder A? *62·5 g*

   b) How much of the mixture does he make if he uses 375 g of Powder B? *600 g*

TARGET   To use ratio notation in the context of scale drawing.

A map or plan is usually drawn to scale.

This means that distances in the map or plan are drawn in proportion to the actual distances.

Scales are shown in two ways, using units or as a ratio.

Examples

	Using units	As a ratio
Scale of plan	1 cm represents 1 m	1 : 100
Scale of map	1 cm represents 1 km	1 : 100 000

Example

A plan is drawn to a scale of 1 : 1000.

A fence is 4.6 cm long on the plan. How long is the actual fence?

$$4.6 \, cm \times 1000 = 4600 \, cm$$

$$= 46 \, m \qquad \textbf{Answer} \quad \textit{The actual fence is 46 m long.}$$

A

Use the scale to work out the real length represented by these lines.

1   1 cm to 1 m   _____

2   1 mm to 1 cm   _____

3   1 cm to 1 km   _____

4   1 cm to 2 m   _____

5   1 cm to 5 km   _____

6   This is the floor plan of a room showing the doorway and the window spaces. All the lengths are in metres. All the walls are perpendicular.

Draw the plan using a scale of:

a)   1 cm to 1 m

b)   2 cm to 1 m.

0·5   2·7   1·3   1·6   0·8   1·4

0·8   1·3

2·0   2·4

3·6

1·7   1·3

4·2

B

Use the scale to work out the real length represented by each line.

1 1 : 100 _____

2 1 : 1000 _____

3 1 : 100 000 _____

4 1 : 20 _____

5 1 : 50 000 _____

6 This is the floor plan of a two-bedroom bungalow. All the lengths are in metres. Copy the plan using a scale of:

a) 1 : 100

b) 1 : 50.

C

1 Give the scale used for each of these lines as a ratio.

a) _____ 65 m _____   b) _____ 4·9 km _____

c) _____ 1·33 km _____

d) ____ 18 m ____   e) _____ 11·6 km _____

f) _____ 2 km _____   g) ____ 1·08 m ____

Find the distance between the towns.

2 Ashbourne – Binley

3 Carford – Dalton

4 Eaden – Fairwell

5 Binley – Carford

6 Fairwell – Dalton

7 Ashbourne – Eaden

Scale 1 : 250 000

TARGET   To solve missing number problems and begin to express such problems algebraically.

Performing the same calculation on both sides of an equation will mean that the sides remain equal. This allows us to find the missing number in an equation.

Examples

$\boxed{} + 7 = 19$

$\boxed{} = 12$

(−7 from both sides)

$\boxed{} \div 6 = 3$

$\boxed{} = 18$

(both sides ×6)

$4 \times \boxed{} - 5 = 23$

$4 \times \boxed{} = 28$ (+5 both sides)

$\boxed{} = 7$ (÷4 both sides)

In algebra we use letters instead of boxes for missing numbers.
In the following examples form an algebraic equation using x and solve the equation to find the value of x.

1 Divide x by 2 and take 5 to give 17.

$\dfrac{x}{2} - 5 = 17$ ($\dfrac{x}{2}$ means $x \div 2$)

$\dfrac{x}{2} = 22$ (+5 both sides)

$x = 44$ (×2 both sides)

2 Multiply x by 3 and add 2 to give 20.

$3x + 2 = 20$ ($3x$ means 3 times x)

$3x = 18$ (−2 both sides)

$x = 6$ (÷3 both sides)

A

Find the missing number.

1 $\boxed{} + 4 = 11$

2 $15 + \boxed{} = 24$

3 $\boxed{} + 0 \cdot 7 = 1 \cdot 3$

4 $\boxed{} + \frac{2}{3} = 1\frac{1}{3}$

5 $0 \cdot 48 + \boxed{} = 1$

6 $\boxed{} - 30 = 26$

7 $\boxed{} - 19 = 88$

8 $\boxed{} - \frac{4}{5} = 2\frac{1}{5}$

9 $\boxed{} - 0 \cdot 37 = 1\frac{1}{4}$

10 $\boxed{} - 0 \cdot 66 = 9 \cdot 5$

11 $45 \times \boxed{} = 90$

12 $3 \times \boxed{} = 24$

13 $0 \cdot 5 \times \boxed{} = 2$

14 $10 \times \boxed{} = 1 \cdot 7$

15 $80 \times \boxed{} = 560$

16 $\boxed{} \div 3 = 12$

17 $\boxed{} \div 5 = 0 \cdot 8$

18 $\boxed{} \div 9 = 30$

19 $\boxed{} \div 10 = 0 \cdot 43$

20 $\boxed{} \div 6 = \frac{1}{4}$

Find the number.

21 Double this number and add 3 to give an answer of 11.

22 Multiply this number by 4 and subtract 7 to give 5.

23 Multiply this number by 5 and subtract 3 to give 7.

24 Multiply this number by 6 and add 2 to give 20.

25 Multiply this number by 3 and subtract 6 to give 9.

26 Double this number and subtract 4 to give 12.

B

Find the missing number by forming an algebraic equation and solving it.

1. $3 \times \boxed{2} + 5 = 11$
2. $9 + 6 \times \boxed{7} = 51$
3. $10 \times \boxed{0.5} - 1.4 = 3.6$
4. $4 \times \boxed{\frac{2}{4}} + \frac{3}{5} = 2\frac{1}{5}$
5. $7 \times \boxed{0.8} + 0.8 = 6.4$
6. $8 = 3 \times \boxed{5} - 7$
7. $50 = 6 \times \boxed{8} + 2$
8. $32 = 10 + 2 \times \boxed{11}$
9. $2\frac{1}{2} = \frac{3}{4} + 7 \times \boxed{\frac{1}{4}}$
10. $2 = 5 \times \boxed{0.5} - 0.5$

11. $\boxed{30} \div 2 + 11 = 26$
12. $\boxed{78} \div 10 - 1.4 = 2.4$
13. $\boxed{54} \div 6 + 8 = 17$
14. $\boxed{208} \div 7 - 29 = 6$
15. $\boxed{3} \div 4 + 0.25 = 1$
16. $2 = \boxed{6} \div 3 - \frac{2}{3}$
17. $8 = \boxed{36} \div 9 + 4$
18. $20 = \boxed{132} \div 12 + 9$
19. $0.6 = \boxed{4.5} \div 5 - 0.3$
20. $0 = \boxed{96} \div 8 - 12$

Form an equation and find the value of x.

21. Multiply x by 5 and add 4 to give 19. $x = 3$
22. Double x and subtract 6 to give 8. $x = 7$
23. Multiply x by 7 and subtract 15 to give 13. $x = 4$
24. Divide x by 3 and subtract 7 to give 5. $x = 36$
25. Multiply x by 9 and subtract 11 to give 7. $x = 2$
26. Divide x by 4 and add 10 to give 16. $x = 24$
27. Multiply x by 4 and add 4 to give 100. $x = 24$

C

Solve the equation.

1. $4x + 2 = 30$ $x = 7$
2. $3p - 0.6 = 3.9$ $p = 1.5$
3. $8t + 2.8 = 10$ $t = 0.9$
4. $7k + 3 = 45$ $k = 6$
5. $12d - 8 = 100$ $d = 9$
6. $\frac{m}{4} + 7 = 32$ $100 = m$
7. $\frac{c}{6} - 2 = 9$ $c = 66$ $z = 16$
8. $\frac{z}{10} + 1.7 = 3.3$
9. $\frac{u}{5} - 5 = 7$ $u = 60$
10. $\frac{n}{3} + 0.4 = 1$ $n = 1.8$

Find the value of x.

11. $2x + 4 = 4x - 2$ 3
12. $3x - 7 = x + 3$ 5
13. $6x + 10 = 10x + 4$ 1.5
14. $7x - 2 = 2x + 28$ 6
15. $x + 3 = 4x - 3$ 2
16. $3x + 1 = 2x + 3$ 2
17. $x + 3 = 2x - 1$ 4
18. $5x - 1 = 4x + 2$ 3
19. $3x + 3 = 4x - 4$ 7
20. $x + 6 = 3x - 14$ 10

Form an equation and find the value of x.

21. Adding 3 to x gives the same answer as doubling it and subtracting 5. $x = 8$
22. Multiplying x by 3 and taking 2 gives the same answer as adding 6 to x. $x = 4$
23. Doubling x and adding 5 gives the same answer as multiplying x by 5 and subtracting 4. $x = 3$
24. Multiplying x by 10 and subtracting 6 gives the same answer as doubling x and adding 6. $x = 1.5$
25. Multiplying x by 5 and taking 1 gives the same answer as trebling x and adding 3. $x = 2$

TARGET   To express and solve a missing number problem algebraically.

Examples

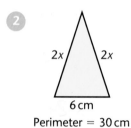

1

$2x + x + 150 = 360$

$3x + 150 = 360$

$3x = 210\ (-150)$

$x = 70\ (\div 3)$

Answer $x = 70°$, $2x = 140°$

3

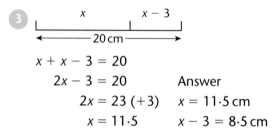

$x + x - 3 = 20$

$2x - 3 = 20$ Answer

$2x = 23\ (+3)$ $x = 11·5$ cm

$x = 11·5$ $x - 3 = 8·5$ cm

2

$2x + 2x + 6 = 30$

$4x + 6 = 30$

$4x = 24\ (-6)$

$x = 6\ (\div 4)$

Side $2x = 12$ cm

Perimeter = 30 cm

4

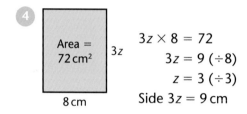

$3z \times 8 = 72$

$3z = 9\ (\div 8)$

$z = 3\ (\div 3)$

Side $3z = 9$ cm

In sections A, B and C Area and Perimeter are shown by the letters A and P.

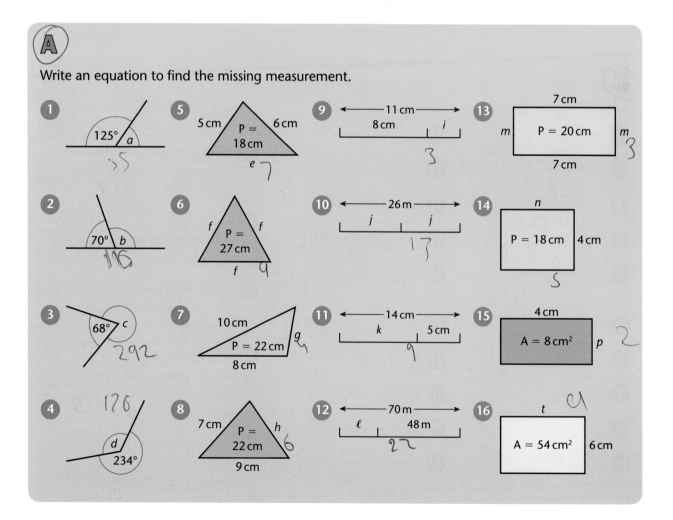

A

Write an equation to find the missing measurement.

1 125° a 55

5 5 cm, 6 cm, P = 18 cm, e 7

9 11 cm, 8 cm, i 3

13 7 cm, m P = 20 cm m, 7 cm   3

2 70° b 116

6 f, f, P = 27 cm, f 9

10 26 m, j, j 17

14 n, P = 18 cm, 4 cm   5

3 68° c 292

7 10 cm, P = 22 cm, 8 cm, g 4

11 14 cm, k, 5 cm   9

15 4 cm, A = 8 cm², p 2

4 126, d, 234°

8 7 cm, P = 22 cm, h, 9 cm   6

12 70 m, ℓ, 48 m   22

16 t, A = 54 cm², 6 cm   9

B

Write an equation to find the missing angles and lengths.

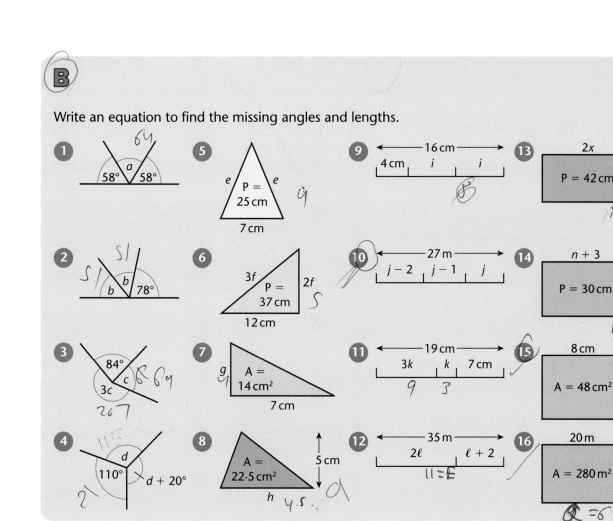

1 64
a
58° 58°

5 e P = 25 cm e
7 cm
9

9 ←16 cm→
4 cm i i
8

13 2x
P = 42 cm x
x = 7

2 51
51 b
b 78°

6 3f P = 37 cm 2f
12 cm
S

10 ←27 m→
j − 2 j − 1 j

14 n + 3
P = 30 cm n
R6 N = 6

3 84°
c 6 6y
3c
207

7 g A = 14 cm²
7 cm

11 ←19 cm→
3k k 7 cm
9 3

15 8 cm
A = 48 cm² 3p
24p = 48
p = 48÷24

4 115
d
110° d + 20°
2

8 A = 22·5 cm² 5 cm
h 4.5

12 ←35 m→
2ℓ ℓ + 2
11 = E

16 20 m
A = 280 m² 2q
46q = 280
q = 280÷40
q = 7

C

Write an equation and solve it to find the missing angles and lengths.

1 2x − 10° 3x x + 40°

2 2x 3x
122° x + 10°

3 P = 52 cm
2x 6x
5x 48m

4 A = 18 cm² x 6
x 6

5 ←26 cm→
a a + 1 a − 2
A = 9

6 ←64 cm→
2y 3y − 5 9 cm
y = 12

7 3v − 4
P = 52 cm 2v
v = 6

8 2z
A = 50 cm² z
z = 5

Answer each question by forming an equation and then solving it.

9 An isosceles triangle has a perimeter of 15 cm. Its longest side is 6 cm long. What is the length of the two equal sides (s)? 4.5

10 A rectangle has a perimeter of 26 cm. It is 3 cm longer than wide. What is its length (l)? 10

11 A rectangle has an area of 36 cm². It is four times as long as it is wide. What is its width (w)? 7.2 cm

12 The shortest side of a right-angled triangle is 6 cm. The triangle has a perimeter of 24 cm and an area of 24 cm². Find the lengths of the other two sides (x and y).

TARGET To use formulae expressed in words and algebraically.

FORMULAE

A formula shows us how to work something out. Formulae can be expressed in words or algebraically.

Example

A formula for working out the number of wheels (w) required for c cars.

In words   The number of wheels required is four times the number of cars.

Algebra $w = 4c$

The advantage of expressing a formula algebraically is obvious.

Some formulae are familiar.

Example

The area (a) of a rectangle is the length times the width.

$$a = lw \quad (lw = \text{length times width})$$

WRITING A FORMULA

Example

Write a formula for the perimeter (p) of this triangle.

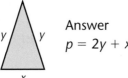

Answer
$p = 2y + x$

USING A FORMULA

A formula for the number of faces (f) in a prism is half the number of vertices (v) plus two.

$$f = \frac{v}{2} + 2 \quad \left(\frac{v}{2} \text{ means } v \div 2\right)$$

How many faces are there in a prism with 12 vertices?

$$v = 12 \qquad f = \frac{12}{2} + 2$$
$$= 6 + 2$$
$$= 8$$

Answer 8 faces.

 A

Write a formula for the perimeter (p) of each shape.

1

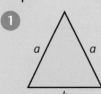

2

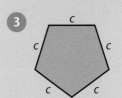

3

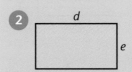

4

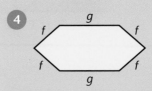

Write a formula for the number of:

5 skis s for p people

6 centimetres c in k kilometres

7 days d in w weeks

8 horseshoes s needed for h horses

9 grams g in k kilograms

10 hours h in d days.

$$m = 60h$$

11 Use the above formula to find the number of minutes in:

  a) 3 hours   **b)** 12 hours

$$a = lw \,(\text{cm}^2)$$

12 Use the above formula to find the area of a rectangle with:

  a) length 6 cm, width 8 cm

  b) length 12 cm, width 10 cm

B

Write a formula for the size of angle *a* in each shape.

 1

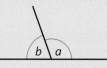

2

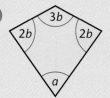

3

4

Draw and label a shape whose perimeter is given by each formula.

5 a quadrilateral $\quad p = 2x + y + z$ (cm)

6 a hexagon $\qquad\quad p = 6a$ (cm)

7 a pentagon $\qquad\; p = 3k + l + m$ (cm)

8 a triangle $\qquad\quad p = 3e$ (cm)

The area of a triangle is half the length of the base times the height.

or $\qquad a = \dfrac{bh}{2}$ (cm²)

9 Use the above formula to find the area of a triangle with:

a) base 9 cm, height 7 cm

b) base 6 cm, height 2·5 cm

10 1 gallon = 4·5 ℓ

Use the above formula to find the number of litres in:

a) 4 gallons

b) 20 gallons

 C

For each shape write a formula for:

a) the perimeter

b) the area.

1

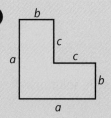

2

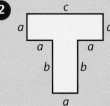

$$v = lwh \text{ (cm}^3)$$

Use the above formula for the volume of a cuboid with dimensions of:

3 length 5 cm, width 4 cm, height 1·5 cm

4 length 40 cm, width 25 cm, height 12 cm

$$\text{sum of angles} = 180(\text{sides} - 2)°$$

Use the above formula to find the sum of the angles of a polygon with:

5 5 sides

6 7 sides

7 An electrician has a call out charge of £25 and he charges a further £50 for every hour worked. Write a formula for how much he would charge (*c*) for working *h* hours.

8 A car begins a journey with a full tank of 40 litres of petrol. It uses one litre of petrol for every 10 miles travelled. Write a formula for the amount of petrol (*p*) in the tank after travelling *m* miles.

9 There are 50 questions in a test. There are 2 marks for each question. Write a formula for the number of marks (*m*) scored by someone who:

a) gets *r* questions right

b) gets *w* questions wrong.

TARGET To find pairs of numbers that satisfy number sentences involving two unknowns.

Examples

Find both possible solutions.

$4x + 3y = 23$ $3a + 2b = 11$

Possible solutions   Possible solutions

$x = 2, y = 5$ $a = 1, b = 4$
$x = 5, y = 1$ $a = 3, b = 1$

Find two possible solutions.

$6x - y = 9$ $2x - 3y = 7$

Solutions   Solutions

$x = 2, y = 3$ $x = 5, y = 1$
$x = 3, y = 9$ $x = 8, y = 3$
and so on   and so on

A

Copy and complete to find all the possible solutions for the equation.

1 $x + y = 4$

$x = 1, y = \boxed{}$
$x = \boxed{}, y = 2$
$x = \boxed{}, y = \boxed{}$

2 $x + 3y = 8$

$x = 2, y = \boxed{}$
$x = \boxed{}, y = \boxed{}$

3 $2x + y = 7$

$x = 3, y = \boxed{}$
$x = \boxed{}, y = 5$
$x = \boxed{}, y = \boxed{}$

Find all the possible solutions for values of both x and y no greater than 10.

4 $2x - y = 7$

$x = 6, y = \boxed{}$
$x = \boxed{}, y = 1$
$x = \boxed{}, y = 9$
$x = \boxed{}, y = \boxed{}$
$x = \boxed{}, y = \boxed{}$

B

Find both possible solutions.

1 $2x + y = 5$

2 $5x + y = 13$

3 $3x + 4y = 30$

4 $2x + 3y = 15$

5 $5a + 2b = 26$

6 $4a + 5b = 52$

7 $7s + 2t = 31$

8 $5s + 3t = 34$

Find two possible solutions.

9 $x - 2y = 11$

10 $3x - 2y = 2$

11 $4x - 2y = 10$

12 $3x - y = 13$

13 $10p - 3q = 1$

14 $5c - 4d = 4$

15 $4m - 3n = 8$

16 $5v - 3w = 5$

C

Find all possible solutions.

1 $6x + y = 29$

2 $4x + 3y = 43$

3 $3x + 2y = 28$

4 $7x + 2y = 46$

5 $9e + 4f = 100$

6 $5y + 3z = 57$

7 $10k + 3l = 98$

8 $5g + 4h = 89$

Find three possible solutions.

9 $6p - 5q = 19$

10 $3d - 2e = 23$

11 $4r - 3s = 22$

12 $7g - 4h = 15$

13 $5w - 3x = 38$

14 $10k - 7m = 12$

15 $8t - 3u = 15$

16 $9z - 4a = 26$

TARGET To list all possible outcomes of combinations of two variables.

Examples

① Adult tickets for a concert cost £5. Children's tickets cost £3. A group of people pay £46 for their tickets. Find all the possible combinations of adult and child tickets for this amount.

Answer
2 adult, 12 child
5 adult, 7 child
8 adult, 2 child

② Find all possible solutions for this equation
$$3x + 4y = 53$$
Answer
$x = 3, y = 11$ $x = 11, y = 5$
$x = 7, y = 8$ $x = 15, y = 2$

A

① A class of 25 children are asked to get into groups of 2 or 3. Copy and complete the list showing all the possible ways this can be done.

2 TWOS, 7 THREES

5 TWOS, ☐ THREES

☐ TWOS, 3 THREES

☐ TWOS, ☐ THREES

② The same 25 children are then asked to get into groups of 3 or 4. List all the possible ways this can be done.

③ Esme has 2p and 5p coins only. She has 39p. List all the possible combinations of 2p and 5p coins which can make 39p.

④ Andy has 46 straws. Find all the possible ways he can use all 46 straws to make squares and triangles.

B

① A farmer has 86 eggs. The eggs are put into boxes of 6 or 8. Find all the possible ways in which all 86 eggs can be put into boxes.

② A baker makes 150 cakes. The cakes are packed in boxes of 4 or 9. Find all the possible ways in which all the cakes can be packed.

For each equation list all the possible values of *x* and *y*.

③ $2x + y = 10$

④ $3x + 2y = 20$

⑤ $x + 4y = 22$

⑥ $5x + 3y = 37$

⑦ $3x + 4y = 38$

⑧ $2x + 5y = 43$

⑨ $6x + y = 34$

⑩ $4x + 5y = 47$

C

① The angles of a quadrilateral are all multiples of 5°. Three of the angles are equal and larger than the fourth angle. Find all the possible combinations of angle sizes of the shape.

② A cinema has 16 or 20 seats in each row. There are 412 seats in the cinema. Find all the possible combinations of rows of 16 and 20 which result in 412 seats.

For each equation list all the possible values of *x* and *y*.

③ $7x + 5y = 94$

④ $3x + 8y = 100$

⑤ $5x + 9y = 132$

⑥ $10x + 3y = 195$

⑦ $2x + 11y = 127$

⑧ $3x + 5y = 81$

⑨ $4x + 7y = 113$

⑩ $12x + 5y = 238$

TARGET To generate and describe number sequences.

A

Pattern 1

Pattern 2

Pattern 3

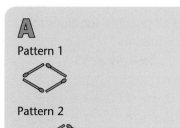

1 Draw the next two diagrams in the above pattern.

2 Copy and complete the table.

Pattern	Matches
1	4
2	
3	
4	
5	

3 Copy and complete this sentence.

The rule for the number of matches is ____ times the pattern number.

4 How many matches would there be in:

a) the 7th pattern

b) the 10th pattern

c) the 30th pattern

d) the 50th pattern?

B

Pattern 1

Pattern 2

Pattern 3

1 Draw the next two diagrams in the above pattern.

2 Copy and complete the table.

Pattern	Dots
1	5
2	
3	
4	
5	

3 Copy and complete.

The rule for the number of dots is ____ times the pattern number plus ____.

4 How many dots would there be in:

a) the 10th pattern

b) the 15th pattern

c) the 43rd pattern?

5 Which pattern has:

a) 23 dots

b) 38 dots

c) 56 dots?

C

Pattern 1

Pattern 2

Pattern 3

1 How many matches would there be in:

a) the 9th pattern

b) the 17th pattern

c) the 28th pattern?

2 Which pattern has

a) 40 matches

b) 67 matches

c) 100 matches?

3 Pattern 1

Pattern 2

Pattern 3

Copy and complete.

The rule for the number of dots is ____ times the pattern number minus ____.

4 How many dots would there be in the 25th pattern?

5 Which pattern has:

a) 60 dots

b) 92 dots?

TARGET   To generate and describe number sequences.

Examples

					The rule is:	The nth term is:
To find the rule that	1	3	5	7	add 2	$2n - 1$
links the numbers	3	0	-3	-6	subtract 3	$6 - 3n$
study the gaps.	$\frac{4}{9}$	$\frac{8}{9}$	$1\frac{3}{9}$	$1\frac{7}{9}$	add $\frac{4}{9}$.	$\frac{4n}{9}$.

A

Write the first six numbers in each sequence.

	Start at	Rule		Start at	Rule		Start at	Rule
1	4	+10	**6**	65	−7	**11**	26	+9
2	38	−2	**7**	15	+20	**12**	30	−3
3	7	+3	**8**	110	−11	**13**	$\frac{1}{2}$	$+\frac{1}{2}$
4	29	−4	**9**	21	+2	**14**	80	−5
5	0·5	+1	**10**	948	−101	**15**	25	+25

B

Complete these sequences by filling in the boxes. Write the rule each time.

1 44   47   50   53   ☐ ☐ ☐

2 89   85   81   77   ☐ ☐ ☐

3 115   140   165   190   ☐ ☐ ☐

4 0·5   0·6   0·7   0·8   ☐ ☐ ☐

5 −2   −4   −6   ☐ ☐ ☐   −14

6 119   114   ☐ ☐ ☐   94   89

7 −9   −6   ☐ ☐ ☐   6   9

8 $\frac{1}{5}$ $\frac{2}{5}$ $\frac{3}{5}$ $\frac{4}{5}$ ☐ ☐ ☐

9 5   3   1   ☐ ☐ ☐   −7

10 37   ☐   55   ☐   73   ☐   91

11 366   316   ☐   216   ☐ ☐   66

12 ☐   −15   −10   ☐ ☐   5   10

13 $1\frac{6}{7}$ ☐ $1\frac{2}{7}$ 1   ☐ ☐ $\frac{1}{7}$

14 ☐ ☐   4·5   5   ☐   6   6·5

15 ☐   182   ☐   380   ☐   578   677

16 10   6   ☐ ☐ ☐   −10   −14

C

Copy these sequences and write the next three numbers. What is the rule for each sequence?
Can you write the rule for the nth term?

1 84   72   60   48

2 64   71   78   85

3 1·1   1·07   1·04   1·01

4 4 $3\frac{5}{8}$ $3\frac{2}{8}$ $2\frac{7}{8}$

5 165   146   127   108

6 −9   −7   −5   −3

7 75   67   59   51

8 0·02   0·04   0·06   0·08

9 15   11   7   3

10 43   55   67   79

11 −20   −14   −8   −2

12 5   4·5   4   3·5

13 135   156   177   198

14 36   28   20   12

15 50   175   300   425

16 1·25   1·5   1·75   2

17 10 $8\frac{3}{4}$ $7\frac{1}{2}$ $6\frac{1}{4}$

18 −11   −8   −5   −2

TARGET   To generate and describe number sequences.

Examples

					The rule is:	The nth term is:
To find the rule that	4	7	10	13	add 3	$n + 3$
links the numbers	1	6	11	16	add 5	$5n - 4$
study the gaps.	0·2	0·4	0·6	0·8	add 0·2	$\frac{n}{5}$ or $\frac{2n}{10}$

A

Write the first six numbers in each sequence.

	Start at	Rule		Start at	Rule		Start at	Rule
1	10	+20	6	6·5	−0·5	11	1	×2
2	0·1	+0·2	7	3	−1	12	2	$-\frac{1}{4}$
3	−8	+2	8	−20	+5	13	158	−21
4	44	−3	9	50	+99	14	10	−4
5	2	$+\frac{1}{2}$	10	0·25	+0·25	15	0·74	−0·01

B

Copy and complete. Write the rule.

1   5·4   5·1   4·8   4·5   ☐   ☐   ☐

2   −5   −4   −3   −2   ☐   ☐   ☐

3   1000   920   840   760   ☐   ☐   ☐

4   1·9   3·8   5·7   7·6   ☐   ☐   ☐

5   ☐   ☐   ☐ $1\frac{1}{3}$ $1\frac{2}{3}$ 2 $2\frac{1}{3}$

6   ☐   ☐   ☐   3   8   13   18

7   ☐   ☐   ☐   1·7   1·62   1·54   1·46

8   ☐   ☐   ☐   125   150   175   200

Write the first 6 terms.

9   nth term = $2n + 1$

10   nth term = $5n - 20$

11   nth term = $3 - n$

12   nth term = $10 - 2n$

13   nth term = $\frac{5n}{2}$

14   nth term = $3n - 1$

15   nth term = $\frac{n}{5} + 0.2$

16   nth term = $4 - 3n$

C

Write the next 4 numbers and the rule for the nth term.

1   19   26   33   40

2   10   8·75   7·5   6·25

3   $\frac{3}{5}$ $1\frac{1}{5}$ $1\frac{4}{5}$ $2\frac{2}{5}$

4   7·7   7   6·3   5·6

5   50   38   26   14

6   0·75   1·5   2·25   3

7   $\frac{5}{8}$ $1\frac{1}{4}$ $1\frac{7}{8}$ $2\frac{1}{2}$

8   1·0   0·99   0·98   0·97

9   −17   −13   −9   −5

10   $\frac{1}{2}$ $1\frac{3}{4}$ 3 $4\frac{1}{4}$

11   1   0·85   0·7   0·55

12   10   8·25   6·5   4·75

Write the first 6 numbers.

13   nth term = $10 - 3n$

14   nth term = $\frac{2n}{3}$

15   nth term = $n^2 + 1$

16   nth term = $\frac{n}{4} - 0.1$

17   nth term = $n^2 - n$

18   nth term = $4.5 - \frac{3n}{2}$

TARGET To generate and describe number sequences.

Examples

$-3 \quad -1 \quad 1 \quad 3 \quad 5 \quad 7$

The rule is add 2.

The nth term is $2n - 5$.

Write the first six terms.

$20 - 4n$	16	12	8	4	0	-4
$3n + 1$	4	7	10	13	16	19
$\dfrac{2n}{10}$	0.2	0.4	0.6	0.8	1.0	1.2

A

Write the first six numbers in each sequence.

	Start at	Rule
1	57	$+9$
2	$2\frac{1}{2}$	$-\frac{1}{4}$
3	3	$+0.5$
4	150	-20
5	-10	$+3$
6	10	-4

Complete each sequence.

7 1·5 1·75 2 ☐ ☐

8 $\frac{1}{2}$ ☐ *1* $1\frac{1}{2}$ ☐ *2* $2\frac{1}{2}$

9 -6 -4 -2 ☐ ☐

10 2 4 6 ☐ *8* ☐ *10*

11 100 ☐ 302 403 ☐

12 ☐ *80* 68 56 44 ☐ *32*

    3 6 9 12 15 18

Look at the above pattern. Write down:

13 the 7th term *21*

14 the 11th term *33*

15 the 20th term *60*

16 a rule for the nth term. *3n*

B

Fill in the boxes. Give the rule for the nth term.

1 -12 -7 -2 ☐ ☐

2 0.1 0.4 0.7 ☐ ☐

3 $\frac{1}{4}$ ☐ $\frac{3}{4}$ ☐ $1\frac{1}{4}$ ☐

4 -1 -3 ☐ ☐ -9 ☐

5 4 ☐ 42 61 80

6 38 28 18 8 ☐ ☐

Write the first six terms for each sequence.

7 $7 - 2n$

8 $\frac{2n}{6}$ *$\frac{1}{3}$, $\frac{2}{3}$, 1, $1\frac{1}{3}$, $1\frac{2}{3}$, 2*

9 $n - 5$

10 $3n + 2$ *5, 8, 11, 14, 17, 20*

11 $\frac{5n}{10}$ *0.5, 1, 0.5, 2, 2.5, 3*

12 $4 - 2n$ *2, 0, -2, -4, -6...*

⬤⬤⬤○○○○○

Look at the pattern of beads. What colour is:

13 the 15th bead *yellow*

14 the 33rd bead

15 the 50th bead *red*

16 the 100th bead?

C

Write the next 3 numbers. Give the rule for the nth term.

1 2·75 3·8 4·85 5·9 *6.95, 8, 9·05*

2 200 178 156 134

3 10 7 4 1

4 100 81 64 49

5 1 $1\frac{3}{5}$ $2\frac{1}{5}$ $2\frac{4}{5}$ *$3\frac{2}{5}$, 4, $4\frac{3}{5}$*

6 6·7 5·2 3·7 2·2 *0.7, -0.8, -2.3*

Write down a formula for the nth term of each pattern.

7 11 22 33 44 55 *11n*

8 4 7 10 13 16 *1 + 3n*

9 -5 -10 -15 -20 -25 *$-5n$*

10 -1 -3 -5 -7 -9

11 0·1 0·6 1·1 1·6 *$\frac{5n - 0.4}{10}$*

12 $1\frac{1}{3}$ $2\frac{2}{3}$ 4 $5\frac{1}{3}$ *$\frac{4n}{3}$*

⬤⬤⬤⬤⬤○○○○○

Look at the pattern of beads. What colour is:

13 the 20th bead *red*

14 the 50th bead

15 the 80th bead *jet blue*

16 the 100th bead?

TARGET To convert between standard units of length, mass and capacity and between miles and kilometres.

UNITS OF LENGTH

$$\xrightarrow{\times1000} \quad \xrightarrow{\times100} \quad \xrightarrow{\times10}$$

km $\quad$ m $\quad$ cm $\quad$ mm

$$\xleftarrow{\div1000} \quad \xleftarrow{\div100} \quad \xleftarrow{\div10}$$

1 mile = 1·6 km
8 km = 5 miles

Examples

3 km 517 m = 3517 m = 3·517 km

2 m 96 cm = 296 cm = 2·96 m

1 cm 4 mm = 14 mm = 1·4 cm

UNITS OF MASS

$$\xrightarrow{\times1000}$$

kg $\quad$ g

$$\xleftarrow{\div1000}$$

Examples

2 kg 700 g = 2700 g = 2·7 kg

6 kg 390 g = 6390 g = 6·39 kg

0 kg 105 g = 105 g = 0·105 kg

UNITS OF CAPACITY

$$\xrightarrow{\times1000}$$

litres $\quad$ ml

$$\xleftarrow{\div1000}$$

Examples

1 litre 250 ml = 1250 ml = 1·25 litres

4 litres 600 ml = 4600 ml = 4·6 litres

5 litres 825 ml = 5825 ml = 5·825 litres

A

Copy and complete.

1. 2 cm 4 mm = ☐ mm = ☐ cm

2. 0 m 76 cm = ☐ cm = ☐ m

3. 15 km 200 m = ☐ m = ☐ km

4. 0 kg 800 g = ☐ g = ☐ kg

5. 1 litre 100 ml = ☐ ml = ☐ litres

6. 0 cm 6 mm = ☐ mm = ☐ cm

7. 3 m 15 cm = ☐ cm = ☐ m

8. 0 km 300 m = ☐ m = ☐ km

9. 8 kg 290 g = ☐ g = ☐ kg

10. 0 litres 900 ml = ☐ ml = litres

11. 110 mm = ☐ cm ☐ mm = ☐ cm

12. 238 cm = ☐ m ☐ cm = ☐ m

13. 4700 m = ☐ km ☐ m = ☐ km

14. 12 600 g = ☐ kg ☐ g = ☐ kg

15. 520 ml = ☐ litres ☐ ml = ☐ litres

16. 359 mm = ☐ cm ☐ mm = ☐ cm

17. 720 cm = ☐ m ☐ cm = ☐ m

18. 2650 m = ☐ km ☐ m = ☐ km

19. 530 g = ☐ kg ☐ g = ☐ kg

20. 9400 ml = ☐ litres ☐ ml = ☐ litres

Change to km. $\qquad$ Change to miles.

21. 9 miles $\qquad$ 25. 32 km

22. 35 miles $\qquad$ 26. 60 km

23. 80 miles $\qquad$ 27. 96 km

24. 67 miles $\qquad$ 28. 44 km

B

Copy and complete.

1 4·35 m = ☐ m ☐ cm = ☐ cm

2 0·027 m = ☐ m ☐ mm = ☐ mm

3 16·88 km = ☐ km ☐ m = ☐ m

4 0·06 kg = ☐ kg ☐ g = ☐ g

5 3·1 litres = ☐ litres ☐ ml = ☐ ml

6 0·7 m = ☐ cm = ☐ m ☐ cm

7 0·18 m = ☐ mm = ☐ m ☐ mm

8 5·296 km = ☐ m = ☐ km ☐ m

9 0·435 kg = ☐ g = ☐ kg ☐ g

10 0·002 litres = ☐ ml = ☐ litres ☐ ml

11 809 cm = ☐ m ☐ cm = ☐ m

12 2536 mm = ☐ m ☐ mm = ☐ m

13 48 m = ☐ km ☐ m = ☐ km

14 1727 g = ☐ kg ☐ g = ☐ kg

15 93 ml = ☐ litres ☐ ml = ☐ litres

16 6 cm = ☐ m = ☐ m ☐ cm

17 374 mm = ☐ m = ☐ m ☐ mm

18 519 m = ☐ km = ☐ km ☐ m

19 68 g = ☐ kg = ☐ kg ☐ g

20 12 130 ml = ☐ litres = ☐ litres ☐ ml

Change to km.

21 22·9 miles

22 9·3 miles

23 157·2 miles

24 314·4 miles

Change to miles.

25 5·4 km

26 180 km

27 17·6 km

28 78 km

C

Copy and complete by putting >, < or = in each box.

1 700 g ☐ 0·007 kg ☐ 70 g

2 900 m ☐ 900 000 mm ☐ 0·009 km

3 0·004 litres ☐ 4 ml ☐ 0·04 litres

4 30 m ☐ 30 000 cm ☐ 0·3 km

5 8000 ml ☐ 0·8 litres ☐ 800 ml

6 0·2 cm ☐ 0·02 m ☐ 200 mm

7 0·06 kg ☐ 60 g ☐ 0·006 kg

8 50 000 mm ☐ 0·05 km ☐ 50 000 cm

Change to km.

9 0·92 miles

10 219·3 miles

11 6·77 miles

12 138·6 miles

Change to miles.

13 155 km

14 41·8 km

15 23·4 km

16 87 km

17 The combined weight of 12 identical bricks is 9·45 kg. What does one brick weigh in grams?

18 France has 1950 miles of coastline and land borders 2889 km long. Give the length of the country's perimeter in:
a) miles
b) kilometres.

19 A serving of custard is 135 ml. How much custard is needed for 18 servings? Give your answer in litres.

TARGET To convert between standard units of length, mass and capacity.

UNITS OF LENGTH

$$km \xrightarrow{\times1000} m \xrightarrow{\times100} cm \xrightarrow{\times10} mm$$
$$km \xleftarrow{\div1000} m \xleftarrow{\div100} cm \xleftarrow{\div10} mm$$

UNITS OF MASS

$$kg \xrightarrow{\times1000} g$$
$$kg \xleftarrow{\div1000} g$$

UNITS OF CAPACITY

$$litres \xrightarrow{\times1000} ml$$
$$litres \xleftarrow{\div1000} ml$$

A

Copy and complete.

1 5000 m = ☐ km
2 1800 m = ☐ km
3 3·5 km = ☐ m
4 2·9 km = ☐ m
5 640 cm = ☐ m
6 25 cm = ☐ m
7 0·48 m = ☐ cm
8 9·36 m = ☐ cm
9 2 mm = ☐ cm
10 71 mm = ☐ cm
11 54 cm = ☐ mm
12 0·8 cm = ☐ mm
13 0·6 kg = ☐ g
14 3·2 kg = ☐ g
15 970 g = ☐ kg
16 4050 g = ☐ kg
17 1·6 litres = ☐ ml
18 8·2 litres = ☐ ml
19 300 ml = ☐ litres
20 7900 ml = ☐ litres

Change to:

	miles		km
21	40 km	25	2 miles
22	72 km	26	30 miles
23	12 km	27	100 miles
24	28 km	28	11 miles

B

Copy and complete.

1 2168 m = ☐ km
2 359 m = ☐ km
3 7·708 km = ☐ m
4 0·063 km = ☐ m
5 29 cm = ☐ m
6 580 cm = ☐ m
7 0·07 m = ☐ cm
8 4·11 m = ☐ cm
9 153 mm = ☐ m
10 8 mm = ☐ m
11 6·49 m = ☐ mm
12 0·072 m = ☐ mm
13 3·456 kg = ☐ g
14 0·002 kg = ☐ g
15 179 g = ☐ kg
16 3 g = ☐ kg
17 0·6 litres = ☐ ml
18 8·01 litres = ☐ ml
19 2400 ml = ☐ litres
20 75 ml = ☐ litres

Change to:

	miles		km
21	36 km	25	4·8 miles
22	50 km	26	62·5 miles
23	124 km	27	8 miles
24	69·2 km	28	250 miles

C

Copy and complete by putting >, < or = in the box.

1 10 cm ☐ 0·09 m
2 1641 mm ☐ 16·41 m
3 50 g ☐ 0·05 kg
4 2288 ml ☐ 2·8 litres
5 3000 mm ☐ 0·003 km
6 1440 cm ☐ 0·04 km
7 25 g ☐ 0·025 kg
8 38 ml ☐ 0·008 litres

Convert to miles

9 47 km   11 73 km
10 9·4 km   12 53·8 km

Convert to kilometres.

13 1562 miles
14 284·6 miles
15 65·77 miles
16 12·29 miles

17 Each nail weighs 3·85 g. There are 24 nails in a packet. What is the total weight of the nails in 60 packets in kilograms?

18 A lorry travels 263 km in Belgium and 172 miles in England. How much longer in miles is the English journey?

TARGET   To read, write and convert between standard metric units.

A

Give the measurement
shown by each arrow as:

a) mm   **b)** cm.

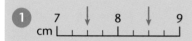

1 7 ↓ 8 ↓ 9 cm

2 10 ↓ 20 ↓ 30 mm

3 35 ↓ 40 ↓ 45 cm

4 50 60 ↓ 70 80 ↓ 90 mm

Give the measurement
shown by each arrow as:

a) ml   **b)** litres.

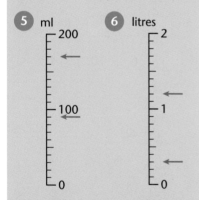

5 ml 200 ← 100 ← 0

6 litres 2 ← 1 ← 0

7 ml 1000 800 ← 600 400 ← 200

8 litres 4 ← 2 ← 0

B

Give the measurement
shown by each arrow as:

a) grams   **b)** kg.

1 g 300 ← 250 ←

2 g 120 ← 100 ← 80

3 kg 23 24 25

4 kg 5 6 7

Give the measurement
shown by each arrow as:

a) cm   **b)** metres.

5 cm 80 ↓ 90 ↓

6 m ↓0·6 0·7 ↓ 0·8

7 cm ↓ 11 12 ↓

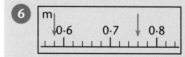

8 mm 40 ↓ 50 60 ↓ 70

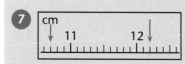

C

Give the difference between
X and Y as:

a) ml   **b)** litres.

1 litres 4 X 3 2 Y

2 litres 0·4 X 0·3 0·2 Y 0·1

3 ml 600 X 500 Y 400

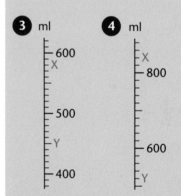

4 ml X 800 600 Y

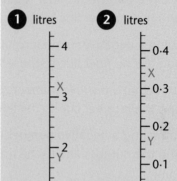

Give the difference between
X and Y as:

a) mm   **b)** metres.

5 mm 4 5 X 6 7 Y

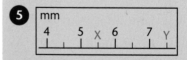

6 cm X 3 4 Y 5

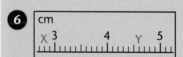

7 mm 80 X 90 Y

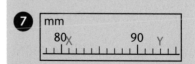

8 m X 0·6 Y 0·65

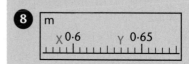

To add and subtract positive and negative numbers including for measures such as temperature.

Negative numbers | Positive numbers

−10 −9 −8 −7 −6 −5 −4 −3 −2 −1 0 1 2 3 4 5 6 7 8 9 10

Examples

Adding a positive number results in a move along the number line to the right.

$6 + 2 = 8$ $-6 + 2 = -4$

Adding a negative number results in a move along the number line to the left.

$6 + (-2) = 4$ $-6 + (-2) = -8$

Subtracting a positive number results in a move along the number line to the left.

$7 - 3 = 4$ $-7 - 3 = -10$

Subtracting a negative number results in a move along the number line to the right.

$7 - (-3) = 10$ $-7 - (-3) = -4$

A

Copy and complete by writing the missing numbers in the boxes

1. −4 −3 −2 ☐ ☐ ☐ 2

2. 10 8 6 4 ☐ ☐ ☐

3. 12 8 ☐ ☐ ☐ −8 −12

4. 10 7 4 ☐ ☐ ☐ −8

5. −6 −4 −2 ☐ ☐ ☐ 6

6. 8 5 ☐ ☐ ☐ −7 −10

7. −13 −8 −3 ☐ ☐ ☐ 17

8. 10 ☐ ☐ ☐ −6 −10 −14

9. What temperatures are shown by the letters on the scale?

10. Which letter shows the coldest temperature?

11. Give the difference in temperature between:
    a) A and B   b) A and C   c) B and C.

12. What would the temperature be if it was:
    a) at A and fell 9°
    b) at C and rose 13°
    c) at B and fell 25°.

13. The temperature is −6°C and it rises by 10°C. What is the new temperature?

14. The temperature is −6°C and it falls by 10°C. What is the new temperature?

°C
— 20
B →
— 10
A → — 0
— −10
C →
— −20

B

1. $3 + (-2)$
2. $5 - (-6)$
3. $-4 + (-9)$
4. $-2 - (-5)$

9. $6 + (-3)$
10. $-1 + 8$
11. $-2 + (-5)$
12. $-3 - 7$

17. $-5 - (-10)$
18. $2 - (-7)$
19. $-2 + (-6)$
20. $-3 + 2$

25. $5 + (-5)$
26. $-3 - (-7)$
27. $1 - (-5)$
28. $-4 - 2$

5. $-5 + 3$
6. $-6 - 5$
7. $4 + (-7)$
8. $-1 - (-1)$

13. $7 - (-2)$
14. $1 + (-8)$
15. $-3 + (-6)$
16. $-4 - (-3)$

21. $4 - (-3)$
22. $-1 - (-4)$
23. $3 + (-5)$
24. $-6 - 8$

29. $-1 + 9$
30. $-5 + (-1)$
31. $2 + (-2)$
32. $-4 - (-5)$

Copy and complete the tables showing changes in temperature.

33.

OLD	CHANGE	NEW
−3°C	+8°C	5°C
9°C	−10°C	
−5°C	−5°C	
−2°C	+12°C	
8°C	+6°C	
11°C	−15°C	

34.

OLD	CHANGE	NEW
8°C	−11°C	−3°C
	+14°C	−6°C
	−7°C	−1°C
	+16°C	13°C
	+9°C	1°C
	−12°C	−15°C

35.

OLD	CHANGE	NEW
−6°C		9°C
−2°C		−14°C
−13°C		7°C
5°C		−1°C
−9°C		−2°C
3°C		−11°C

C

Work out

1. $2 + (-6) + (-12)$
2. $-7 - 4 - (-3)$
3. $5 - (-3) + (-6)$
4. $-4 + (-8) - (-9)$

5. $3 - (-1) - (-5)$
6. $-2 + 3 + (-8)$
7. $6 + (-5) - (-3)$
8. $-5 + (-7) + (-4)$

9. $-3 - (-11) + (-14)$
10. $-9 + 4 - (-6)$
11. $-6 - 2 + (-7)$
12. $-1 - (-2) - (-5)$

13. $-8 + 10 - (-4)$
14. $-4 - (-1) + (-12)$
15. $1 - (-6) - (-3)$
16. $-10 + (-4) + (-7)$

17. $-2 - 2 - (-2)$
18. $7 + (-10) + (-6)$
19. $-5 + (-3) - (-14)$
20. $8 - (-5) + (-9)$

21. $-12 + 7 + (-8)$
22. $-6 - (-4) - (-5)$
23. $4 + (-8) - (-10)$
24. $-1 - 11 + (-7)$

25. The amount of money in a bank account is the balance. Banks often allow customers to have a negative balance. Copy and complete this table showing balances at the start and end of May.

BALANCE 1st May	CHANGE	BALANCE 31st May
−£300	+£50	−£250
−£120		£80
£70		−£190
£64	−£105	
−£20	−£90	
−£49	+£36	
£17	−£78	
	−£40	−£60
	+£57	−£81
	−£135	£429
	−£110	−£26

TARGET To find the areas and perimeters of rectangles using the formulae.

The area of a shape is the amount of surface it covers. It is measured in squares, usually square metres (m^2) or square centimetres (cm^2).

The perimeter of a shape is the distance around its edges. It is a length and is measured in units of length such as metres and centimetres.

The area and perimeter of a rectangle can be found using these formulae:

Area = lw

Perimeter = $2(l + w)$

(l = length, w = width)

Example 1

Area
　= (9×7) cm^2
　= 63 cm^2

Perimeter
　= $2(9 + 7)$ cm
　= 2×16 cm
　= 32 cm

Example 2

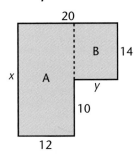

All lengths are in metres.
Find:

a) unknown lengths x and y

b) area of hexagon

c) perimeter of hexagon

x = 24 m (14 + 10)
y = 8 m (20 − 12)

Area of A = (24×12) m^2 = 288 m^2

Area of B = (14×8) m^2 = $\underline{112\ m^2}$

　　Area of hexagon = $\underline{400\ m^2}$

Perimeter of hexagon = 88 m
　　$(24 + 20 + 14 + 8 + 10 + 12)$ m

For each of the following shapes find:

a) the area　　　**b)** the perimeter.

All lengths are in cm.

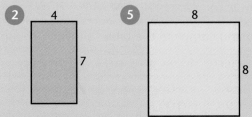

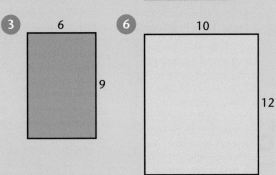

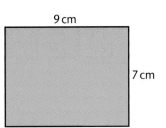

For each of the following shapes find:

a) the area　　　**b)** the perimeter.

7 square
sides 4 cm

9 square
sides 10 cm

8 rectangle
sides 7 cm 5 cm

10 rectangle
sides 8 cm 3 cm

Use squared paper.

11 Draw a square with a perimeter of 28 cm. Work out the area.

12 Draw two different rectangles each with an area of 28 cm^2. Work out the perimeters.

13 Draw two different rectangles each with a perimeter of 28 cm. Work out the areas.

B

1 Copy and complete the table showing the measurements of rectangles.

Length	Width	Perimeter	Area
8 cm	5 cm		
7 cm			21 cm²
	6 cm	32 cm	
9 cm		26 cm	
	10 m		200 m²
12 m			24 m²
	7 m	36 m	
	8 m		120 m²

For each of the following shapes work out:

a) the perimeter

b) the area.

All lengths are in centimetres.

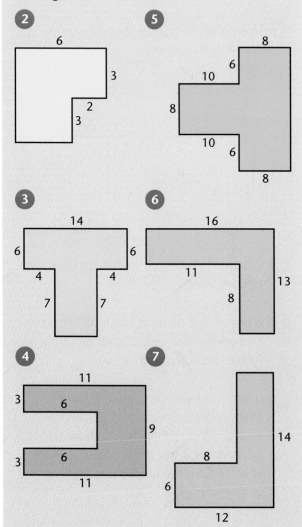

 C

For each of the following shapes work out:

a) the perimeter   **b)** the area.

All lengths are in centimetres.

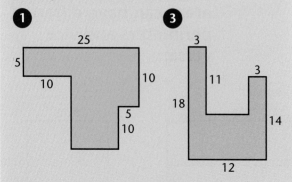

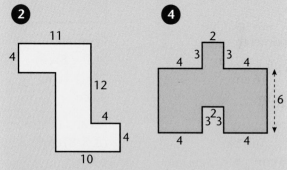

5

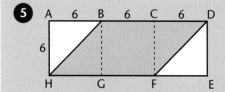

Look at the above diagram.
Work out the area of:

a) rectangle ADEH

b) square ABGH

c) triangle ABH

d) parallelogram BDFH.

6 A rectangular room is 7·6 m long and has a perimeter of 23·2 m.

   a) What is the area of the room?

   b) Square carpet tiles are 40 cm long. How many are needed to cover the floor of the room?

7 A rectangular field is three times as long as it is wide. The fence around it is 240 m long. What is the area of the field?

TARGET To recognise that shapes with the same areas can have different perimeters and vice versa.

Examples

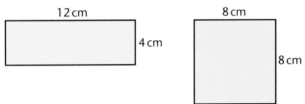

Perimeter
2(12 + 4) cm
2 × 16 cm
32 cm

Perimeter
2(8 + 8) cm
2 × 16 cm
32 cm

Area
(12 × 4) cm²
48 cm²

Area
(8 × 8) cm²
64 cm²

The square and the rectangle have the same perimeter but different areas.

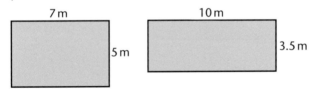

Perimeter
2(7 + 5) m
2 × 12 m
24 m

Perimeter
2(10 + 3·5) m
2 × 13·5 m
27 m

Area
(7 × 5) m²
35 m²

Area
(10 × 3·5) m²
35 m²

The rectangles have the same area but different perimeters.

A

Use 1 cm squared paper.

1 Using only the grid lines draw different shapes each with an area of 16 cm².

Work out the perimeter of each shape.

Examples

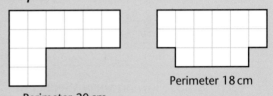

Perimeter 20 cm   Perimeter 18 cm

2 Which of all the possible shapes has the smallest perimeter?

3 Using only the grid lines find ways of drawing shapes with a perimeter of 16 cm.

Work out the area of each shape.

Examples

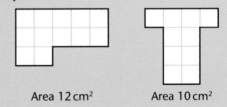

Area 12 cm²   Area 10 cm²

4 Which of all the possible shapes has the largest area?

5 A farmer has 40 m of fence. What is the maximum area he can enclose using four straight lengths of fence?

6 Using 1 cm squared paper, Pabel and Melissa both draw rectangles with an area of 48 cm². Pabel's rectangle is 12 cm long. Melissa's rectangle is 4 cm shorter. Give the length and width of both rectangles.

B

1 **a)** Draw this rectangle.

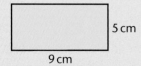
5 cm
9 cm

Work out the area.

b) Draw a different rectangle with the same perimeter but a smaller area.

c) Draw another rectangle with the same perimeter but this time with a larger area.

d) Label the dimensions and areas of each rectangle.

2 **a)** Draw this rectangle.

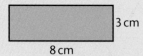
3 cm
8 cm

Work out the perimeter.

b) Draw a different rectangle with the same area but a longer perimeter.

c) Draw another rectangle with the same area but a shorter perimeter.

d) Label the dimensions and write down the perimeter of each rectangle.

3 **a)** Draw a square with a perimeter of 16 cm.

b) Draw two different rectangles with the same perimeter as the square.

c) Work out the area of each shape.

d) Which shape has the largest area?

4 **a)** Draw a square with an area of 36 cm².

b) Draw two different rectangles with the same area as the square.

c) Work out the perimeters of each shape.

d) Which shape has the shortest perimeter?

C

1 A factory is 60 m long and has an area of 3000 m². Its warehouse has the same perimeter but is 15 m longer. What is the area of the warehouse?

2 Letitia's bedroom is 6 m long and 3·6 m wide. Brandon's room has the same area but is 40 cm wider. How long is Brandon's room?

3 Copy this table showing the measurements of rectilinear shapes with a perimeter of 20 cm.

Length	Width	Area
5 cm	5 cm	25 cm²
6 cm		
7 cm		
8 cm		
9 cm		

4 Describe how the area of the rectangles changes with the length by completing this sentence:

The longer the rectangle, the .... the area.

5 Repeat the table for other rectangles which have the same perimeter as a square (24 cm, 28 cm, 32 cm, etc). Can you see a pattern in the areas of the rectangles? Describe it.

6 Investigate the area of rectangles with the same perimeter but which do not share that perimeter with a square (18 cm, 22 cm, 26 cm, etc). Do you find the same relationship between length of rectangle and size of area?

Is there a pattern in the areas of the rectangles? Describe it.

TARGET To use formulae to calculate the area of triangles and parallelograms.

The area of a triangle is half the base times the height.

$$A = \frac{bh}{2}$$

Why this formula works is apparent when considering a right-angled triangle.

Example 1

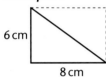

Area of rectangle
$(8 \times 6)\,cm^2 = 48\,cm^2$

Area of triangle
$\frac{(8 \times 6)}{2}\,cm^2 = \frac{48}{2}\,cm^2$
$= 24\,cm^2$

Considering a scalene triangle as two right-angled triangles, it is apparent why the formula applies to all triangles.

Example 2

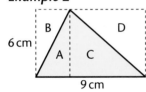

The areas of triangles:
A and B are equal
C and D are equal.

Therefore, the yellow triangle's area is half that of the rectangle or half the triangle's base times its height.

$$Area = \frac{(6 \times 9)}{2}\,cm^2 = \frac{54}{2}\,cm^2 = 27\,cm^2$$

The area of a parallelogram is the base times the height. ($A = bh$)

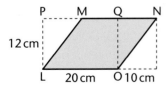

The areas of triangles LPM and OQN are equal.

Therefore, the area of the parallelogram equals that of rectangle LPQO or the base of the parallelogram times its height.

$$Area = (20 \times 12)\,cm^2 = 240\,cm^2$$

A

All lengths are in cm. Find the area of:
a) the rectangle   **b)** the coloured triangle.

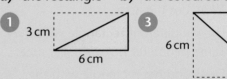

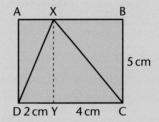

5 Find the area of:

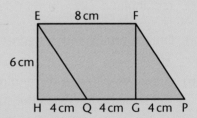

a) rectangle AXYD   **b)** triangle DXY
c) rectangle XBCY   **d)** triangle XCY
e) rectangle ABCD   **f)** triangle DXC

6

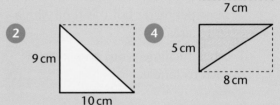

Find the area of:
a) rectangle EFGH
b) triangle EQH
c) triangle FPG
d) parallelogram EFPQ.

Find the area of each triangle.

7   **8**

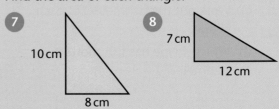

B

All lengths are in centimetres.

Find the area of each triangle.

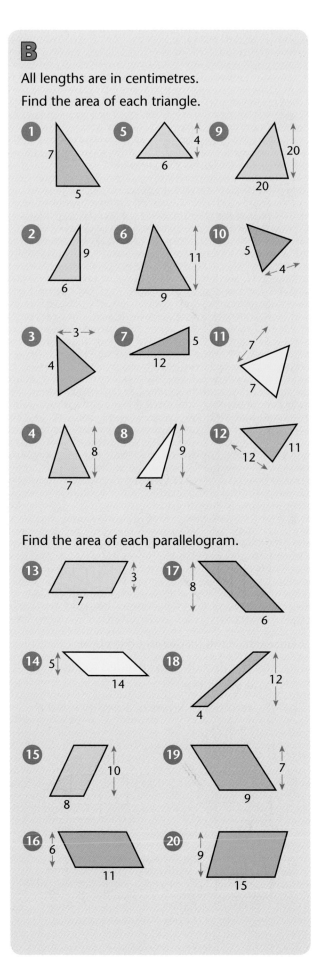

Find the area of each parallelogram.

C

All lengths are in centimetres.

Find the total area of each coloured shape.

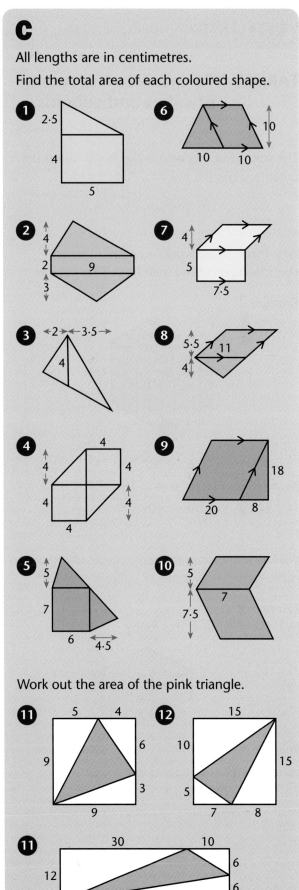

Work out the area of the pink triangle.

TARGET   To calculate the volume of cubes and cuboids.

The volume of a cuboid is the length times the breadth times the height.

$$V = lbh$$

Why this formula works is apparent when considering a cuboid built from 1 cm³ blocks.

Example 1

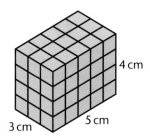

Blocks in one layer = 3 × 5 = 15
Blocks in four layers = 4 × 15 = 60
Volume = 60 cm³

Volume is always measured in cubic units such as cubic centimetres (cm³) or cubic metres (m³).

Example 2
Find the volume of this room.

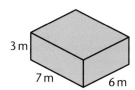

Volume = lbh
Volume = (7 × 6 × 3) m³
= (42 × 3) m³
= 126 m³

A

Find the volume of each of the following cubes/cuboids. All the cubes are 1 cm³.

1   5

2 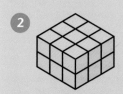   6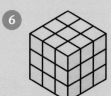

3 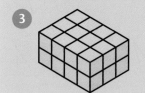   7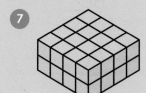

4 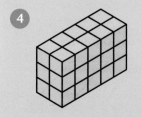   8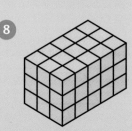

For each of the following boxes find:

a) the number of 1 cm³ needed to cover the base of the box

b) the number of layers of 1 cm³ needed to fill the box

c) the volume of the box.

9 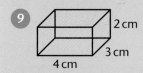   11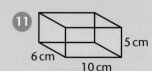

10 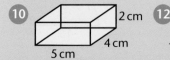   12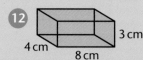

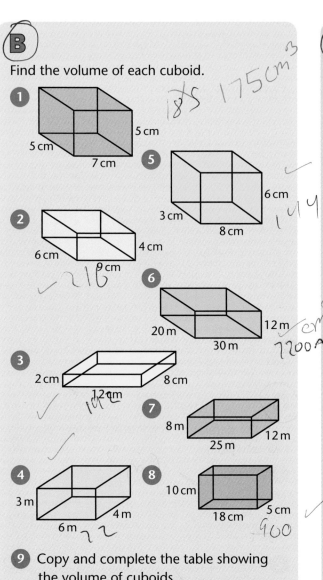

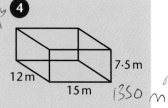

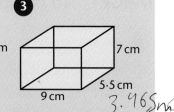

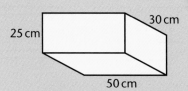

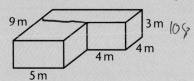

B

Find the volume of each cuboid.

1 5 cm, 5 cm, 7 cm *1×5 175 cm³*

2 6 cm, 4 cm, 9 cm *✓216*

3 2 cm, 8 cm, 12 cm *✓ 16m*

4 3 m, 4 m, 6 m *72*

5 3 cm, 6 cm, 8 cm *✓ 144*

6 20 m, 12 m, 30 m *7200 cm³ Am*

7 8 m, 25 m, 12 m *✓*

8 10 cm, 18 cm, 5 cm *✓ 900*

9 Copy and complete the table showing the volume of cuboids.

Length	Breadth	Height	Volume
15 cm	4 cm	8 cm	*480*
7 cm	3 cm	5 cm	*105* ✓
20 cm	13 cm	*2*	520 cm³
6 ✓	6 cm	3 cm	108 cm³
12 cm	*10*	6 cm	720 cm³
22 cm	5 cm	*9*	990 cm³
8 ✓	6 cm	4 cm	192 cm³
16 cm	8 cm	*5*	640 cm³

10 How many 1 cm cubes would fit into this box? 10 cm, 10 cm, 10 cm *1000 ✓*

11 What is the volume of a cube with:
 a) 2 metre edges *8*
 b) 5 cm edges? *125 ✓ cm³*

C

Find the volume of each cuboid.

1 24 cm, 20 cm, 35 cm *16 800* *168m*

2 6 m, 2·5 m, 6 m *× 90m³* *88*

3 7 cm, 5·5 cm, 9 cm *3.465m cm³*

4 7·5 m, 12 m, 15 m *1350 m³*

5 How many one centimetre cubes would fit into a one metre cube? *30 000 ×*

6 A cube has edges of 16 cm. What is its volume? *4098 ✓ cm³*

7 A cube has a volume of 343 cm³. How long is each of its edges? *7 ✓ cm³*

8 A game is packaged in a box with these dimensions. 25 cm, 30 cm, 50 cm

 a) What is the volume of the box? *37500 cm³*
 b) How many boxes would fit into a cubic container with edges of 1·5 m?
 c) How many boxes would fit into a cuboid box 3 m long, 2 m wide and 2 m high?

9 Find the volume of the air space in this L-shaped room. 9 m, 3 m, 4 m, 4 m, 5 m *168 × 183m³* *108*

TARGET   To compare volumes of cubes and cuboids.

A

For each pair of cuboids find:

a) which has the greater volume

b) the difference in their volumes.
   (All cubes are 1 cm³.)

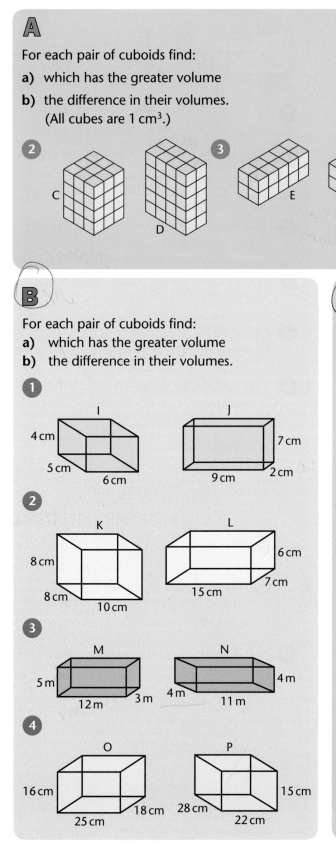

B

For each pair of cuboids find:

a) which has the greater volume

b) the difference in their volumes.

1

I   4 cm   5 cm   6 cm

J   7 cm   9 cm   2 cm

2

K   8 cm   8 cm   10 cm

L   6 cm   7 cm   15 cm

3

M   5 m   12 m   3 m

N   4 m   4 m   11 m

4

O   16 cm   25 cm   18 cm

P   15 cm   28 cm   22 cm

C

Find the difference in volume between each pair of shapes.

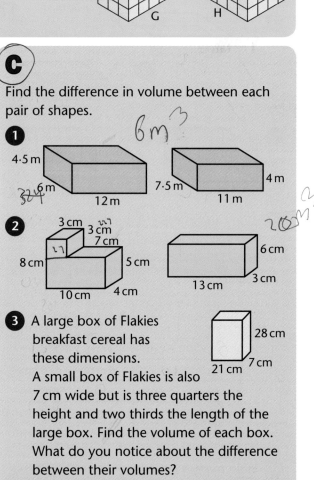

1   4·5 m   6 m   12 m   7·5 m   4 m   11 m

2   3 cm   3 cm   7 cm   8 cm   5 cm   10 cm   4 cm   6 cm   13 cm   3 cm

3 A large box of Flakies breakfast cereal has these dimensions.
A small box of Flakies is also 7 cm wide but is three quarters the height and two thirds the length of the large box. Find the volume of each box. What do you notice about the difference between their volumes?

28 cm   21 cm   7 cm

4 How many cubic millimetres fit into one cubic centimetre?

5 How many cubic metres fit into one cubic kilometre?

TARGET   To solve word problems involving measures.

Example

An apple pie weighs 0·8 kg.
It is cut into five equal slices.
Two are eaten. What is the
weight of the remaining pie?

0·8 kg = 800 g
800 ÷ 5 = 160
160 × 3 = 480
Answer   *480 g is left.*

A

1. Stella has a 6 m ball of string. One quarter is cut off. How much does she have left?

2. Norris buys three sacks of potatoes, a large one holding 45 kg and two smaller ones holding 27·5 kg each. What is the total weight of the potatoes he has bought?

3. The temperature is 3°C. It falls 8°C and then rises 2°C. What is the new temperature?

4. A motor mower has 700 ml of petrol. 2·5 litres is added. 0·6 litres is used. How much petrol is in the mower?

5. The wall of a room is 4 m long. A radiator 1·6 m long is to be placed exactly in the centre of the wall. How far should it be from each side of the wall to the radiator?

B

1. A packet of cereal weighs 1·2 kg. 450 g is used. One third of the rest is used. How much is left?

2. A water bottle holds 2·6 litres. 1·9 litres is used. 750 ml is added. How much water is in the bottle?

3. Ceri buys six 80 cm ribbons and seven 50 cm ribbons. What is the total length of the ribbons bought in metres?

4. The temperature at 6 pm is 9·3°C. By midnight it falls to 3·6°C and it falls as much again by 6 am. What is the temperature at 6 am?

5. A recipe for eight people requires one kilogram of meat. How much is needed for three people?

6. Claire buys a 2 litre bottle of milk. Seven tenths is used. A quarter of what is left is used. How much milk is left?

C

1. A crate of 24 empty bottles weighs 6·4 kg. The crate weighs 2·8 kg. What does each bottle weigh?

2. Three fifths of a bottle of cooking oil is used. 450 ml is left. How much oil does a full bottle hold in litres?

3. A machine makes 320 staples from a 10 m length of wire. Each staple uses 15 mm of wire. How much of the wire is left?

4. A can of fruit weighs 425 g. There are eight cans in each box. What is the total weight in kilograms of the cans in four boxes?

5. Nancy makes 1·2 litres of lemon squash. She pours two fifths into a jug and the rest is shared equally between six glasses. How much squash is in each glass?

6. Brian needs 250 lengths of tape, each 60 cm long. Tapes are 30 m long. How many will he need to buy?

TARGET   To solve word problems involving decimal notation of measures.

Example

A watering can has a capacity of 3·75 litres.
It is filled and emptied six times.
How much water has been used?

$$\begin{array}{r} 3\cdot75 \\ \times \quad 6 \\ \hline 22\cdot50 \\ {\scriptstyle 4\ 3} \end{array}$$

Answer   *22·5 litres has been used.*

A

1. A greengrocer has 83·5 kg of potatoes. 56·2 kg are sold. How much is left?

2. On Monday Joyce used 78·9 litres of water. On Tuesday she used 13·6 litres more than she had the day before. How much water did she use on Tuesday?

3. Jack is driving 63 km. He is halfway. How far has he driven?

4. One coin weighs 7·4 g. What do six coins weigh?

5. David's fish tank holds 52·8 litres of water. He drains off 10 per cent. How much is left?

6. The annual rainfall in the Scottish Highlands was 3·12 m. In the next year it is 69 cm less. What was the rainfall in the second year?

7. Lydia runs 6·4 km every day for a week. How far does she run altogether?

B

1. Each roll of wallpaper is 6·25 m. Maxine buys eight rolls. What is the total length of her wallpaper? **50**

2. Robert earns £2779 in four weeks. What does he earn each week? **794.75**

3. A baby weighs 7·8 kg. The next time she is weighed her weight has increased by 5 per cent. What is the baby's new weight? **8.1a   39C**

4. The planned length of a tunnel is 2·47 km. 875 m still needs to be dug. How long is the tunnel which has been dug? **1.595**

5. Five identical bricks weigh 6·3 kg. What does one brick weigh? **1.26**

6. One pot of soup holds 0·58 litres. What do nine pots hold? **5.22**

7. A large bag of peas weighs 1·35 kg. A small bag weighs 685 g. How much heavier is the large bag? **665**

C

1. Seven refrigerators are loaded onto a lorry. Each weighs 78·42 kg. What is the total weight of the load? **548·a4**

2. A saucepan holds 2·37 litres of water. 568 ml is poured away. How much water is left?

3. At 8 am the shadow of a tree is 50·4 m long. By midday it is a quarter as long. How long is the shadow at midday? **12·6**

4. A dishwasher uses 238·5 litres of water in six washes. How much does it use in each wash? **39·75**

5. A sheep weighs 26·32 kg before shearing. 1465 g of wool is removed. How much does the sheep weigh now? **l·485**

6. Lloyd throws the javelin 67·5 metres. The winning throw is 6 per cent longer. What is the winning throw? **5**

TARGET To solve word problems involving the calculation and conversion of units of measure.

Example

An avenue of trees is 2·16 km long. The trees are evenly spaced 15 m apart. How many are there on each side of the avenue?

2·16 km = 2160 m

2160 ÷ 15 = 144

Answer   *There are 145 trees on each side of the avenue.*
(144 spaces plus the final tree.)

A

1. A park has a perimeter of 1700 m. Kylie runs round the park five times. How far has she run altogether in kilometres?

2. A cafe has 7·8 litres of soup. It provides 30 equal servings. How much is each serving in millilitres?

3. One can of peas weighs 200 g. The cans on the shelves of a shop weigh 7·4 kg altogether. How many cans are on the shelves?

4. One gallon is 4·5 litres. What is nine gallons in litres?

5. A lawn is 18·4 m wide. A mower cuts strips of grass 80 cm wide. How many times will the mower need to be pushed the length of the lawn in order to cut the grass?

6. Each bag of chips weighs 1500 g. What is the total weight of six bags?

B

1. One bottle of vinegar holds 350 ml. How much vinegar is in eighteen bottles in litres? *6·3*

2. One pound is 1·6 US *6·3* dollars.
   a) How many dollars is £8·30? *13·30*
   b) How many pounds is 72 dollars? *45*

3. Each pin is made from 3·4 cm of wire. How much wire is needed for 4000 pins in metres? *136*

4. Pots of mustard hold 190 ml. How many pots can be filled from 4·75 litres? *25*

5. A patio is 7 m long and 5·46 m wide. What is the area of the patio? *38·22*

6. A small jar of hand cream holds 50 ml. How many jars can be filled from 3·8 litres? *76*

C

1. A pot of gold fish food holds 13 g. How much food is there in 175 pots in kilograms? *2·275*

2. Each magazine in a stack is 18 mm thick. The stack is 61·2 cm tall. How many magazines are there? *34*

3. Bottles of washing up liquid each hold 435 ml. There are 24 bottles in a box. How much washing up liquid is there in a box in litres? *10·44*

4. One kilogram is 2·2 pounds weight (lbs). An American footballer weighs 277·2 lbs. What is this in kilograms? *126*

5. The perimeter of a rectangular room is 22 m. The longest side is 6·5 m. What is the area of the room? *29·25*

6. Each can of fruit weighs 350 g. How many cans would have a total weight of 15·4 kg? *42*

44

350 | 15400
    1400
        1340

TARGET   To solve word problems involving the calculation and conversion of units of measure.

Example

In 25 days a sunflower plant grows 84 cm. What is its mean growth rate per day in millimetres?

84 cm = 840 mm
840 ÷ 25 = 33·6

Answer   *Mean growth rate is 33·6 mm per day.*

A

1 North Street is 1·16 km long. South Street is 329 metres shorter. How long is South Street?

2 The total weight of the cans in a box is 3·6 kg. Each can weighs 300 g. How many cans are in the box? 12 ✓

3 There are 200 straws in a box. Each straw is 16 cm long. What is the total length of the straws?

4 Lena has a 2·5 litre can of paint and a 675 ml can. How much paint does she have altogether? 3·175 ✓

5 A pot noodle weighs 90 g. What is the total weight of 24 pots?

6 A tub of ice cream holds 1·2 litres. Sharon eats 450 ml. How much ice cream is left? 750ml ✓

B

1 The perimeter of a football pitch is 286 metres. To warm up for training the players jog round the pitch four times. How far has each player run in kilometres?

2 Davina's bottle of perfume holds 0·12 litres. One fifth is used. How much is left in millilitres? 9·6 ✓

3 Ryan's suitcase and contents weigh 24·36 kg. He takes out a guide book weighing 485 g. What is the weight of his luggage now? 23·071 ✓

4 Asha walks 864 metres to school every day. When she transfers to Secondary School her journey will be 2·37 km further. How far is it from Asha's home to her Secondary School?

5 Ewan buys sixteen lollies for £7·20. How much does each lolly cost? -0 45

6 A mug holds 230 ml. A cafe serves fifty mugs of tea. How much tea is served in litres? 1150 ✓

C

1 A bottle of flavouring holds 38 ml. How many bottles can be filled from 9·5 litres? 12456

2 One packet of peanuts weighs 175 g. What is the total weight of 74 packets? 12·95kg ✓

3 One staple uses 24 mm of wire. How many staples can be made from 7·8 metres?

4 One Brasilian real is worth 28p. Marsha buys reals for £182. How many reals does she buy? + 650 5096

5 A petrol pump delivers 595 ml every second. How much is pumped in one minute in litres? ✓ 35700

6 There are 32 tiles in a pack. They have a total weight of 7·68 kg. What does one tile weigh in grams? 240 ✓

7 Each length of rail on a railway track is 24 m long. The track is 51·3 km long. How many lengths of rail have been used to build the railway?

TARGET To solve multi-step word problems involving measures.

A

1 A rectangular room is 4·6 m long and 3·8 m wide. What is the perimeter of the room? *16·*

2 Joanna takes 20 ml of medicine every day. One bottle holds 100 ml. How many bottles will she need for sixty days? *12*

3 A crate with 24 empty bottles weighs 6 kg. Each bottle weighs 200 g. What does the crate weigh? *1·2 kg*

4 A plane is due to arrive at 19:25 but take off is delayed by 4 hours 45 minutes and the flight time is 35 minutes longer than expected. When does the plane land? *am 00·45*

5 Mario buys three shelves 1·4 m long and two shelves 85 cm long. What is the total length of shelving Mario has bought? *6·5·9*   *4·2*

B

1 Cheese costs £5·60 for 1 kg. How much does 450 g cost? *2·52*

2 Alex weighs 38·95 kg. Rodney weighs three quarters of a kilogram more than Alex. Bryant weighs 560 g more than Rodney. What does Bryant weigh? *40·26 kg*

3 A CD lasts eighty minutes. It is played continuously for 24 hours. How many times is it played? *18*

4 A bottle holds two litres of drink. 800 ml is poured into a jug. The rest is shared equally between five glasses. How much drink is in each glass? *240*

5 A piece of wood is 3 m long. It is cut into five equal lengths. Anjali takes one of these lengths and cuts three eighths off. What are Anjali's two lengths of wood? *85*

6 A carpet costs £18 per square metre. How much does it cost to carpet a room 6 m long and 4·5 m wide? *50·y*   *£486*

C

Alicia 73·423
Sanjay 44·198
g

1 Alicia and Sanjay have a combined weight of 87·62 kg. Sanjay weighs 774 g more than Alicia. What do they each weigh? *50·6*   *£52·62*

2 Rolls of weed control fabric are 8 m long and 1·5 m wide. They can be cut to fill any shape. How many rolls are needed to cover a piece of ground 26 m long and 6 m wide? *13*

3 One pound is worth 1·4 Euros and 6·7 Danish kroner. How many Danish kroner can be bought with 196 Euros? *938*

4 Cans of beans cost 39p each. Sylvia pays for some cans with a £20 note and receives £9·47 change. How many cans has she bought? *27*   *24*

5 A box of cereal holds 0·875 kg. Each day for two weeks Rufus eats one 35 g portion. How much cereal is left? *385*

6 Maria buys two 2 litre tubs of ice cream. Three fifths of the vanilla tub is eaten and three eighths of the chocolate tub. How much more chocolate ice cream is left than vanilla? *450 ml*

TARGET   To solve multi-step word problems involving measures.

A

1. A box holding twenty cans of fish weighs 3 kg. The box weighs 200 g. What is the weight of each can?

2. A rectangular table has a perimeter of 3·2 m. The two shorter sides are each 65 cm long. How long is the table?

3. A drink is made by adding 350 ml of juice to 1·4 litres of water. The drink is equally poured into ten glasses. How much drink is in each glass?

4. Isaac buys three sandwiches for £1·85 each and two drinks for 79p each. He pays £10. How much change does he receive?

5. Pansy has two ribbons, both 5 m long. One quarter of her blue ribbon is used. 65 cm of her red ribbon is used. How much longer is her red ribbon than her blue?

6. How many 2 litre tubs of ice cream are needed to provide sixty 100 ml servings?

B

1. Four nights at a hotel costs £275. What does it cost to stay at the hotel for seven nights?

2. The tea in a tea bag weighs 2·5 g. How many boxes of 480 bags can be made from 18 kg of tea?   *15*

3. Alice wants to hang a painting exactly in the centre of her wall. The wall is 4·2 m long. The painting is 86 cm wide. How far should the distance be from each side wall to the painting?

4. Forty grams of seed is needed for every square metre of lawn. How much seed is needed for a lawn 35 m long and 27 m wide? Give your answer in kilograms.   *37.8*

5. Three fifths of a 2 litre carton of milk is left. A further 185 ml is used. How much milk is left now?

6. Chicken needs to be cooked for 40 minutes per kilogram plus 20 minutes. Morris works out that his chicken needs to be cooked for two and a half hours. What does his chicken weigh?   *3.2m*

C

1. Five exercise books weigh 700 g. The books in a packet weigh 4·48 kg. How many books are in the packet?

2. One and a half kilograms of brown flour is mixed with 750 g of white flour. The mixture is used to make fifty rolls. How much flour is used in each roll?   *45g*

3. Square floor tiles are 30 cm long. How many are needed to cover a floor 7·5 m long and 4·8 m wide?

4. A machine makes pins using 36 mm of wire for each pin. 15 m of wire is fed into the machine. When it is switched off there is 60 cm of wire left. How many pins have been made?   *400*

5. A sprinkler uses 225 ml of water every second. How much does it use in seven and a half minutes in litres?

6. Nuts cost £4·80 per kilogram. Gary buys 375 g. How much does he pay?   *£1·80*

TARGET To solve practical measurement problems by dividing whole numbers and decimals by 10 and 100.

Examples

100 sheets of paper are 2·5 cm thick. How thick is one sheet?

Answer 0·025 cm (2·5 ÷ 100)

80 matches weigh 16 g. What does one match weigh?

Answer 0·2 g

(16 ÷ 80) g
(16 ÷ 8 ÷ 10) g
(2 ÷ 10) g
0·2 g

A

1. Ten identical nails weigh 67 g. What does one nail weigh?

2. A stack of 100 photographs is 3 cm thick. How thick is one photograph?

3. A bottle of eyedrops holds 12 ml. It provides twenty drops. How much is each drop?

4. A car driving at a steady speed travels 18 km in 10 minutes. How far does it travel in one minute?

5. There are 100 nuts in a 350 g packet. How much does one nut weigh?

6. Measure the weight of ten identical pairs of scissors. Estimate the weight of one pair.

7. Measure the distance you walk in ten paces. Estimate the length of one stride.

8. Estimate the length of time it takes you to write your name.

B

1. There are twenty slices in a loaf of bread. The loaf is 22 cm long. How thick is one slice?

2. There are fifty identical sweets in a box. Altogether they weigh 240 g. What does one sweet weigh? *4·8 g*

3. Running at a steady pace an athlete runs 400 m in 48 seconds. How long does it take him to run one metre?

4. A leaking pipe loses 2·7 litres of water in thirty minutes. How much does it lose in one minute? *90 ml*

5. The total weight of the 100 pills in a packet is 25 g. What does one pill weigh?

6. Estimate the width of one pencil crayon. *2mm* *0·2m*

7. Estimate the weight of one 2p coin. *1·8 g*

8. Estimate the length of time it takes you to read one line of a book. Choose a page with no pictures and little dialogue.

C

1. The fifty tic tacs in a box weigh 18 g. What does one tic tac weigh?

2. A train travels 180 km in one hour. How far in kilometres does it travel in one second? *0·05k m*

3. A packet of eighty envelopes is 3·6 cm thick. What is the thickness of one envelope?

4. Forty identical pins weigh 5 g. How much does one pin weigh? *0·125 g*

5. A sprinkler uses 1620 litres of water in three hours. How much water does it use in one second? *150*

6. Estimate the thickness of one sheet of card or sugar paper. *0·5cm*

7. Estimate the length of time it takes you to walk 1 cm. *1 milSecond*

8. Estimate the weight of one counter.

TARGET   To estimate the size of angles.

A

1 Estimate the size of each angle in the triangle to the nearest 10°.

2 Measure the angles.

3 Use a ruler only. Try to draw these angles.

a) 55°   c) 85°   e) 25°
b) 135°   d) 105°   f) 155°

4 Now use a protractor to measure your angles. If any of the angles are 10° or more too large or too small draw it again.

B

1 Estimate the size of each angle in the quadrilateral to the nearest 5°.

2 Measure the angles to the nearest degree.

3 Use a ruler only. Try to draw these angles.

a) 72°   c) 18°   e) 36°
b) 149°   d) 93°   f) 174°

4 Now use a protractor. Measure your angles.
If any of your angles are 5° or more too large or too small have another try.

C

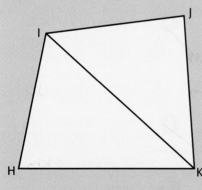

1 Estimate and then measure to the nearest degree the angles of:

a) triangle HIK   c) quadrilateral HIJK.
b) triangle IJK

2 Draw these angles, using a ruler only.

a) 201°   c) 253°   e) 228°
b) 304°   d) 276°   f) 337°

3 Measure your angles. Award yourself:

3 points   0°–1° out
2 points   2°–3° out
1 point   4°–5° out.

4 Try again. Can you beat your first score?

TARGET   To find unknown angles in triangles and quadrilaterals.

The sum of the angles in a triangle is 180°.

The sum of the angles in a quadrilateral is 360°.

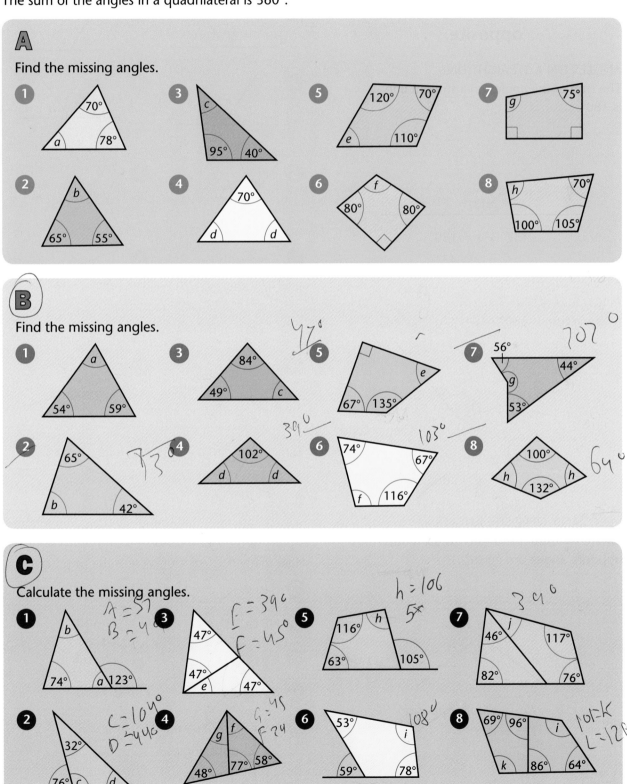

TARGET To find missing angles:
- on a straight line
- at a point
- which are vertically opposite.

ANGLES ON A STRAIGHT LINE
The sum of the angles on a straight line is 180°.

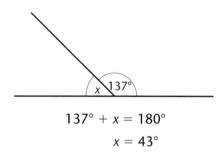

$$137° + x = 180°$$
$$x = 43°$$

ANGLES AT A POINT
A whole turn is 360°.

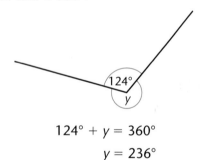

$$124° + y = 360°$$
$$y = 236°$$

VERTICALLY OPPOSITE ANGLES
Where two straight lines cross each other opposite angles are equal.

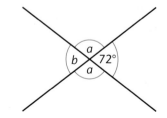

$$b = 72° \text{ (vertically opposite)}$$
$$a + 72° = 180°$$
$$a = 108°$$

A

Find the angles marked with letters.

1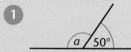

3

2

4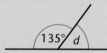

5

7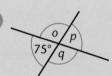

6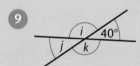

8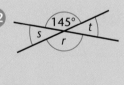

9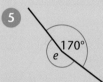

11

10

12

How many degrees clockwise is the turn from:

13 S to W

17 N to NW

14 NE to SW

18 SE to NE

15 E to SE

19 NW to S

16 NW to E

20 W to NE?

21 How many degrees is:
   a) $2\frac{1}{2}$ right angles
   b) $1\frac{1}{3}$ right angles?

B

Find the angles marked with letters.

1 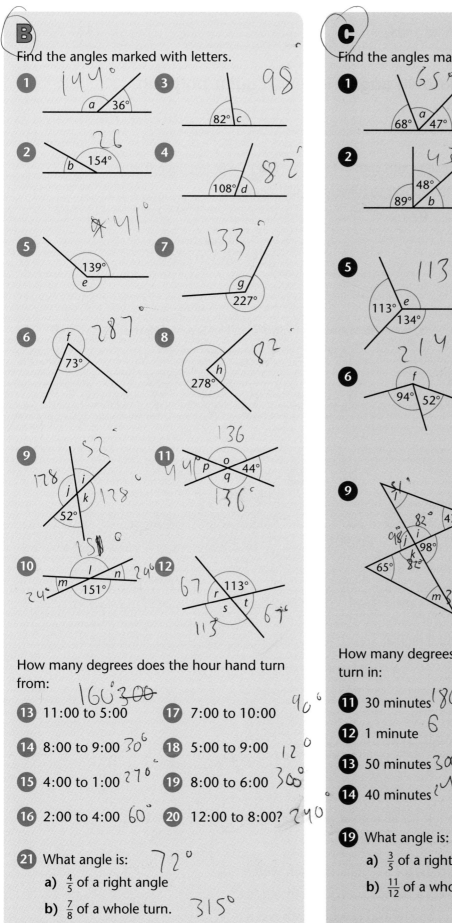 144° a 36°

3 98 82° c

2 26 b 154°

4 82 108° d

5 41° 139° e

7 133 g 227°

6 f 287 73°

8 82 278° h

9 52 178 i j k 128 52°

11 136 44 p o q 44° 136

10 158 24 m l n 240 151°

12 67 113° r s t 67 113

How many degrees does the hour hand turn from:

160 ~~300~~

13 11:00 to 5:00

17 7:00 to 10:00 90°

14 8:00 to 9:00 30°

18 5:00 to 9:00 12°

15 4:00 to 1:00 27°

19 8:00 to 6:00 300°

16 2:00 to 4:00 60°

20 12:00 to 8:00? 240

21 What angle is: 72°
 a) $\frac{4}{5}$ of a right angle
 b) $\frac{7}{8}$ of a whole turn. 315°

C

Find the angles marked with letters.

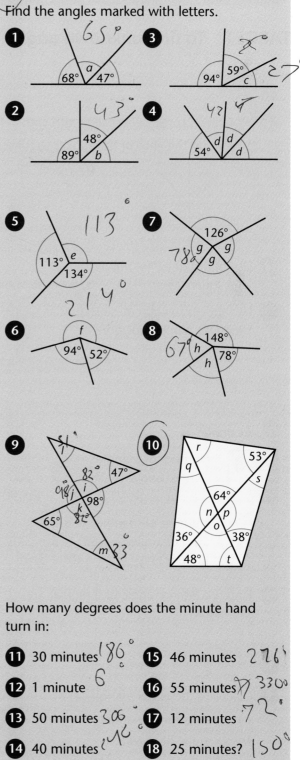

1 65° 68° a 47°

3 8° 94° 59° c 27°

2 43 48° 89° b

4 42 54° d d d

5 113 113° e 134°

7 126° 78 g g g

6 214 94° f 52°

8 67 148° h 78° h

9 51 82 47° 98 j i 98° k 82 65° m 33

10 r 53° q s 64° n p o 36° 38° 48° t

How many degrees does the minute hand turn in:

11 30 minutes 186°

15 46 minutes 276°

12 1 minute 6

16 55 minutes 330°

13 50 minutes 306°

17 12 minutes 72°

14 40 minutes 246°

18 25 minutes? 150°

19 What angle is:
 a) $\frac{3}{5}$ of a right angle 54°
 b) $\frac{11}{12}$ of a whole turn. 330°

TARGET To find unknown angles in any regular polygon.

A

1 **a)** Draw 8 spokes of equal length with a 45° angle (360° ÷ 8) between them.

b) Join up the ends of the spokes to make a regular octagon.

a) 　　　　**b)**

2 Use this method to draw:

a) a square (360° ÷ 4)　**b)** a regular pentagon (360° ÷ 5)　**c)** a regular hexagon (360° ÷ 6)

3 Use spokes to copy these shapes, based on regular polygons

B

Examples

Number of triangles = 2
Sum of angles = 180° × 2 = 360°
Interior angle (i) = 360° ÷ 4 = 90°

Number of triangles = 3
Sum of angles = 180° × 3 = 540°
Interior angle (i) = 540° ÷ 5 = ☐

1 Find the interior angle of a regular pentagon.

2 Copy and complete the table for regular polygons with 10 or fewer sides.

Number of sides	Sum of angles	Interior angle
3		
4	360°	90°
5	540°	

C

1 Calculate the exterior angle (e) of:

a) an equilateral triangle

b) a regular hexagon.

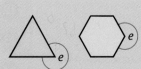

2 Calculate the exterior angle for all regular pentagons with 10 or fewer sides.

3 Write a formula for:

a) the sum of the angles (s) for a regular polygon with *n* sides

b) the interior angle (i) of a regular polygon with *n* sides

c) the exterior angle (e) of a regular polygon with *n* sides.

TARGET To draw quadrilaterals accurately, using appropriate markings for lines and angles.

Construct the quadrilaterals.
Measure and record unknown lengths (*x*) and angles (*z*).
Show all parallel sides, equal sides, right angles and equal angles.

All measurements are in cm.

Show:
parallel sides with arrows
equal sides with dashes
equal angles with arcs.

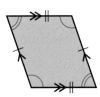

A

1 square
sides 3·8 cm

2 rectangle
sides 4·7 cm, 2·5 cm

3

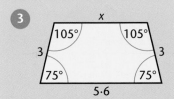

4
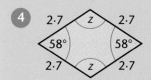

5
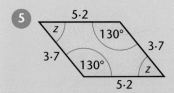

6
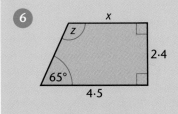

B

1 parallelogram
sides 4·6 cm, 3·1 cm
angles 45°, 135°

2 rhombus
sides 5·4 cm
angles 81°, 99°

3
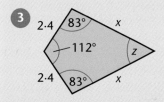

4
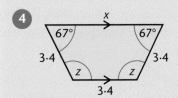

5
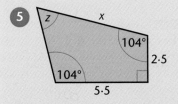

6
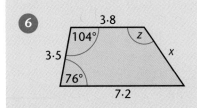

C

1 parallelogram
sides 5·6 cm, 2·3 cm
one angle of 124°

2 rhombus
sides 3·7 cm
one angle of 38°

3 symmetrical trapezium
ABCD
AB = 4·6 cm
BC = 2·9 cm
angle ABC = 61°

4

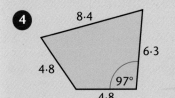

5
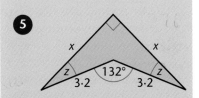

6
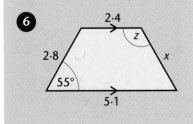

Examples

Construct triangle ABC where ∠A = 55°, ∠B = 42° and AB = 5·6 cm.

① Measure 5·6 cm along base line and locate A and B.

② Measure a 55° angle at point A and draw line AC.

③ Measure a 42° angle at point B and draw line BC.

④ Locate C where the lines AB and AC cross.

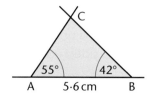

Construct triangle DEF where ∠D = 35°, DE = 7·5 cm and DF = 5·5 cm.

① Measure 7·5 cm along base line and locate D and E.

② Measure a 35° angle at point D and draw line DF.

③ Measure 5·5 cm along DF from point D and locate F.

④ Draw line EF.

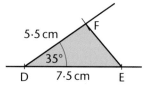

Construct triangle HIJ where HI = 8 cm, HJ = 6 cm and IJ = 4·8 cm.

① Measure 8 cm along base line and locate H and I.

② Draw an arc of radius 6 cm from point H.

③ Draw an arc of radius 4·8 cm from point I.

④ Locate J where the arcs cross.

⑤ Draw lines HJ and IJ.

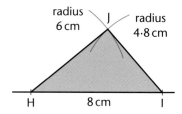

A For each of the following: **a)** construct the triangle
b) label the angles and given measurements
c) measure and record the length of side *x* to the nearest mm.

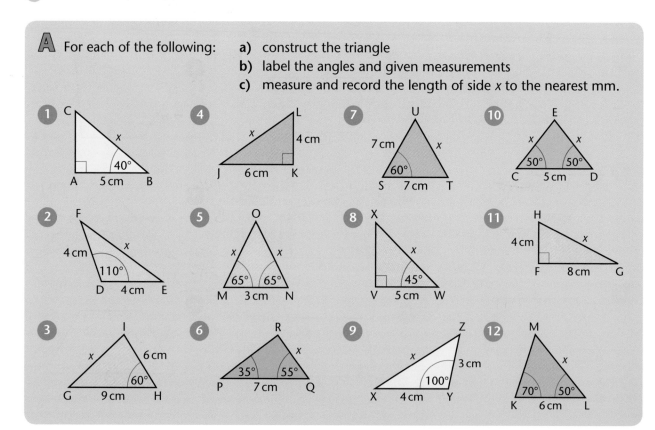

B

Construct each triangle.
Label the angles and given measurements.
Measure and record the length of side *x* to the nearest mm.
All lengths are in cm.

1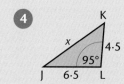

4

2

5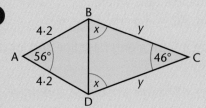

3

6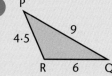

Construct the following triangles.
Label all given angles and measurements.

7 A right angled triangle ABC where ∠A = 90°, AB is 8·5 cm and AC is 4·2 cm.

8 A triangle STU where ∠S = 60°, ∠U = 55° and SU = 5·8 cm.

9 An isosceles triangle XYZ where ∠X = 48° and both XY and XZ are 4 cm.

10 A triangle FGH where ∠F = 40°, ∠G = 75° and FG = 7·5 cm.

11 Use a ruler and a pair of compasses only. Construct an equilateral triangle with sides of 4·7 cm.

12 Use a ruler and a protractor only. Construct an equilateral triangle with sides of 3·9 cm.

C

Construct each shape.
Label the angles and given measurements.
Measure and record the unknown angle *x* and side *y*.
All lengths are in cm.

1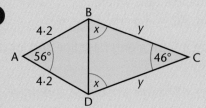

2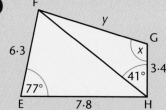

3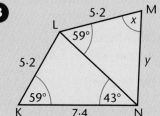

Construct the following triangles.
Label all measurements.

4 A right angled triangle with an angle of 35° and a longest side of 7·4 cm.

5 An isosceles triangle with a shortest side of 5·7 cm opposite an angle of 52°.

6 A triangle with sides of 9·3 cm, 3·9 cm and 6·6 cm.

7 A right angled triangle with an angle of 49° and a shortest side of 3·8 cm.

8 A triangle with angles of 79° and 65° and a longest side of 8·8 cm.

9 An isosceles triangle with one angle of 84° and a longest side of 6·1 cm.

TARGET To practise constructing 2-D shapes

Examples

Construct triangle ABC where
AB = 2·9 cm, AC = 4·5 cm, ∠A = 67°

1. Measure 4·5 cm along base line and locate A and C.

2. Measure 67° angle at point A and draw line AB.

3. Measure 2·9 cm along AB and locate B.

4. Draw line BC.

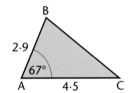

Construct triangle KLM where
KL = 2·6 cm, LM = 4·2 cm, KM = 3·4 cm

1. Draw base line LM (4·2 cm).

2. Draw an arc of radius 2·6 cm from L.

3. Draw an arc of radius 3·4 cm from M.

4. Locate K where arcs cross.
   Draw KL and KM.

Construct quadrilateral WXYZ.

1. Draw WZ (5·4 cm).

2. Measure 83° at W. Draw WX.

3. Measure 112° at Z. Draw ZY (4·3 cm). Locate Y.

4. Measure 64° at Y. Draw YX.

5. Locate X where WX and YX cross.

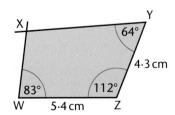

A

Construct each shape.
Measure and record unknown lengths *x* and angles *z*. All lengths are in cm.

1.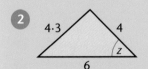

4.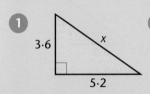

2.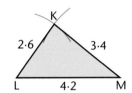

5.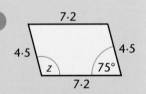

3.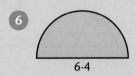

6.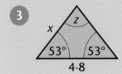

Construct the following shapes.
Show all equal sides, parallel sides, right angles and equal angles.

7. equilateral triangle
   sides 3 cm.

8. right-angled isosceles triangle
   shorter sides 2·5 cm.

9. triangle ABC
   AB = 4·1 cm, AC = 3·7 cm, ∠A = 43°.

10. rhombus
    sides 2·8 cm
    angles 60°, 120°.

11. rectangle
    sides 5·3 cm, 1·4 cm.

12. quadrant (quarter circle)
    radius 4 cm.

B

Construct each shape. All lengths are in cm.
Measure and record unknown lengths *x* and
angles *z*.

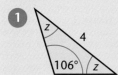

1

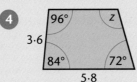

4

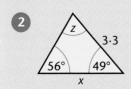

2

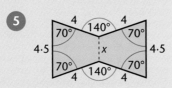

5

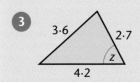

3

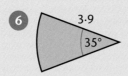

6

Construct the following shapes.
Show all equal sides, parallel sides, right angles
and equal angles.

7 triangle ABC
   AB = 4·6 cm, ∠A = 93°, ∠C = 58°

8 isosceles triangle DEF
   DE = 5·1 cm, ∠D = 46°, ∠E = 67°

9 parallelogram GHIJ
   GH = 3·4 cm, GI = 2·6 cm, ∠G = 124°

10 symmetrical trapezium
   sides 4·3 cm, 2.1 cm
   angles 107°, 73°

11 regular hexagon
   sides 2·2 cm

12 sector of circle
   radius 3·7 cm
   angle at centre 115°

C

Construct each shape.
Measure and record unknown lengths *x*
and angles *z*. All lengths are in cm.

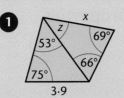

1

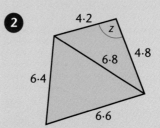

2

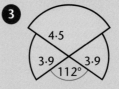

3

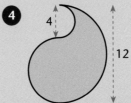

4

Construct the following shapes.
Show all equal sides, parallel sides, right
angles and equal angles.

5 a right angled triangle with the two
   shortest sides 3·3 cm and 2·5 cm

6 an isosceles triangle with an angle of
   92° and a longest side of 6·2 cm

7 a rhombus KLMN
   KL = 4·7 cm, ∠NKL = 28°

8 symmetrical trapezium PQRS
   PQ = 3·5 cm, QR = 2·4 cm, ∠RSP =
   96°

9 regular decagon (10 sided polygon)
   sides 1·8 cm

10 a sector which is three eighths
   of a circle
   radius 3·6 cm

TARGET **To compare and classify 2-D shapes and describe their properties.**

TRIANGLES
equilateral
isosceles
right-angled
scalene

QUADRILATERALS
square
rectangle
rhombus
parallelogram
trapezium
kite

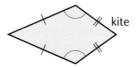

kite

OTHER POLYGONS
5 sides – pentagon
6 sides – hexagon
7 sides – heptagon
8 sides – octagon

REGULAR POLYGONS
Regular polygons have all sides equal and all angles equal.
equilateral triangle
square
regular pentagon
regular hexagon etc.

PROPERTIES CHECKLIST
number of sides
number of parallel sides
number of perpendicular sides
number of equal angles
types of angles
number of lines of symmetry
properties of diagonals

Square
Diagonals are perpendicular and bisect (cut each other in half).

A

1 Write the name of each shape.

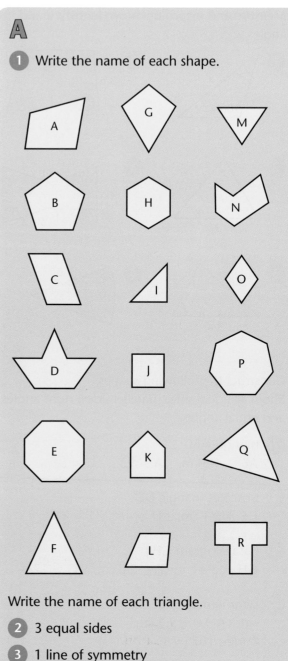

Write the name of each triangle.

2 3 equal sides

3 1 line of symmetry

4 1 pair of perpendicular lines

5 2 angles of 45°

Write the name of the quadrilateral.

6 4 right angles but not 4 equal sides

7 opposite sides equal and no right angle

8 one pair of parallel sides

9 4 equal sides, no perpendicular sides

B

Which of the shapes A–R in Section A:

1. are regular

2. have no lines of symmetry

3. have 2 or more pairs of parallel sides

4. have 1 or more reflex angles

5. have 1 or more pairs of perpendicular sides

6. have 2 or more lines of symmetry.

Identify the shape from the clues and describe other properties it possesses.

7. 4 sides
   opposite angles equal
   no lines of symmetry

8. 6 sides
   3 pairs of parallel sides

9. sum of angles is 180°
   3 equal sides

10. 2 pairs of parallel sides
    diagonals are perpendicular
    no right angle

11. all sides equal
    sum of angles is 540°

12. sum of angles is 360°
    diagonals are equal and bisect
    but are not perpendicular.

Describe the properties of each shape.

13. square

14. isosceles triangle

15. regular octagon

16. symmetrical trapezium.

C

Give the sum of the angles of the following shapes.

1. an equilateral triangle

2. a square

3. a regular pentagon

4. a regular hexagon.

5. Write a formula for the sum of the angles (a) of a regular polygon with n sides.

6. Use your formula to work out the sum of the angles of:
   a) a regular heptagon
   b) a regular decagon (10 sides)
   c) a regular dodecagon (12 sides).

7. Which quadrilaterals have diagonals which:
   a) are of equal length
   b) are perpendicular
   c) bisect (cut each other in half)?

8. Investigate the largest possible number of pairs of:
   a) parallel sides in different polygons
   b) perpendicular sides in different polygons.

   Record your results in a table.

Shape	// Sides Possible	⊥ Sides Possible
quadrilateral	2	4
pentagon		
hexagon		
heptagon		
octagon		
nonagon		
decagon		

9. Describe any patterns in your results.

TARGET To describe the properties of 3-D shapes.

POLYHEDRA

A polyhedron is a 3-D shape with straight edges.

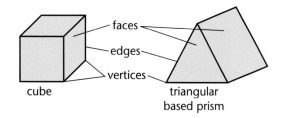

faces
edges
vertices
cube
triangular based prism

A prism has two identical end faces and the same cross section throughout its length.

PARALLEL AND PERPENDICULAR FACES/EDGES

Parallel and perpendicular faces and edges can be identified by placing one face of a shape on a flat surface.

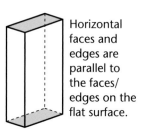

Horizontal faces and edges are parallel to the faces/ edges on the flat surface.

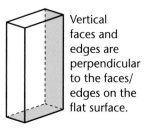

Vertical faces and edges are perpendicular to the faces/ edges on the flat surface.

Ⓐ

1 Match each of the shapes A to L with one of the names of 3-D shapes.

cone	hemisphere	pentagonal based prism
cube	hexagonal based prism	square based pyramid
cuboid	octagonal based prism	tetrahedron
cylinder	octahedron	triangular based prism

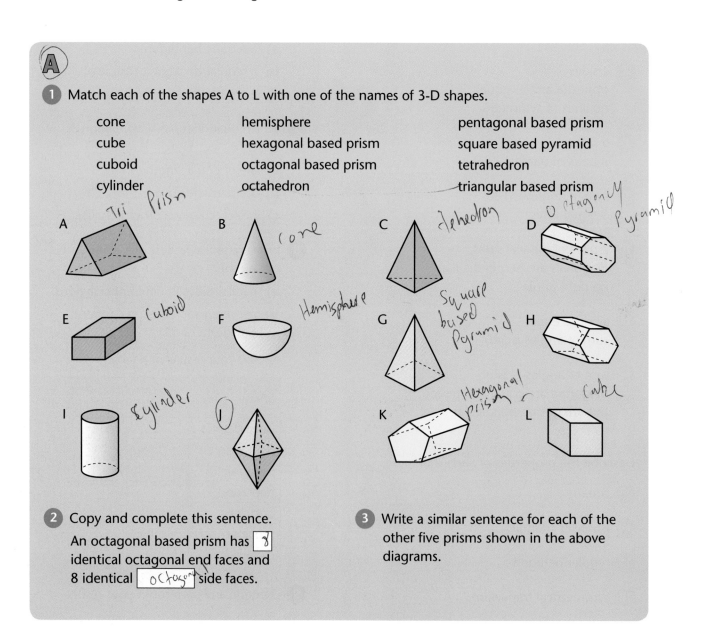

A — Tri Prism

B — cone

C — dehedron

D — Octagonal Pyramid

E — Cuboid

F — Hemisphere

G — Square based Pyramid

H

I — Cylinder

J

K — Hexagonal prism

L — cube

2 Copy and complete this sentence.

An octagonal based prism has ☐8 identical octagonal end faces and 8 identical ☐octagon side faces.

3 Write a similar sentence for each of the other five prisms shown in the above diagrams.

B

1 Copy and complete this table showing the properties of nine different polyhedra.

Shape	Sides	Edges	Vertices
Pentagon prism	7	15	10
Tehedron	7	6	4
Octagonal prism	10	24	16
cube	6	12	8
triangle prism	5	9	6
Octahedron	8	12	6
Hexagonal prism	8	18	12
Cuboid	6	12	8
Square base pyramid.	5	8	5

2 For each of the shapes in the above table write down:

a) how many pairs of parallel faces there are in the shape

b) how many pairs of perpendicular faces there are in the shape?

C

Copy and complete the following formulae where:

S = number of sides of end face of prism

F = number of faces of a prism

E = number of edges of a prism

V = number of vertices of a prism

1 $F = S + \boxed{S} + 2$

2 $E = \boxed{3} S$

3 $V = \boxed{2} S$

4 $E = F + V - \boxed{S} + 2$

Use your formulae to find:

5 the number of faces and edges of a prism with 24 vertices Octagonal prism
Faces =   Edges = 10

6 the number of vertices and edges of a prism with 12 faces

7 the number of faces and vertices of a prism with 45 edges.

For each of the following shapes write down how many faces have:

a) pairs of parallel edges

b) pairs of perpendicular edges.

8 a heptagonal prism 15

9 a hexagonal pyramid

10 a 10 sided (decagonal) prism

11 a pentagonal pyramid

12 a 9 sided (nonagonal) prism

13 an octagonal pyramid

14 Look at the shapes in Section A.

a) Which shape has parallel edges in the shape but not in any face?

b) How many pairs of parallel faces does this shape have?

15 How many edges are there on the end face of a prism with:

a) 20 faces with parallel edges

b) 20 faces with perpendicular edges.

TARGET To make nets for 3-D shapes.

A net is a 2-D representation of a 3-D shape. It shows the faces of the 3-D shape arranged so that they can be folded to build the shape.

The simplest nets to build are those of 3-D shapes with regular faces.

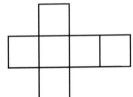

A net for a cube is easily constructed using square paper.

Similarly, triangular paper can be used to make a net for a tetrahedron.

When constructing nets for 3-D shapes which do not have regular faces you need to be very careful that your shape will fit together precisely.

A good way to understand how to draw nets is to unfold actual boxes, such as cereal boxes or Toblerone packets, and study which lengths of the net match each other.

A

All lengths are in cm.

1 Copy this net onto squared paper. Cut it out and fold it to make an open cube.

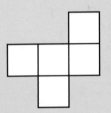

2 Copy this net. Cut it out. Cut off one square and fold it to make a net for a closed cube.

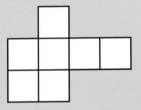

3 Copy this net onto square paper. Cut it out and make the cuboid.

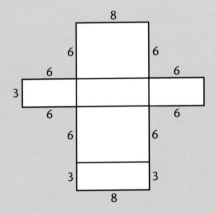

4 Make a net for a closed cube with edges 2 cm long.

5 Make a net for this cuboid.

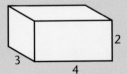

B

All lengths are in cm.

1. Make a net for this open cuboid.

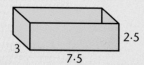

2·5
3
7·5

2. Make a net for this closed cuboid.

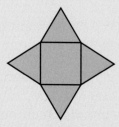

3·5
4·5
4

3. Copy this net onto squared paper. Cut it out and make the pyramid.

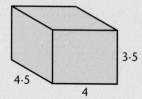

4. Copy this net onto squared paper. Cut it out and make the triangular based prism.

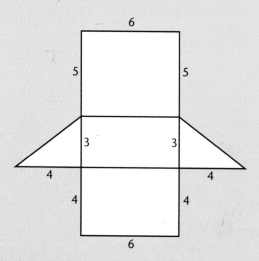

6
5   5
3   3
4   4
4   4
6

5. There are 11 different nets for a closed cube.
   Can you find them all?

C

All lengths are in cm.

1. Make a net for a square based pyramid with a base area of 16 cm² and a height of 2·5 cm for each triangular face.

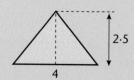

2·5
4

2. Make a net for this triangular based prism. Cut it out and build the shape.

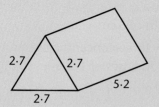

2·7   2·7
5·2
2·7

3. A prism is 4·9 cm long. Its end face is a regular hexagon with 1·6 cm sides. Make a net for the prism. Cut it out and build the shape.

4. Make a net for a tetrahedron with edges of 3·4 cm.

5. Make a net for this hexagonal based prism. Cut it out and make the prism.

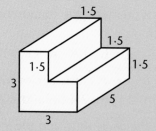

1·5
1·5
1·5   1·5
3
5
3

6. Copy this net onto triangular paper, cut out and make a tetrahedron.

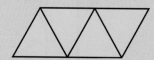

7. Work systematically to find all the possible nets for a tetrahedron.

TARGET　To illustrate and name parts of circles and know that the diameter is twice the radius.

A

The radius is the distance from the centre of the circle to the perimeter (circumference).

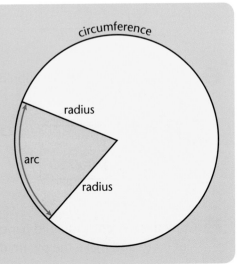

1. Draw a circle with a radius of 3·5 cm. Draw and label a radius.
2. Draw a semicircle with a length of 5 cm.
3. Draw a quarter circle (quadrant) with a length of 3 cm.

4. Draw three concentric circles with radiuses of 1·5 cm, 2 cm and 2·5 cm.

B

1. Draw a circle with a radius of:
   a) 2·9 cm　b) 3·3 cm　c) 1·6 cm　d) 2·2 cm
2. a) Draw and label a radius for each circle.
   b) Draw and label a diameter for each circle.
   c) Write the length of each diameter.
3. Draw a semicircle with a length of:
   a) 5·0 cm　b) 3·4 cm　c) 4·6 cm　d) 6·2 cm
4. Draw a quarter circle (quadrant) with a length of:
   a) 2·8 cm　b) 1·9 cm　c) 3·7 cm　d) 2·6 cm
5. Draw four concentric circles with radiuses of 1·8 cm, 2·1 cm, 2·4 cm and 2·7 cm.
6. Draw the circle touching the insides of the square by finding the centre of the square. Complete the pattern.

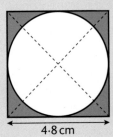

4·8 cm

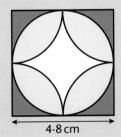

4·8 cm

C

1. Draw five concentric circles with radiuses of 1·5 cm, 1·7 cm, 1·9 cm, 2·1 cm and 2·3 cm.

Draw the patterns.

2. a)

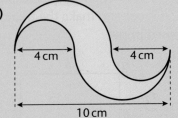

4 cm　　4 cm

10 cm

   b) Draw the same pattern with a length of 5 cm.

3. Draw the large circle with a radius of 3·2 cm.

4. Use the points where each circle touches its square to form another square. How many circles can you draw? Start with a large square.

TARGET   To name parts of circles and construct arcs and sectors.

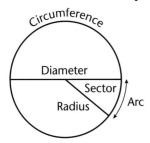

The circumference is the perimeter of a circle.
The radius is the distance from the centre of the circle to the circumference.
The diameter is a straight line connecting two points on the circumference and passing through the centre of the circle.

A

1. Draw a circle with a radius of:
   a) 2·3 cm   c) 3·5 cm
   b) 1·7 cm   d) 2·8 cm

2. Draw and label the diameter and circumference of each circle.

3. Draw a circle with a diameter of:
   a) 3 cm   c) 5·2 cm
   b) 6·4 cm   d) 8·2 cm

4. Draw and label the radius and circumference of each circle.

5. A semicircle is half a circle. Draw a semicircle with a length of:
   a) 5 cm   b) 7·8 cm

6. A quadrant is a quarter circle. Draw a quadrant with a length of:
   a) 4·4 cm   b) 9 cm

B

1. What is the diameter of a circle with a radius of:
   a) 5·3 cm   c) 8·9 cm
   b) 4·6 cm   d) 6·7 cm

2. What is the radius of a circle with a diameter of:
   a) 15 cm   c) 9·6 cm
   b) 10·8 cm   d) 12·4 cm

Construct the following sectors.

3. 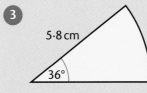 5·8 cm 36°

4. 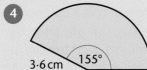 3·6 cm 155°

5. 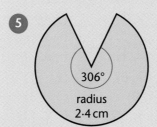 306° radius 2·4 cm

6. 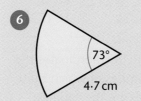 73° 4·7 cm

C

Draw a sector with the following angle and radius.

1. 229°   2·1 cm
2. 54°   5·3 cm
3. 148°   4·9 cm
4. 281°   1·6 cm
5. 27°   6·8 cm

6. Copy the pattern. Draw the large circle with a radius of 7·6 cm.

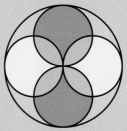

7. Copy the pattern. Make each petal 2·6 cm long.

8. Did you use a protractor to draw the pattern in 7? It can be done using a compass only. Can you work out how?

TARGET   To describe positions on the full co-ordinate grid.

The position of a point on a grid is given by its *x* and *y* co-ordinates.

The *x* co-ordinate always comes first.

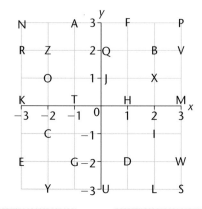

Examples

Point O is (−2, 1)   Point X is (2, 1)

Point C is (−2, −1)   Point I is (2, −1)

A

Use the above grid.

Which letter is at:

1 (3, 4)   **5** (4, 3)

2 (5, 5)   **6** (3, 1)

3 (0, 3)   **7** (2, 2)

4 (1, 1)   **8** (5, 0)?

Give the position of:

9 G   **13** V

10 C   **14** P

11 O   **15** L

12 K   **16** Q.

Use the grid to write:

17 your name

18 your school

19 your favourite colour

20 your favourite meal.

B

Use the above grid.
Which letter is at:

1 (3, 2)   **5** (−2, 2)

2 (−3, −2)   **6** (1, −2)

3 (0, 1)   **7** (−1, 0)

4 (2, −3)   **8** (−2, −1)?

Give the position of:

9 W   **13** K

10 Y   **14** P

11 Q   **15** U

12 G   **16** C.

Each set of co-ordinates spells out the name of a European capital city, but one letter has been moved. Find the city.

17 (3, −3)   **19** (−2, 1)
(−2, 1)   (3, 0)
(2, −3)   (−3, −2)
(−2, 1)   (−3, 2)

18 (−1, 0)   **20** (2, −1)
(1, 0)   (3, −3)
(−3, −2)   (−2, 1)
(−3, 3)   (1, 3)
(−1, 3)   (−1, 3)
(3, −3)

21 Write in co-ordinates the countries of which these cities are the capitals.

C

Use the above grid. Find the European capital cities.

1 (2, −3)   **3** (3, −3)
(0, 1)   (−3, 0)
(0, −3)   (−2, 1)
(2, 2)   (3, 3)
(2, −3)   (0, 1)
(0, 1)   (−3, −2)
(−1, 3)
(−3, 3)   **4** (−3, 2)
(−1, 3)   (−3, −2)
(−2, −3)
2 (3, 2)   (−3, 0)
(−1, 3)   (0, 1)
(1, −2)   (−1, 3)
(0, −3)   (3, 2)
(−2, 2)   (2, −1)
(−3, 0)

5 Write in co-ordinates the countries of which these cities are the capitals.

6 A (−3, 1), B (1, 3) and C (3, −1) are three vertices of square ABCD. Draw a grid like the one above, plot the points and complete the square.

7 Find the midpoint of line:
   a) AB   c) CD   e) BD
   b) BC   d) AD   f) AC.

TARGET To draw shapes on the full co-ordinate grid.

Examples

Join the following points in the order given to form a rhombus.

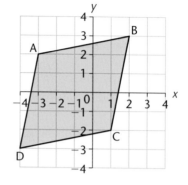

1. A (−3, 2)
2. B (2, 3)
3. C (1, −2)
4. D (−4, −3)
5. A (−3, 2)

A

1. Copy the above grid. Draw and complete:
   a) square ABCD
   b) parallelogram EFGH.

Draw a grid like the one above. Plot the points for each shape and join them up in the order given.

2. (2, 0)
   (0, 2)
   (3, 3)
   (2, 0)

3. (5, 6)
   (6, 4)
   (5, 2)
   (4, 4)
   (5, 6)

Draw a new grid and form the shapes.

4. (3, 6)
   (4, 4)
   (0, 2)
   (3, 6)

5. (2, 1)
   (5, 4)
   (6, 3)
   (3, 0)
   (2, 1)

6. Label each shape.

B

Draw a grid like the one above. Plot the points for each shape and join them up in the order given. Use a different colour for each shape.

1. (−4, 4)
   (0, 3)
   (1, −1)
   (−3, 0)
   (−4, 4)

2. (4, −2)
   (−2, −4)
   (−3, −1)
   (3, 1)
   (4, −2)

Draw a new grid and form the shapes.

3. A (−4, 1)
   B (0, 3)
   C (2, −1)
   D (−2, −3)
   A (−4, 1)

4. E (−1, 4)
   F (4, 2)
   G (3, −2)
   H (−2, 0)
   E (−1, 4)

5. Label each shape.

6. Write down the mid-point of each line.
   a) AB
   b) BC
   c) CD
   d) AD

7. Write down the point where the diagonals intersect in:
   a) shape ABCD
   b) shape EFGH

C

1. Draw a grid with both *x* and *y* axes labelled from −6 to 6. Plot the following points:
   L (−4, −1)
   M (2, 1)
   R (0, −2)

2. LM is the longest line in an isosceles triangle KLM. Give the co-ordinates of both possible positions of K.

3. LMN is an isosceles triangle. Give both possible positions for N if:
   a) LM = MN
   b) LM = LN

4. L, M and R are three vertices of a parallelogram LMRQ. Give the co-ordinates of all three possible positions for Q.

TARGET To draw and translate shapes on the first quadrant of the co-ordinate grid.

To translate a shape means to slide it into a new position.
The shape is not rotated (turned).

Example

Translate the blue triangle:

1 Up 3 Left 2 (U3 L2)

2 Right 4 Down 2 (R4 D2)

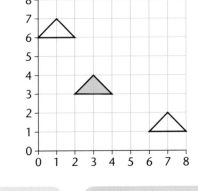

A

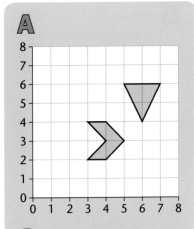

1 Copy the grid and triangle.
Translate the triangle three times.

a) U2 (up 2)

b) L5 (left 5)

c) D3 (down 3)

2 Draw a new grid and the hexagon.
Translate the hexagon three times.

a) R3 (right 3)

b) U4 (up 4)

c) L2 (left 2)

3 Give the co-ordinates for the new position of each of the translated shapes.

B

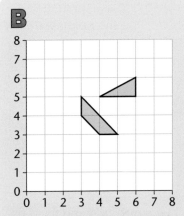

1 Give the co-ordinates of the new position of the above triangle after a translation of:

a) L3 D4   c) L4 U1

b) R2 U2   d) R1 D3.

Copy the grid and draw the translations to check.

2 Predict the co-ordinates of the new position of the above trapezium after a translation of:

a) L1 U1   c) R2 D2

b) R3 U2   d) L2 D3.

Draw a new grid and translate the trapezium to check.

C

1 Draw a new grid.
Plot these points.
(3, 4) (5, 6) (6, 3)
Join them up to make a triangle.

2 Predict the co-ordinates of the triangle after a translation of:

a) L3 D2   c) L3 U1

b) R2 U2   d) R1 D3

Draw the translations to check.

3 Draw a new grid.
Plot these points and join them up in the order given.
(2, 2) (3, 4) (5, 5) (4, 3) (2, 2)

4 Predict the co-ordinates of the rectangle after a translation of:

a) R1 D1   c) L2 U2

b) R2 U3   d) R3 D2

Draw the translations to check.

TARGET   To reflect a shape on the first quadrant of the co-ordinate grid.

Example

① The blue trapezium is reflected in a mirror line (0, 3) to (6, 3).

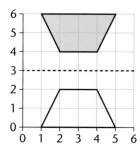

② Reflect the blue hexagon in the mirror line. Give the co-ordinates of the reflection.

Answer (3, 4) (3, 5) (4, 5) (5, 4) (5, 3) (4, 3)

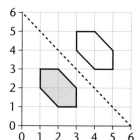

A

Copy the grid, the shape and the mirror line. Sketch the reflection.

①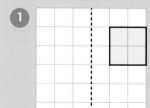

②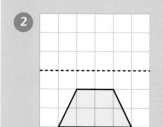

③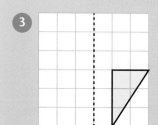

④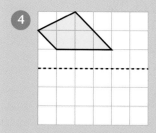

B

Copy the grid, the shape and the mirror line. Sketch the reflection.

①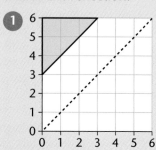

②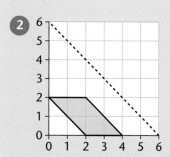

Plot these co-ordinates on a 6 × 6 grid and join them up in the order given to form a shape. Draw the mirror line and sketch the reflection.

③ (0, 0) (2, 2) (5, 2) (4, 0) (0, 0)
Mirror line (0, 3) to (6, 3)

④ (4, 3) (4, 6) (6, 6) (6, 5) (4, 3)
Mirror line (3, 0) to (3, 6)

C

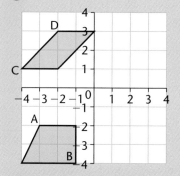

① Copy the above grid and the trapezium. Sketch the reflection:
a) in the *x* axis
b) in the *y* axis
c) in a mirror line (−4, 4) to (4, −4)

② Copy the above grid and the parallelogram. Sketch the reflection:
a) in the *x* axis
b) in the *y* axis
c) in a mirror line (−4, −4) to (4, 4)

③ For each of the points A–D in the above shapes give the co-ordinates of its position:
a) in the original shape
b) in each reflection.

TARGET   **To translate a shape on the full co-ordinate grid.**

To translate a shape means to slide it into a new position.

Example

Translate the blue triangle:

1️⃣ Left 2 Up 3

2️⃣ Right 3 Down 1

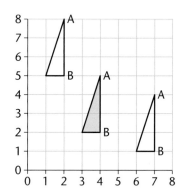

Translate the yellow triangle:

3️⃣ Left 3 Up 2

4️⃣ Right 1 Down 3

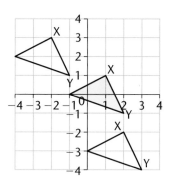

The shape is not rotated (turned).

Each line of the translated shape is parallel to the equivalent line in the original shape.

AB is parallel to the *y* axis in the blue triangle and in both translations.

XY in the yellow triangle is parallel to XY in each translation.

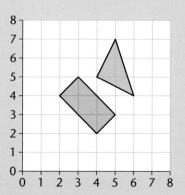

1️⃣ Copy the grid and the triangle.
Translate the triangle:

  a) Left 2 Down 3

  b) Right 1 Down 2

  c) Left 4 Up 1

2️⃣ Copy the grid and the rectangle.
Translate the rectangle:

  a) Right 2 Up 3

  b) Left 2 Down 1

  c) Right 3 Down 2

3️⃣ Draw a new grid. Plot these co-ordinates and join them up in the order given.
(2, 5) (3, 6) (5, 5) (4, 4) (2, 5)

Translate the parallelogram:

  a) Left 2 Down 2

  b) Right 3 Up 2

  c) Right 1 Down 4

4️⃣ Draw a new grid. Plot these co-ordinates and join them up in the order given.
(2, 2) (2, 4) (3, 4) (3, 3)
(5, 3) (5, 2) (2, 2)

Translate the hexagon:

  a) Left 2 Down 2

  b) Right 3 Up 3

  c) Left 1 Up 4

B

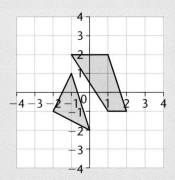

1 Copy the grid and the trapezium.
Translate the trapezium:
 a) Left 2 Down 2
 b) Left 3 Up 2
 c) Right 2 Down 3

2 Copy the grid and the triangle.
Translate the triangle:
 a) Right 3 Up 2
 b) Left 1 Up 3
 c) Right 4 Down 2

3 Draw a new grid.
Plot these co-ordinates and join them up
in the order given.
$(-1, 0)$ $(0, 2)$ $(2, 1)$ $(1, -1)$ $(-1, 0)$

4 Translate the square:
 a) Left 2 Down 3
 b) Left 3 Up 1
 c) Right 2 Down 2

5 Draw a new grid.
Plot these co-ordinates and join them up
in the order given.
$(-1, 2)$ $(0, 0)$ $(-1, -2)$ $(-2, 0)$ $(-1, 2)$

6 Translate the rhombus:
 a) Right 4 Up 1
 b) Left 2 Up 2
 c) Right 3 Down 2

C

For each of the following draw a grid with
both x and y axes labelled from -6 to 6.
Plot the co-ordinates and join them up in
the order given to form a shape.

1 $(-4, -3)$ $(-2, -1)$ $(-3, 0)$ $(0, 0)$
$(0, -3)$ $(-1, -2)$ $(-3, -4)$ $(-4, -3)$

Translate the heptagon:
 a) Right 4 Up 4
 b) Left 2 Up 5
 c) Right 6 Down 2

2 $(2, 4)$ $(2, 2)$ $(4, 2)$ $(1, -1)$ $(1, 1)$
$(-1, 1)$ $(2, 4)$

Translate the hexagon:
 a) Left 3 Down 4
 b) Left 4 Up 2
 c) Right 2 Down 5

3 $(3, -3)$ $(0, -2)$ $(-1, -4)$ $(0, 0)$ $(3, -3)$

Translate the quadrilateral:
 a) Right 2 Up 5
 b) Left 3 Up 6
 c) Left 5 Down 2

4 $(-3, 2)$ $(-1, 4)$ $(-1, 2)$ $(1, 1)$ $(-1, 0)$
$(-3, 2)$

Translate the pentagon:
 a) Right 4 Up 1
 b) Left 3 Down 3
 c) Right 5 Down 6

5 $(-1, -1)$ $(-2, 3)$ $(1, 2)$ $(-1, -1)$

Translate the triangle:
 a) Right 5 Down 4
 b) Right 4 Up 3
 c) Left 2 Down 5

TARGET To reflect shapes on the co-ordinate plane.

Examples

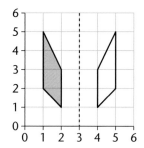

The orange shape is reflected in a mirror line (3, 0) to (3, 6).

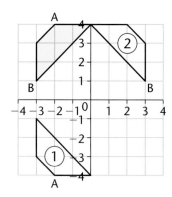

The yellow trapezium is reflected:

① in the *x* axis

② in the *y* axis.

Each point in the reflected shape matches a point in the original shape.

Matching points are an equal distance from the mirror line.

For example, look at the yellow trapezium.

A (−2, 4) becomes (−2, −4) in reflection ①.

B (−3, 1) becomes (3, 1) in reflection ②.

A

Copy the grid, the shape and the mirror line. Sketch the reflection.

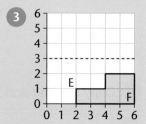

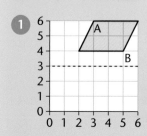

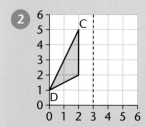

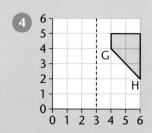

5 Give the co-ordinates of points A–H:

a) in the above shapes

b) in the reflected shapes.

Plot the co-ordinates for each of the following on a 6 × 6 grid and join them up in the order given to form a shape. Draw the mirror line and sketch the reflection.

6 (3, 0) (1, 2) (5, 2) (3, 0)
Mirror line (0, 3) to (6, 3)

7 (4, 2) (4, 4) (6, 2) (6, 0) (4, 2)
Mirror line (3, 0) to (3, 6)

8 (0, 6) (4, 6) (3, 4) (1, 4) (0, 6)
Mirror line (0, 3) to (6, 3)

9 (0, 2) (0, 3) (1, 4) (2, 4) (2, 1) (1, 1) (0, 2)
Mirror line (3, 0) to (3, 6)

10 (3, 4) (1, 4) (2, 6) (3, 6)
Plot the above co-ordinates and join them up in the order given to form one half of a symmetrical trapezium. Complete the shape and draw its reflection in a mirror line (0, 3) to (6, 3).

Copy the grid, the shape and the mirror line.
Sketch the reflection:

a) in the mirror line   b) in the *x* axis.

 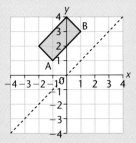

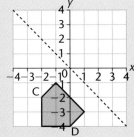

Copy the grid, the shape and the mirror line.
Sketch the reflection:

a) in the mirror line   b) in the *y* axis.

 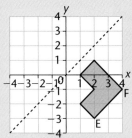

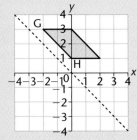

 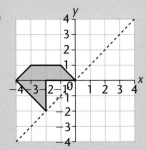

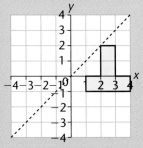

5 Give the co-ordinates of point A–H:

a) in the above shape

b) in the reflection in the mirror line

c) in the reflection in the *x* or *y* axis.

Draw an 8 × 8 grid with both axes labelled −4 to 4 as above.
Plot the points and join them up in the order given to form a shape.
Draw the mirror line and sketch the reflection:

a) in the mirror line

b) in the *x* axis.

6 (−2, −4) (1, −1) (1, −3)
(0, −4) (−2, −4)
Mirror line (−4, −4) to (4, 4)

7 (1, 1) (−1, 3) (1, 3) (2, 4)
(4, 4) (1, 1)
Mirror line (−4, 4) to (4, −4)

C

Copy the grid, the shape and the mirror line.
Sketch the reflection:

a) in the mirror line

b) in the *y* axis.

3 Give the co-ordinates of the reflection of the hexagon:

a) in the mirror line

b) in the *y* axis.

4 Give the co-ordinates of the reflection of the octagon:

a) in the mirror line

b) in the *y* axis.

For each of the following draw an 8 × 8 grid with both axes labelled −4 to 4 as above. Plot the points and join them up in the order given to form a shape. Draw the mirror line and sketch the reflection:

a) in the mirror line

b) in the axis indicated.

5 (2, 0) (−1, 2) (2, 4) (1, 2) (2, 0)
a) Mirror line (−4, 4) to (4, −4)
b) *x* axis.

6 (0, −2) (−1, −2) (−1, −1) (2, −1)
(2, −4) (1, −4) (1, −3) (0, −3) (0, −2)
a) Mirror line (−4, −4) to (4, 4)
b) *x* axis.

7 (−4, 0) (−3, 0) (−3, 1) (−1, 1)
(−1, −1) (−2, −1) (−2, −2) (−4, 0)
a) Mirror line (−4, 4) to (4, −4)
b) *y* axis.

8 (−1, 2) (−1, −1) (−4, −1) (−3, 0)
(−4, 1) (−3, 2) (−2, 1) (−1, 2)
a) Mirror line (−4, −4) to (4, 4)
b) *y* axis.

TARGET   To interpret and construct pie charts.

Example 1

The pie chart shows the 350 votes cast for the three candidates in an election.

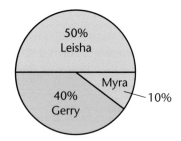

How many votes did each candidate receive?

Leisha	Myra	Gerry
50% of 350	10% of 350	40% of 350
350 ÷ 2	350 ÷ 10	(350 ÷ 10) × 4
175 votes	35 votes	35 × 4
		140 votes

Example 2

Draw a pie chart to show the 200 runners taking part in a fun run.

Men	100	Boys	20
Women	60	Girls	20

A. Find the angle at the centre of each sector.

Boys/Girls	Men	Women
$\frac{20}{200}$ $\frac{1}{10}$	$\frac{100}{200}$ $\frac{1}{2}$	$\frac{60}{200}$ $\frac{3}{10}$
360° ÷ 10	360° ÷ 2	(360° ÷ 10) × 3
36°	180°	36° × 3
		108°

B. Draw the pie chart.

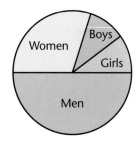

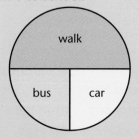

A

1. The pie chart shows how the 28 children in one class come to school.

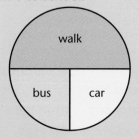

   a) How many children travel by bus?
   b) How many children walk?
   c) How many children travel by car?
   d) What is the angle at the centre of the yellow sector?

2. The pie chart shows the number of votes received by candidates for a local council. 750 people voted.

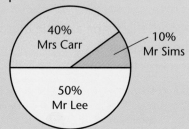

   How many people voted for each candidate?

3. The pie chart shows the 240 members of the audience at a cinema.

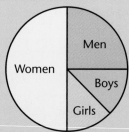

   a) How many women were in the audience?
   b) How many men?
   c) How many girls?
   d) What is the angle at the centre of the blue sector?

B

1 The votes of 20 children choosing a name for their village football team.

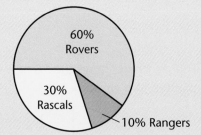

a) How many children voted for each name?

b) What is the angle at the centre of the red sector?

2 The size of shoe worn by the 90 children in Year 5.

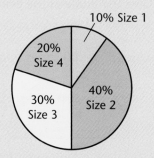

a) How many children wear each size of shoe?

b) What is the angle at the centre of each sector?

3 The first 300 vowels in a book.

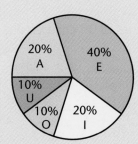

a) How many are there of each vowel?

b) Construct the pie chart.

C

1 The instruments played by the 60 members of an orchestra.

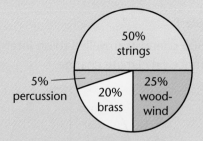

a) How many players are there in each section of the orchestra?

b) What is the angle at the centre of the green sector?

2 How 500 people prefer to eat eggs.

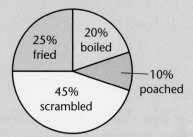

a) How many of the people asked preferred each of the four ways of cooking eggs?

b) Give the angle at the centre of each sector.

3 Eighty golfers played in a tournament. These are the scores they made at the most difficult hole on the course.

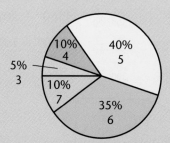

a) How many golfers made each score?

b) Construct the pie chart.

TARGET   To interpret and construct pie charts.

Example 1

How 500 scientists travelled to an international conference on climate change.

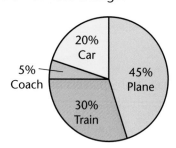

How many people used each form of transport?

Car	100 people	(500 ÷ 10) × 2
Coach	25 people	(500 ÷ 10) ÷ 2
Train	150 people	(500 ÷ 10) × 3
Plane	225 people	(500 ÷ 100) × 45

Example 2

Construct a pie chart to show the time given to each subject in Year 6 on Tuesdays.

Maths	60 mins	**A.**	Find the angle at
English	75 mins.		the centre of each
P.E.	45 mins.		sector.
Science	90 mins.	**B.**	Construct the pie
Music	30 mins.		chart.
Total	300 mins.		

A. Maths $\frac{60}{300}$ $\frac{1}{5}$ 360° ÷ 5 = 72°

English $\frac{75}{300}$ $\frac{1}{4}$ 360° ÷ 4 = 90°

P.E. $\frac{45}{300}$ $\frac{3}{20}$ (360° ÷ 20) × 3 = 54°

Science $\frac{90}{300}$ $\frac{3}{10}$ (360° ÷ 10) × 3 = 108°

Music $\frac{30}{300}$ $\frac{1}{10}$ 360° ÷ 10 = 36°

B.

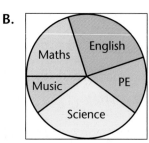

A

1 The pie chart shows the 56 new trees planted in a wood.

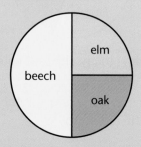

a) How many of each type of tree were planted?
b) Give the angle at the centre of the brown sector.

2 The colours of 200 shoes sold in a shop.

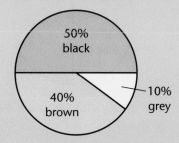

a) How many shoes of each colour were sold?
b) Give the angle at the centre of the yellow sector.

3 The ages of 30 children at a party.

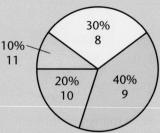

a) How many children of each age were at the party?
b) Give the angle at the centre of the pink sector.

B

Lindy's holiday cost £1500. The pie chart shows how the money was spent.

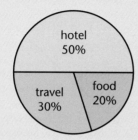

1. How much did Lindy spend on:
   a) her hotel   b) food   c) travel?

2. Give the angle at the centre of each sector.

3. The number of people travelling in each of 120 cars.

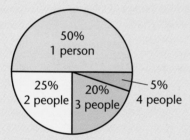

   a) How many cars carried each number of people?

   b) Construct the pie chart.

4. This table shows the 80 main courses served in an Italian restaurant.

Course	Servings
Fish	10
Pasta	20
Pizza	40
Meat	10

   a) Find the proportion of the 80 courses served represented by each type of course.

   b) Work out the angle at the centre of each sector of a pie chart showing these proportions.

   c) Construct the pie chart.

C

1. The pie chart shows what 160 people chose to be served with their apple pie.

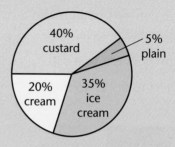

   a) How many people chose each accompaniment?   *cream*

   b) Give the angle at the centre of each sector.   *72* *144* *18* *126*

2. The 40 members of a hockey club were asked to choose their best position. These are the results.

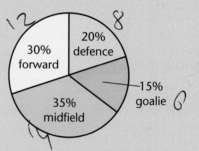

   a) How many members chose each position?

   b) Construct the pie chart.

3. This table shows the 3000 books in a library.

Categories	Books
Fiction	1350
Non-fiction	900
Children's	600
Reference	150

   a) Find the proportion of the total number of books represented by each category. $\frac{9}{20}$ $\frac{13}{20}$ *Fic* *Non*

   b) Work out the angle at the centre of each sector of a pie chart showing the proportions. $\frac{2}{10}$ *children*

   c) Construct the pie chart.

   1:4:6:9

TARGET   To interpret conversion graphs involving measures.

This graph converts pounds into kilograms and vice versa.

2 kilograms converts to 4·4 lb.

2 lb converts to 0·9 kg to the nearest 100 g.

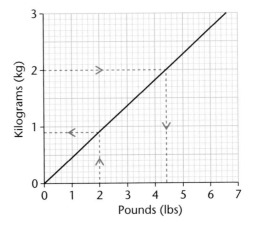

A

This graph converts kilometres to miles.

1 Use the graph to convert to the nearest mile:

   a) 16 km   **e)** 72 km

   b) 40 km   **f)** 48 km

   c) 32 km   **g)** 14 km

   d) 56 km   **h)** 26 km

2 Use the graph to convert to the nearest kilometre:

   a) 50 miles   **e)** 5 miles

   b) 15 miles   **f)** 34 miles

   c) 40 miles   **g)** 19 miles

   d) 21 miles   **h)** 46 miles.

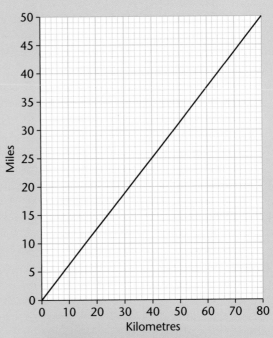

3 A marathon course is 42 km long. How long is the race to the nearest mile?

4 Two French villages are 9 miles apart. What is this distance as shown in km on a road sign?

B

This graph converts ounces to grams.

1 Convert to the nearest 10 grams:

a) 5 oz   e) 23 oz

b) 28 oz   f) 19 oz

c) 9 oz   g) 14 oz

d) 35 oz   h) 33 oz.

2 Convert to the nearest ounce:

a) 600 g   e) 200 g

b) 320 g   f) 540 g

c) 740 g   g) 980 g

d) 460 g   h) 60 g.

3 A rubber weighs 30 oz. What does it weigh in grams?

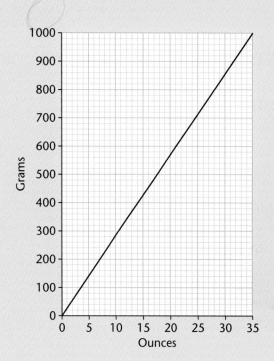

C

1 Draw a graph to convert litres to gallons.

a) Label the horizontal axis (litres) in 5s to 45.

b) Label the vertical axis (gallons) in 1s to 10.

c) Plot the points (0, 0) and (45, 10).

d) Join the points with a straight line.

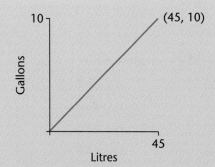

2 Use your graph to convert to the nearest tenth of a gallon:

a) 36 litres   d) 43 litres

b) 23 litres   e) 9 litres

c) 1 litre   f) 13 litres.

3 Use your graph to convert to the nearest litre:

a) 6 gallons   d) 4 gallons

b) 8·2 gallons   e) 5·6 gallons

c) 2·4 gallons   f) 1·8 gallons.

4 Draw a graph to convert feet and inches to centimetres. (1 foot = 12 inches)

a) Label the horizontal axis (inches) in 5s to 40.

b) Label the vertical axis (centimetres) in 10s to 100.

c) Join points (0, 0) and (40, 100) with a straight line.

5 Use your graph to convert to the nearest centimetre:

a) 10 inches   d) 4 inches

b) 2 feet   e) 3 ft 2 inches

c) 1 ft 4 inches   f) 2 ft 8 inches.

6 Use your graph to convert to feet and inches:

a) 50 cm   d) 8 cm

b) 20 cm   e) 72 cm

c) 90 cm   f) 30 cm.

TARGET To interpret conversion graphs involving currencies.

The currency used in South Africa is the rand. This graph converts pounds into rands.

60 rand converts to £4.

£6·40 converts to 96 rand.

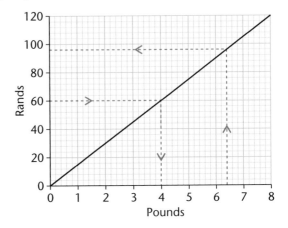

 A

This graph converts pounds to US dollars.

1 Convert to the nearest dollar.

   a) £36   **e)** £56

   b) £16   **f)** £24

   c) £60   **g)** £4

   d) £28   **h)** £48

2 Convert to the nearest pound.

   a) 60 dollars   **e)** 30 dollars

   b) 12 dollars   **f)** 36 dollars

   c) 48 dollars   **g)** 18 dollars

   d) 78 dollars   **h)** 66 dollars

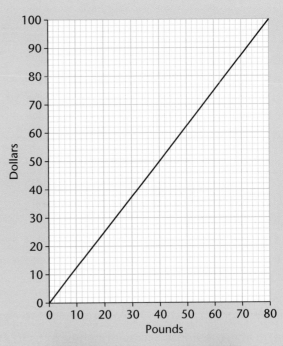

3 In New York a yellow cab fare was 10 dollars. How much would this be in pounds to the nearest 50 pence?

4 An American tourist in London pays his hotel bill of £72 in dollars. What does he pay?

B

This graph converts pounds to Euros.

1 Convert to the nearest Euro.

a) £24   e) £29
b) £36   f) £12
c) £4   g) £32
d) £15   h) £19

2 Convert to the nearest pound.

a) 50 Euros   e) 35 Euros
b) 25 Euros   f) 6 Euros
c) 39 Euros   g) 20 Euros
d) 10 Euros   h) 44 Euros

3 Sharon buys a handbag in Spain for 23 Euros. How much would this be in pounds to the nearest 50p?

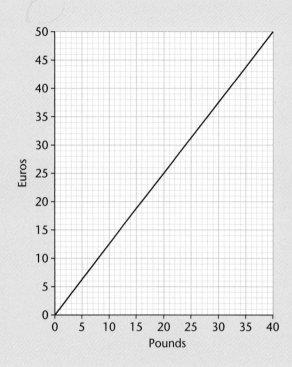

C

1 Currency exchange rates often change. Draw a new conversion graph for converting pounds to Euros.

a) Label the horizontal axis (pounds) in 10s to 100.
b) Label the vertical axis (Euros) in 10s to 120.
c) Plot the points (0, 0) and (100, 120).
d) Join the points with a straight line.

2 Use your graph to convert to the nearest Euro:

a) £40   d) £68
b) £80   e) £10
c) £50   f) £90

3 Use your graph to convert to the nearest pound:

a) 24 Euros   d) 84 Euros
b) 120 Euros   e) 36 Euros
c) 72 Euros   f) 90 Euros

4 Draw a conversion graph for converting pounds to Danish kroner.

a) Label the horizontal axis (pounds) in 10s to 100.
b) Label the vertical axis (kroner) in 100s to 1000.
c) Join the points (0, 0) and (100, 920) with a straight line.

5 Use your graph to convert to the nearest 10 krone:

a) £62   c) £10   e) £12
b) £38   d) £74   f) £88.

6 Use your graph to convert to the nearest pound:

a) 500 kroner   d) 280 kroner
b) 680 kroner   e) 340 kroner
c) 100 kroner   f) 580 kroner.

TARGET   To interpret line graphs showing journeys and use them to solve problems.

Example

This line graph shows a car journey from the driver's home to Camford.

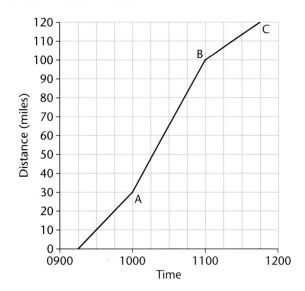

1. When does the journey begin?

   Answer   *09:15*

2. How far is it from the driver's home to A?

   Answer   *30 miles*

3. How far had the car travelled at:

   a) 9:30   Answer   *10 miles*

   b) 10:30?   , Answer   *65 miles*

4. At what time does the car reach B?

   Answer   *11:00*

5. What is the distance from B to C?

   Answer   *20 miles*

6. Give the car's speed between A and B.

   Answer   *70 miles per hour*

 A

This graph shows Katina's car journey from Leeds to Stoke.

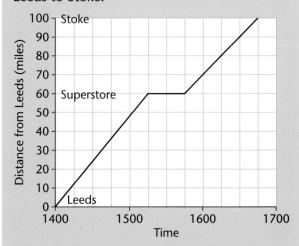

1. How far is it from Leeds to Stoke?

2. How far is it from the superstore to Stoke?

3. At what time does Katina:

   a) arrive at the superstore

   b) arrive at Stoke?

4. How long does she stop at the superstore?

5. How long does the journey take:

   a) from Leeds to the superstore

   b) from the superstore to Stoke?

6. How far has Katina travelled at 4pm?

7. At what time does Katina pass a sign which tells her it is 10 miles to Stoke?

8. Give the speed of the car from the superstore to Stoke.

9. How long does the journey take altogether?

B

Cosmo cycles to the base of a tall hill (Point A), rides up to the summit (Point B), enjoys the view and then returns home.

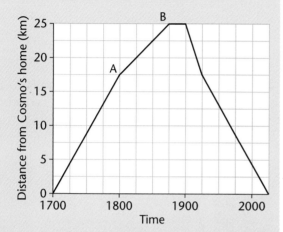

1 How far is it from Cosmo's house:
   a) to the base of the hill (A) *17·5*
   b) to the summit of the hill (B)? *25km*

2 At what time did Cosmo:
   a) begin the return journey *19.00*
   b) arrive back at home? *20;15*

3 How long did he spend enjoying the view? *15*

4 How long did it take him to cycle:
   a) from his home to the base of the hill *1H*
   b) from the base of the hill to the summit? *45 min*

5 Give the speed in kilometres per hour at which Cosmo cycled on his return journey:
   a) from the summit to the base of the hill *30km*
   b) from the base of the hill to his house? *17.5km*

C

This graph shows the journeys made by groups of football fans travelling from London to Manchester by coach or train.

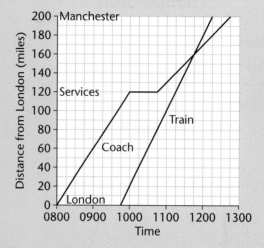

1 At what time did:
   a) the coach arrive at the motorway services *10·00*
   b) the train leave London? *9·45*

2 How far had the coach travelled before it stopped at the services? *120*

3 How long did the coach stop? *45*

4 How far had the train travelled when: *26*
   a) the coach arrived at the services *2n (12m)*
   b) the coach left the services? *80*

5 How far apart were the coach and the train:
   a) when the coach left the services *40*
   b) at 12:00 *10*
   c) when the train arrived at Manchester? *20*

6 At what time had both coach and train travelled the same distance? *1145*

7 What was the speed in mph of:
   a) the coach from London to the services *80*
   b) the coach from the services to Manchester *40*
   c) the train? *80*

T **To interpret and construct line graphs involving changes in temperature.**

Example

This graph shows the temperature in a 24 hour period from midnight to midnight.

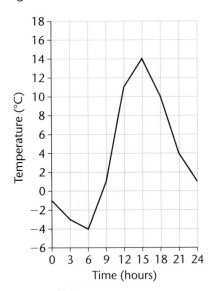

① What is the temperature at 03:00?

Answer −3°C

② How much does the temperature rise between 06:00 and 09:00?

Answer 5°C

③ When is a temperature of 14°C recorded?

Answer *15:00*

④ How much does the temperature fall between 18:00 and 21:00?

Answer 6°C

⑤ Estimate two times when the temperature is 6°C.

Answer *10:30, 20:00*

This graph shows the temperature of a saucepan of water heated until it is boiling and then left to cool.

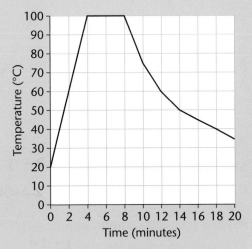

① What is the temperature of the water before it is heated?

② How long does it take for the temperature to reach 100°C?

③ After how many minutes does the water begin to cool?

④ Give the two times when the water temperature is 60°C.

⑤ How much does the water temperature fall between the 18th and 20th minute?

⑥ Estimate the water temperature at:

a) 1 minute   b) 13 minutes.

⑦ Vicki tested the thermal insulating effectiveness of three containers, A, B and C. Draw a line graph to show her results for all three containers.

Time (minutes)	0	5	10	20	25	30
Water Temp. °C (A)	100	70	50	40	35	30
Water Temp. °C (B)	100	85	75	65	55	50
Water Temp. °C (C)	100	50	35	30	25	25

B

This line graph shows the average daily maximum temperature in Helsinki for one year.

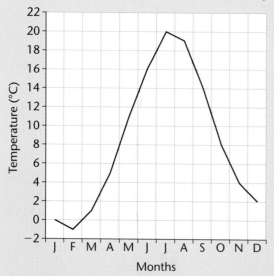

Months

1. What was the temperature in:
   a) September 11   b) April? 8

2. In which month was the temperature:
   a) 1°C May   b) 19°C? August

3. What was the highest temperature? 20

4. In which month was the temperature below zero? February

5. How much did the temperature:
   a) rise between May and June 4
   b) fall between November and December? 1

6. Between which two months was there:
   a) the largest rise in temperature April – May
   b) the largest fall in temperature? Agust Sept

7. Use the table below to draw a line graph showing the average daily maximum temperature in Moscow in one year.

Month	J	F	M	A	M	J	J	A	S	O	N	D
Temperature (°C)	−6	−5	3	11	19	22	26	23	17	9	2	−3

C

This line graph shows the daily maximum and minimum temperatures in Aberdeen for the first 10 days of January.

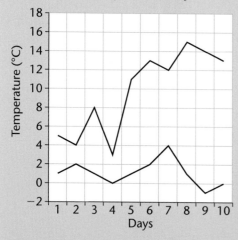

Days

1. On which day was there:
   a) the highest maximum temperature 15
   b) the lowest minimum temperature? −1

2. What was:
   a) the lowest maximum temperature 3
   b) the highest minimum temperature? 4

3. What was the difference between the maximum and minimum temperatures on:
   a) 3rd January   b) 8th January?

4. On which day was the difference between the maximum and minimum temperatures:
   a) largest 9   b) smallest? 4

5. Use the table below to draw a line graph showing the daily maximum and minimum temperatures in New York for the first 10 days of January.

Days	1	2	3	4	5	6	7	8	9	10
Max. Temp. (°C)	4	1	2	2	0	3	4	5	5	3
Min. Temp. (°C)	1	−2	−3	−4	−5	−8	−11	−9	−10	−8

TARGET   To calculate the mean of a set of data.

The mean or average of a set of data is the total divided by the number of items in the set.

Example

The number of hours worked
by a plumber each day.

11 8 5 9 6 10 7 9 4 6

Total hours	75 hours
No. of days	10
Mean	7·5 hours (75 ÷ 10)

A

Find the mean of each set of data.

1 The ages of the five children in a family.

5 5 8 12 15

2 The shoe sizes worn by eight women.

3 5 3 4 6 3 5 3

3 The marks out of 10 of nine children in a spelling test.

7 10 10 7 9
9 8 2 10

4 The number of people entering a shop each minute.

8 4 2 7 8 3
6 3 8 4 5 2

5 The daily maximum temperature in one week in November.

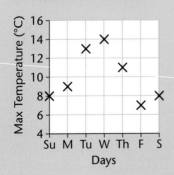

B

Find the mean of each set of data.

1 The estimated heights in metres of a rock face made by the climbers.

90 80 100 150 70
100 110 90 80 100

2 The ages of the eleven players in a football team.

26 24 17 20 26 28
19 30 25 17 21

3 The number of buses stopping each hour at a bus stop.

1 3 5 5 4 2 3 4
5 4 2 3 2 1 1

4 The number of people sitting at each table of a cafe.

4 1 0 2 1 4 1
1 4 3 4 1 0

5 The daily maximum temperatures in °C for one week in May.

20 16 19 14
13 18 19

C

Find the mean of each set of data.

1 The heights in metres of the nine members of a family.

1·3 1·6 1·2 1·9
1·1 0·9 1·7 1·2 1·7

2 The number of passengers getting off a bus at each of its first eight stops.

0 1 3 1 4 1 4 6

3 The average daily maximum temperature in °C for each month of a year.

5 6 9 12 15 17
19 18 14 13 9 7

4 The daily maximum temperatures in °C for one week in February.

4 5 1 −2 −1 4 3

5 The number of people living in each of the 100 houses in a road.

People	3	4	5	6
Houses	20	35	30	15

TARGET   To interpret the mean of a set of data.

The mean is the total divided by the number of items in the set.

Examples

6 classes
174 children
Find the mean class size.

Answer   *29* (174 ÷ 6)

4 classes
Mean class size 26
How many children?

Answer   *104* (26 × 4)

Mean class size 30
210 children
How many classes?

Answer   *7* (210 ÷ 30)

 A

Find the mean for each set of data.

1. Football matches 8
   Total goals 40
   Mean goals per game?

2. Dogs 3
   Total weight 21 kg
   Mean weight per dog?

3. Restaurant tables 10
   Diners 25
   Mean diners per table?

4. Library users 12
   Books borrowed 36
   Mean books per person?

5. Swimming sessions 5
   Total lengths 100

6. Darts 3
   Total score 51

7. Dice 2
   Total score 7

8. Tests 4
   Total marks 320%

 B

Find the mean.

1. Flights 5
   Total distance 12 000 km

2. Cars 100
   Passengers 280

3. Boxes of apples 8
   Total apples 1000

Find the total.

4. Car journeys 12
   Mean distance 45 miles

5. Buses 2
   Mean passengers 56·5

6. Trees 3
   Mean number of apples 269

Find the number of items.

7. Distance cycled (km)
   Total 257   Mean 25·7

8. Train passengers
   Total 720   Mean 180

9. Bags of apples
   Total 150   Mean 7·5

C

Find the mean.

1. Adults 4
   Total weight 263·2 kg

2. Pages read 15
   Time 36 minutes

3. Shop customers 20
   Total takings £355

Find the total.

4. Cans 500
   Mean weight 435 g

5. Pages read 26
   Mean time 3 mins. 30 secs.

6. Customers 12
   Mean takings £4·60

Find the number of items.

7. Weight of fish
   Total 1·8 kg
   Mean 225 g

8. Time per page (minutes)
   Total 57   Mean 1·9

9. Takings per customer
   Total £2·85
   Mean 57p

TARGET   To calculate and interpret the mean of a set of data.

The mean or average of a set of data is found by dividing the total of the values by the number of items in the set.

MEAN = TOTAL ÷ ITEMS

Examples

1 The number of letters delivered in the post each morning.

M	Tu	W	Th	F	Sat
4	7	6	3	8	2

Total of letters = 30.
Number of deliveries = 6.
Mean number of letters in each delivery
5 = (30 ÷ 6).

2 The ten anglers on a riverbank caught the following number of fish each.

8 11 5 9 6 10 7 9 4 ☐

The mean number of fish caught by each angler was 7·5. How many fish were caught by the tenth angler?

Total of fish caught by:
1st nine anglers = 69
All ten anglers = 75 (7·5 × 10)
10th angler   = 6 (75 − 69)

A

For each set of data find:

a) the total of the values
b) the number of items in the set
c) the mean.

1 The number of tries scored by a rugby team in each of their first nine games.

2 4 1 7 1 3 2 6 1

2 The weight of five packets of cheese.

220 g 260 g 210 g 220 g 240 g

3 The speed in miles per hour of seven cars.

65 55 40 50 55 75 45

4 The number of minutes taken by a barber to cut the hair of eleven customers.

10 12 11 13 7 12
13 6 14 10 13

5 The marks of ten children in their weekly spelling tests.

7 10 9 10 6
8 10 6 9 10

6 The number of hours of sunshine each day in one week.

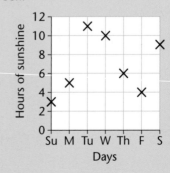

B

1 The opening batsman in a cricket team scored the highest number of runs in his team's innings. The other ten batsmen made the following scores.

1   35   17   0   15   40   0   8   1   0

The mean score for the eleven batsmen was 20. Find the opening batsman's score.

2 The first 12 customers at a booking office each bought the following number of cinema tickets.

2   1   3   16   1   4
1   5   4   1   7   2

After the 13th customer the mean number of tickets for each customer was 4. Find the number of tickets bought by the 13th customer.

3 The daily maximum temperatures recorded for six days in January.

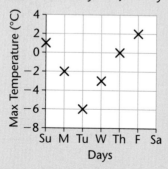

When the temperature on Saturday was included the mean temperature for the week was −1°C. Find the Saturday temperature.

C

Investigating friction, Chloe let a marble roll down a ramp onto different surfaces to see how far it would roll. These are her results.

Test Number	Distance rolled on		
	Carpet	Wood	Plastic
1	1·5 m	4·7 m	3·3 m
2	1·3 m	4·5 m	?
3	1·1 m	5·0 m	2·9 m
4	1·7 m	4·3 m	3·5 m
5	1·4 m	4·8 m	3·1 m

1 Find the mean distance the marble rolled on:

a) carpet   **b)** wood.

2 The mean distance rolled on plastic was 3·24 m. Find the missing result.

3 The monthly rainfall recorded in millimetres in one year in Jerusalem.

J	F	M	A	M	J	J	A	S	O	N	D
100	110	80	20	10	0	0	0	0	10	60	?

Including the missing December total, the mean rainfall for each month was 40 mm. Find the rainfall for December.

4 Louis rolled a dice 100 times. The table shows his scores.

Score	1	2	3	4	5	6
Frequency	14	20	18	15	16	17

Find the mean score.

TARGET   To solve number problems involving addition and subtraction.

In an arithmagon the pair of numbers at the end of
each line are added together to give the number
between them.

Example

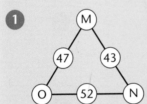

45 + 27 = 72
27 + 16 = 43
16 + 45 = 61

Find the missing numbers in these arithmagons.

A

1

2
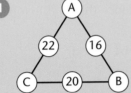

3
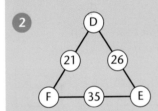

4
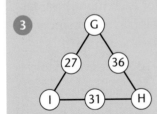

B

1

2
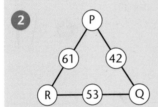

3
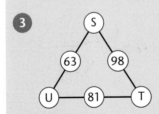

4
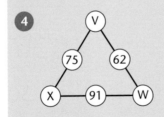

C

1
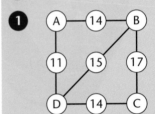

2
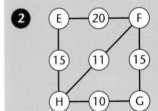

3
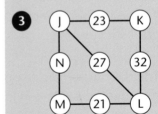

4
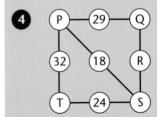

TARGET   To solve number puzzles involving multiplication and division.

In a multiplication pyramid pairs of numbers are
multiplied together to make the number above them.

Use jottings to help complete the multiplication pyramids.

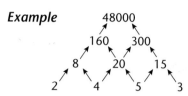

Example

```
              48000
          160      300
        8      20      15
      2    4      5      3
```

A

1

```
        □
      □     □
    8     3     10
```

2

```
        □
     15     35
   □     5     □
```

3

```
        □
     72      □
   9     □     5
```

4

```
        □
     □     12
   11     2     □
```

5

```
     384
   24      □
  6     □     □
```

6

```
     252
   □     18
  7     □     □
```

B

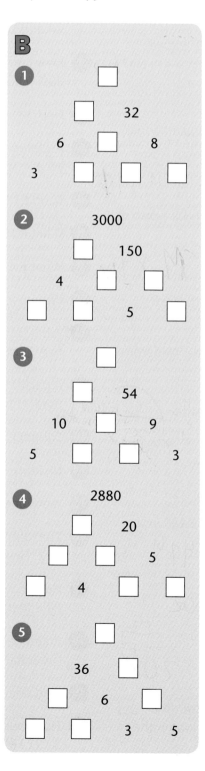

1

```
        □
      □     32
    6     □     8
  3    □    □    □
```

2

```
     3000
       □     150
     4    □    □
   □    □    5    □
```

3

```
        □
      □     54
   10     □     9
  5    □    □    3
```

4

```
     2880
       □     20
    □    □    5
  □    4    □    □
```

5

```
        □
     36      □
   □     6     □
  □    □    3    5
```

C

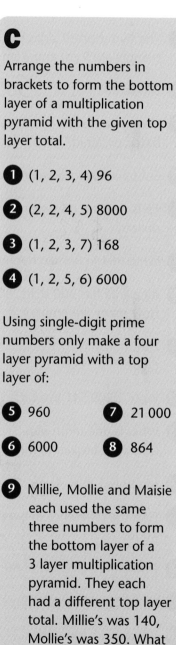

Arrange the numbers in
brackets to form the bottom
layer of a multiplication
pyramid with the given top
layer total.

1 (1, 2, 3, 4) 96

2 (2, 2, 4, 5) 8000

3 (1, 2, 3, 7) 168

4 (1, 2, 5, 6) 6000

Using single-digit prime
numbers only make a four
layer pyramid with a top
layer of:

5 960   **7** 21 000

6 6000   **8** 864

9 Millie, Mollie and Maisie
each used the same
three numbers to form
the bottom layer of a
3 layer multiplication
pyramid. They each
had a different top layer
total. Millie's was 140,
Mollie's was 350. What
was Maisie's total?

TEST 1

1. What number is 1000 times greater than 0·29? *290*

2. Write 4·017 as a mixed number. *4 17/1000*

3. Add 2 005 000 to 48 369. *2 053 369*

4. The two shortest sides of a right-angled triangle are 9 cm and 3 cm. What is its area? *13·5*

5. Divide 4000 by 8. *500*

6. How many edges are there in a pentagonal based pyramid? *10*

7. Subtract 59 from one million. *999,941*

8. £5 is worth 8 US dollars. What is £2 worth in dollars? *$3 2*

9. Write 964 in Roman numerals. *CMLXIV*

10. A cinema has 300 seats. 60% are filled. How many are empty? *128*

11. How many 150 ml bottles can be filled from 6 litres? *40*

12. Write 1 209 541 in words. *One million, two hundred and nine thousand five hundred and forty one*

13. What is one tenth of 6·5 km? Give your answer in metres. *0·65km 650 m*

14. Multiply 5·8 by 4. *23·2*

15. Find the difference between 712 480 and 4006. *708474*

16. Find eleven twelfths of 60. *55*

17. Write 20 millilitres as litres. *0·02*

18. What is −5 more than 2? *−3*

19. Write one fifth as a percentage. *20%*

20. A cuboid has a volume of 480 cm³. It is 12 cm tall and 5 cm wide. How long is the cuboid? *8 m*

TEST 2

1. Write five million three hundred and eighty thousand and twenty in figures. *5 380 020*

2. Divide 308 by 1000.

3. The temperature is 3°C. It falls 9°. What is the new temperature? *−6*

4. How many boxes of 16 can be filled from 2000 chocolates? *125*

5. Find 30% of £2·60. *78*

6. A square has a perimeter of 52 cm. What is its area? *156 16cm*

7. Round 1·555555 to two decimal places. *1·66 1·5*

8. What is the total of 0·19, 0·038 and 0·5? *0·728*

9. What is 0·8 multiplied by 7? *5·6*

10. Write 6·01 litres as millilitres. *6001 6010*

11. What is the radius of a circle with a diameter of 8·7 cm? *4·35cm*

12. A packet of cereal holds 0·75 kg. 10% is used. How much is left in grams? *0·675kg*

13. Subtract −4 from −6. *−2*

14. Multiply 1·1 by 11. *12·1*

15. Write one twentieth as a decimal. *0·05*

16. The ratio of boys to girls in a class of 30 is 3 : 2. How many girls are there in the class? *12*

17. How many faces are there in a prism with 24 edges? *Octagon 10*

18. Round 2 195 360 to the nearest ten thousand. *2 200 000*

19. Find one sixth of 4·2. *0·7*

20. How much greater is 3 206 189 than 3 197 189? *9000*

Write in figures.

1 six hundred and seven thousand three hundred and fifty

2 one million forty-eight thousand and ninety

3 three million two hundred thousand seven hundred and five

4 six million one thousand and twenty-eight

Write in words.

5 59 300

6 401 027

7 2 980 604

8 4 067 090

9 1 700 513

10 520 089

11 8 040 701

12 5 306 002

Write each group of numbers in order, smallest first.

13
176 167
176 176
167 617
167 716

14
294 292
249 922
249 299
294 229

15
3 558 835
3 583 385
3 583 835
3 558 388

16
1 101 144
1 104 114
1 100 414
1 101 411

Give the value of the underlined digit.

17 7̲2 059

18 604 3̲80

19 8 2̲59 600

20 3 016 7̲43

21 5̲ 943 008

22 7 139 2̲10

23 560 19̲6

24 9 3̲85 020

25 1 7̲27 962

26 6 491 4̲85

27 2 808 730

28 4 015 0̲74

Write the answer only.

29 Add 70 000 to 2 159 476.

30 Add 3 004 000 to 26 703.

31 Take 400 000 from 9 244 185.

32 Take 6000 from 1 700 390.

Copy and complete.

33 $1\,632\,109 + \boxed{} = 2\,132\,109$

34 $6\,498\,350 + \boxed{} = 6\,506\,355$

35 $2\,805\,462 - \boxed{} = 2\,804\,762$

36 $3\,029\,517 - \boxed{} = 2\,939\,517$

Round to the nearest:
a) 10 000   b) 100 000

37 807 405

38 1 292 730

39 8 615 374

40 5 074 962

41 2 581 950

42 6 836 409

43 249 386

44 9 053 720

Round to:
a) 1 decimal place   b) 2 decimal places.

45 0·283

46 25·907

47 4·0625

48 37·4753

49 9·5192

50 0·35481

51 12·836

52 53·0684

53 Copy and complete the table showing changes in temperature.

OLD	CHANGE	NEW
−4°C	+12°C	
−1°C	−19°C	
3°C		−5°C
−32°C	+25°C	
	+11°C	4°C
28°C	−40°C	
	+37°C	16°C
−8°C		−31°C

Work out

1 $3\frac{1}{2} + 1\frac{3}{8}$

2 $1\frac{3}{4} + 2\frac{7}{12}$

3 $4\frac{1}{3} + 3\frac{2}{5}$

4 $2\frac{9}{10} + 4\frac{1}{4}$

5 $5\frac{2}{3} - 4\frac{4}{9}$

6 $7\frac{4}{5} - 2\frac{3}{10}$

7 $3\frac{1}{2} - 1\frac{1}{3}$

8 $6\frac{3}{4} - 3\frac{1}{6}$

Work out

9 $\frac{1}{4} \times \frac{2}{7}$

10 $\frac{1}{10} \times \frac{5}{6}$

11 $\frac{1}{3} \times \frac{3}{8}$

12 $\frac{1}{5} \times \frac{7}{12}$

13 $\frac{8}{9} \times \frac{3}{4}$

14 $\frac{5}{6} \times \frac{3}{7}$

15 $\frac{11}{12} \times \frac{2}{5}$

16 $\frac{2}{3} \times \frac{7}{100}$

Work out

17 $\frac{4}{5} \div 4$

18 $\frac{5}{8} \div 10$

19 $\frac{3}{4} \div 3$

20 $\frac{6}{11} \div 2$

21 $\frac{2}{3} \div 5$

22 $\frac{3}{8} \div 12$

23 $\frac{4}{9} \div 8$

24 $\frac{9}{10} \div 6$

Use a calculator to find the decimal equivalent. Round to 3 decimal places where necessary.

25 $\frac{1}{6}$

26 $\frac{7}{8}$

27 $\frac{3}{11}$

28 $\frac{5}{9}$

29 $\frac{2}{7}$

30 $\frac{11}{12}$

31 $\frac{2}{3}$

32 $\frac{9}{11}$

Copy and complete.

33 $\frac{1}{3}$ of ☐ = 24 cm

34 $\frac{1}{10}$ of ☐ = 600 g

35 $\frac{1}{5}$ of ☐ = 40p

36 $\frac{1}{8}$ of ☐ = 2·5 litres

Give the value of the underlined digit.

37 1·32<u>8</u>

38 2<u>6</u>·57

39 0·9<u>4</u>3

40 4·6<u>1</u>

41 <u>3</u>·402

42 7·03<u>5</u>

43 35·1<u>9</u>

44 2·8<u>6</u>7

Write the answer only.

45 0·25 × 10

46 1·369 × 100

47 0·014 × 1000

48 5·073 × 10

49 0·8 × 100

50 2·31 × 1000

51 97 ÷ 10

52 4·4 ÷ 100

53 1060 ÷ 1000

54 802 ÷ 10

55 750 ÷ 100

56 326 ÷ 1000

Work out

57 0·08 × 3

58 0·12 × 9

59 2·5 ÷ 2

60 0·91 ÷ 7

61 3·46 × 5

62 1·73 × 8

63 12·8 ÷ 4

64 2·79 ÷ 6

Round to the nearest:

a) 1 decimal place

b) 2 decimal places

65 0·846

66 3·378

67 0·692

68 1·045

69 2·453

70 0·527

71 0·965

72 7·084

73 Copy and complete the table.

Fraction	Decimal	Percentage
$\frac{1}{10}$	0·1	10%
$\frac{3}{4}$		
$\frac{2}{5}$		
	0·61	
	0·9	
		3%
		25%

Find

74 $\frac{2}{3}$ of £39

75 $\frac{5}{8}$ of 400 ml

76 $\frac{4}{5}$ of 60 cm

77 10% of 2·4 kg

78 1% of 5 litres

79 30% of £1·80

80 5% of £95.

Copy and complete.

1. 138 mm = ☐ cm
2. 7·2 cm = ☐ mm
3. 245 cm = ☐ m
4. 0·07 m = ☐ cm
5. 40 m = ☐ km
6. 8·169 km = ☐ m
7. 20 miles = ☐ km
8. 20 km = ☐ miles
9. 533 g = ☐ kg
10. 2 g = ☐ kg
11. 7·426 kg = ☐ g
12. 0·6 kg = ☐ g
13. 85 ml = ☐ litres
14. 2070 ml = ☐ litres
15. 1·918 litres = ☐ ml
16. 0·304 litres = ☐ ml

Write the measurement shown by each arrow as:
a) g b) kg.

17. ↓700 ↓800 g

18. 100 ↓200 300↓ g

19. ↓ 0·5 0·6 ↓0·7 kg

20. 3 ↓ 4 ↓ kg

21. 3 cm / 8 cm

Work out:
a) the area of the rectangle **24 cm²**
b) the perimeter. **22 cm**

22. Draw a rectangle with the same area but:
a) a shorter perimeter
b) a longer perimeter
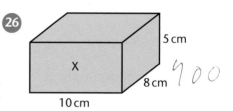

23. Draw a rectangle with the same perimeter but:
a) a smaller area
b) a larger area.
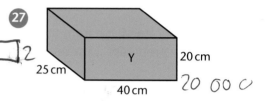

24. Label the dimensions, area and perimeter of all four rectangles.

25. Find the area of each shape. (All lengths are in centimetres.)

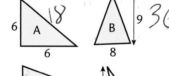
6 / A / 6 **18**
B / 9 **36** / 8

17·5 5 / C / 7
15 / D **48** / 6

80 20 / E / 8

12 / F / 5 **30**
G / 40 / 20 **400** / 8

H **48** **12** **60** / 8 / 4 / 6

Find the volume of each cuboid.

26. 5 cm / X / 8 cm / 10 cm **400**

27. Y / 20 cm / 25 cm / 40 cm **20 000**

28. How many of cuboid X would fit into cuboid Y? **50**

29. One staple is made from 15 mm of wire. How many staples can be made from 2·4 m of wire? **1·5 cm** **160**

30. Three 225 ml glasses are filled from a jug holding 1·5 litres of drink. How much is left in the jug in litres? **0·825 L**

31. Winston's walk to school is 1·26 km long. Crystal's journey is 592 m shorter. How long is Crystal's walk to school in metres? **1260 − 592 = 668** **668**

32. A small packet of flour weighs 850 g. A larger packet weighs 90% more. What is the weight of the larger packet in kilograms? **1·615 kg**

33. A field is twice as long as it is wide. It has a perimeter of 540 m. What is its area? **180 90 180** **16200**

18 × 9 = 16200

Describe the properties of each shape.

1 equilateral triangle *3 equal sides, some angle*

2 parallelogram *4 side, quadriateral*

3 pentagonal prism *5 sides faces*

4 octahedron *10 side, all same angle*

Identify the shape from the clues and describe other properties it possesses.

5 3 sides
2 equal angles *Isosceles triangle*

6 all sides equal
sum of angles of 540° *Pentagon*

7 4 equal sides
no right angle *Rombus*

8 a prism with 9 edges *triangle prism*

9 6 square faces *Cube*

10 4 vertices *Square*

11 Draw a circle with a radius of 2·7 cm. Label the radius, diameter and circumference.

12 What is the radius of a circle with a diameter of:

 a) 11 cm *5·5cm* **b)** 7·8 cm *3·9cm* **c)** 15·3 cm. *7·65cm*

13 What is the diameter of a circle with a radius of:

 a) 9·5 cm *19cm* **b)** 6·8 cm *13·6cm* **c)** 2·95 cm.

14 Make a net for:

 a) a cube with sides 2·4 cm

 b) a closed cuboid 3·2 cm long, 2·6 cm wide and 1·5 cm tall

 c) a square base pyramid with a base of 16 cm² and 3 cm in height.

For each shape write down:

a) the name

b) the number of faces, edges and vertices

c) the number of faces which are parallel or perpendicular to the base.

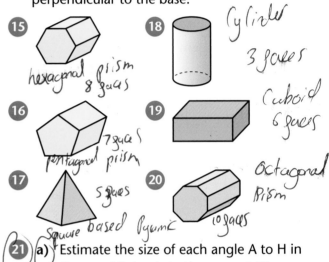

15 *hexagonal prism 8 faces*

18 *Cylinder 3 faces*

16 *pentagonal prism 7 faces*

19 *Cuboid 6 faces*

17 *Square based Pyramid 5 faces*

20 *Octagonal Prism 10 faces*

21 **a)** Estimate the size of each angle A to H in the quadrilaterals to the nearest 5°.

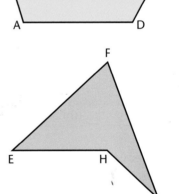

 b) Measure each angle to the nearest degree.

 c) Work out the difference between your estimate and the actual size.

22 Using a ruler only draw angles of:

 a) 254° b) 148° c) 306°.

Measure each angle and work out the difference between your angle and the actual angle.

Find the missing angles.

23

a   147°
33

28

124
g   51°

24

165°
b
195

29

288°
h
72

25
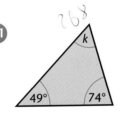
96°
c   c
d
84   84
96

30
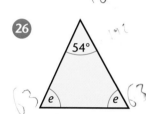
46   134°   46
i   i
j
134

26
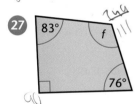
54°
e   e
63   63

31
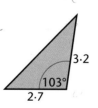
268
k
49°   74°

27
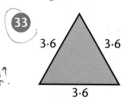
83°
f
111
76°
90

32
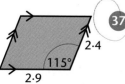
96
x
122°
46°
x
90   96   168
80
74
74

Construct the following shapes.
All lengths are in cm.

33

3·6   3·6
3·6
Book?

36
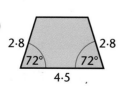
3·2
103°
2·7

34
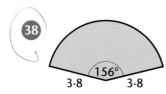
2·4
115°
2·9

37

2·8   2·8
72°   72°
4·5

35
43°
5·1

38
156°
3·8   3·8

---

39 Give the co-ordinates of:

a) the rectangle   **b)** the triangle

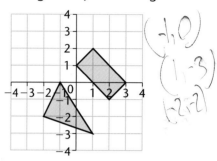

(2,1) (3,0)
(0,1)
(1,2)

(1,0)
(1,-3)
(-2,-2)

40 Copy the grid and the rectangle.
Translate the shape:

a) Left 3   Up 2

b) Left 2   Down 3.

41 Give the co-ordinates of both new positions.

42 Copy the grid and the triangle.
Translate the shape:

a) Right 2   Up 1

b) Left 1   Up 3.

43 Give the co-ordinates of both new positions.

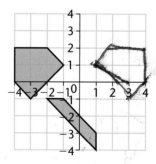

44 Copy the grid and the pentagon.
Sketch the reflection of the shape:

a) in the y axis

b) in the mirror line (−4, −4) to (4, 4).

45 Copy the grid and the trapezium.
Sketch the reflection of the shape:

a) in the x axis

b) in the mirror line (−4, 4) to (4, −4).

46 Give the co-ordinates of both new positions
for each shape.

This pie chart shows the favourite breakfast of 60 Year 6 pupils.

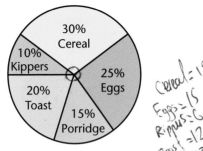

Cereal = 18
Eggs = 15
Kippers = 6
Toast = 12
Porridge = 9

1 How many children chose each breakfast?

2 Work out the angle at the centre of each sector.

3 This table shows the audience in a cinema.

Women	120
Men	75
Girls	60
Boys	45

Construct a pie chart to show the data.

4 Draw a graph to convert miles to kilometres.

  a) Label the horizontal axis (miles) in 5s to 50.

  b) Label the vertical axis (kilometres) in 5s to 80.

  c) Draw a straight line to connect (0, 0) and (50, 80).

5 Use your graph to convert to the nearest kilometre:

  a) 25 miles   **b)** 10 miles   **c)** 45 miles.

6 Use your graph to convert to the nearest mile:

  a) 8 km   **b)** 64 km   **c)** 20 km.

This line graph shows the daily maximum temperature recorded for the first 10 days of May.

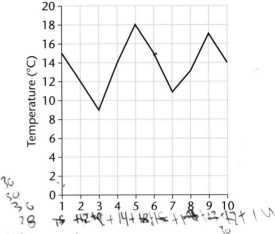

7 What was the temperature on:

  a) 5th May   **b)** 7th May?

8 On which two days was the temperature:

  a) 14°C   **b)** 15°C?

9 By how much did the temperature

  a) rise between 8th May and 9th May

  b) fall between 2nd May and 3rd May

10 Between which two days was there:

  a) the largest fall in temperature

  b) the largest rise in temperature?

11 Find the mean temperature for the first 10 days of May.

12 Use the table below to draw a line graph showing the daily maximum temperature for one week in January.

Day	Su	M	Tu	W	Th	F	Sa
Temp (°C)	8	5	−1	−3	1	0	4

13 Find the mean temperature for the above week.

When a number is multiplied by itself you get a square number.

The number which is multiplied by itself is the square root. ($\sqrt{}$)

Examples

$3^2 = 3 \times 3 = 9$

$\sqrt{9} = 3$

$4^2 = 4 \times 4 = 16$

$\sqrt{16} = 4$

A

1 Copy and complete this table for 12 lines.

$\sqrt{1} = 1 \div 1 = 1$

$\sqrt{4} = 4 \div 2 = 2$

$\sqrt{9} = 9 \div 3 = 3$

HINT: Work from right to left and multiply.

Work out the length of the sides of each square.

2 Area 4 cm² *2*

8 Area 64 cm² *8*

3 Area 81 cm² *9*

9 Area 16 cm² *4*

4 Area 25 cm² *5*

10 Area 144 cm² *12*

5 Area 49 cm² *7*

11 Area 36 cm² *6*

6 Area 100 cm² *10*

12 Area 121 cm² *11*

7 Area 9 cm² *3*

13 Area 1 m²

B

Work out

1 $\sqrt{36} + \sqrt{9}$ *7*

2 $\sqrt{81} + \sqrt{4}$ *11*

3 $\sqrt{144} + \sqrt{49}$ *19*

4 $\sqrt{100} - \sqrt{4}$ *8*

5 $\sqrt{121} - \sqrt{25}$ *6*

6 $\sqrt{81} - \sqrt{64}$ *1*

7 $\sqrt{49} \times \sqrt{121}$ *77*

8 $\sqrt{36} \times \sqrt{81}$ *54*

9 $\sqrt{64} \times \sqrt{16}$ *32*

10 $\sqrt{144} \div \sqrt{4}$ *6*

11 $\sqrt{100} \div \sqrt{25}$ *2*

12 $\sqrt{81} \div \sqrt{9}$ *3*

Work out

13 $\sqrt{100}$ *10*

19 $\sqrt{1600}$ *40*

14 $\sqrt{400}$ *20*

20 $\sqrt{4900}$ *70*

15 $\sqrt{2500}$ *500*

21 $\sqrt{8100}$ *90*

16 $\sqrt{6400}$ *80*

22 $\sqrt{3600}$ *60*

17 $\sqrt{900}$ *30*

23 $\sqrt{10\,000}$ *100*

18 $\sqrt{12\,100}$ *110*

24 $\sqrt{14\,400}$ *120*

C

Example

Which two-digit number has a square root of 3844?

Step 1 – The 10s Digit

3844 comes between:

60^2 and 70^2

$3600 < 3844 < 4900$

The 10s digit is 6.

Step 2 – The Units Digit

3844 ends in a 4.

The units digit must be $2 (2 \times 2 = 4)$ or $8 (8 \times 8 = 64)$

3844 is closer to 60^2 than 70^2.

The units digit is 2.

Therefore $\sqrt{3844} = 62$

Use the above method to predict the square root of these numbers.

1 289 *17*

7 3364 *8*

2 8464 *92*

8 4096 *64*

3 1156 *34*

9 2809 *53*

4 625 *25*

10 6241 *70*

5 2401 *49*

11 3721 *61*

6 5776 *76*

12 7744 *88*

13 Check each answer by squaring your prediction.

TARGET   To use the language of probability and to describe the likelihood of an event.

The probability of an event can be placed on a scale.

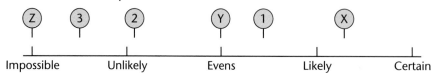

On the way home from school Joe will see:

① a police car

② a fire engine

③ a horse.

The probability of each of these events is not quantifiable. They might be placed on the scale as above but this would depend upon the circumstances. For example, whether Joe's school is in a village or a city centre.

You roll a standard dice and score:

Ⓧ less than 6

Ⓨ an even number

Ⓩ 7

The probability of each of these events is quantifiable and can be expressed as a fraction.

Score	Ways	Outcomes	Probability
less than 6	5	6	$\frac{5}{6}$
even number	3	6	$\frac{3}{6} = \frac{1}{2}$
7	0	6	$\frac{0}{6} = 0$

Each probability can be placed precisely on the scale.

 A

For each of these statements write one of these probabilities.

certain   even chance   impossible

likely   unlikely

① The next person to win the National Lottery will be a bus driver.

② You roll a dice and score more than 2.

③ You spin a coin and get a tail.

④ Next week will have a Tuesday in it.

⑤ You roll a dice and score 6.

⑥ You will eat fish in the next week.

⑦ You will represent Peru in the Olympic Games.

⑧ A word chosen at random from a book will have an e in it.

---

⑨ Using this spinner describe the probability of landing on:

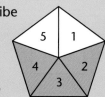

a) red   e) below 6

b) white   f) an odd number

c) 2   g) an even number

d) 6   h) not 5.

The probability of the above spinner landing on red is:

$\frac{3}{5}$ – the number of red sides
     – the total number of sides

⑩ Write down the probability as a fraction for each of the above outcomes **a–h**.

⑪ Write down as a percentage the probability for each of the above outcomes **a–h**.

B

Place the probabilities of these events on a scale like that on page 164.

1. It will rain tomorrow.

2. You will see a fire engine on the way home from school.

3. Snow will fall next year in Edinburgh in February.

4. Your teacher will smile.

5. The sun will rise tomorrow.

6. The next baby born at a hospital is a girl.

7. A word chosen at random from a book has four letters.

8. The Prime Minister had an egg for breakfast this morning.

9. Next year you will pass your driving test.

10. A cyclist will have a puncture in the next 12 months.

For questions **11** to **15** write down the probability of each event as a fraction.

11. Spinning a coin and getting a head.

12. Spinning two coins and getting two heads.

13. Drawing a card from a full pack of 52 and it is:

    a) a club
    b) black
    c) an ace
    d) the 7 of hearts.

14. The President of the USA was born on:

    a) a Wednesday
    b) a day beginning with a T
    c) a day with 6 letters in its name.

15. A month chosen at random from a calendar:

    a) has an r in its name
    b) has 8 letters in its name
    c) has 31 days.

C

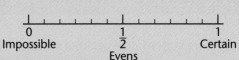
0   Impossible $\frac{1}{2}$ Evens   1   Certain

Work out each of these probabilities as a fraction and place the letters on the above scale.

1. You spin two coins and get:

    a) two tails
    b) at least one tail
    c) a head and a tail
    d) a head or a tail.

2. You roll two dice and score:

    a) 9
    b) less than 5
    c) more than 7.

3. You play Paper, Scissors, Stone and:

    a) win or lose
    b) draw
    c) win.

4. In her pencil case Polly has one green pen, two red pens, four black pens and three blue pens. She takes out a pen at random.
   Work out the probability that it is:

    a) red   c) not green
    b) black   d) red or blue.

   Place the probabilities on a probability scale.

5. Copy this table for 60 rolls of a dice. Complete the second row.

No. of rolls	12	24	36	48	60
6s Expected					
Actual No. of 6s					

Keep a tally of the number of rolls and 6s. Fill in the third row after every 12 rolls.

Our numbers system, the decimal system, is based on groups of 10. In binary the numbers system is based on 2. Instead of units, 10s, 100s, 1000s and so on, the column values in binary numbers are units, 2s, 4s, 8s, 16s, etc.

Examples

16s	8s	4s	2s	Units		
	1	0	0	1	= 9	(one eight and one unit)
		1	1	0	= 6	(one four and one two)
1	0	0	0	0	= 16	(one sixteen)

A

Write in binary.

1. 10
2. 5
3. 13
4. 2
5. 12
6. 7
7. 16
8. 3
9. 14
10. 8
11. 1
12. 11
13. 6
14. 15
15. 4
16. 9

Write in decimal.

17. 1111
18. 11
19. 1001
20. 110
21. 1101
22. 1
23. 101
24. 1011
25. 111
26. 100
27. 1100
28. 10000
29. 10
30. 1010
31. 1110
32. 1000

B

Write the answer in binary.

1. 5 + 7
2. 15 − 13
3. 12 − 6
4. 6 + 9
5. 11 + 3
6. 14 − 4
7. 7 + 6
8. 11 − 8

Convert to decimal.
Work out and write the answer in binary.

9. 11 + 1010
10. 1100 − 100
11. 1001 + 101
12. 10000 − 1001
13. 1000 + 10
14. 1111 − 110
15. 100 × 10
16. 1111 ÷ 11

C

Write in decimal.

1. 11010
2. 10101
3. 11110
4. 10011
5. 100000
6. 110000
7. 11011
8. 101110
9. 10111
10. 110100
11. 100010
12. 110001
13. 11100
14. 111001
15. 100111
16. 111110
17. Work out some other binary numbers and write their decimal equivalents.